A Birder's Guide

to the

Rio Grande Valley of Texas

Library of Congress Catalog Card Number: 91-73556

ISBN Number: 1-878788-01-9

Second Edition

1 2 3 4 5 6 7 8 9

Printed in the United States of America

Publisher

ABA / William J. Graber, III, Chairman, Publications Committee

Series Editor

Paul J. Baicich

Associate Editors

Cindy Lippincott and Bob Berman

Copy Editor

Hugh Willoughby

Layout and Typography

Bob Berman; produced using Ventura Publisher Gold, GEM Edition

Maps

Cindy Lippincott; produced using CorelDRAW version 2

Cover Photography

front cover: Golden-fronted Woodpecker; Vernon Eugene Grove, Jr.
back cover: Green Jays; Vernon Eugene Grove, Jr.

Illustrations

Shawneen Finnegan
Charles H. Gambill
Gail Diane Luckner

Distributed by

American Birding Association Sales
PO Box 6599
Colorado Springs, Colorado
80934-6599 USA

(800) 634-7736 (U.S. & Canada) or (719) 578-0607
Fax: (800) 247-3329 (U.S., Canada, & Mexico) or (719) 471-4722

A BIRDER'S GUIDE

TO THE

RIO GRANDE VALLEY OF TEXAS

by
Harold R. Holt

1992

A Complete Revision of the Guide
Originally Written by
James A. Lane

American Birding Association, Inc.

American Birding Association, Inc.

Since 1969, the American Birding Association has served the North American birding community by helping birders hone their field identification skills and telling them where to find birds. This membership organization exists to promote the recreational observation and study of wild birds, to educate the public in the appreciation of birds and their vital role in the environment, to assist in the study of birds in their natural habitat, and to contribute to the development of improved bird population studies. The organization also keeps North American birders informed about valuable resources, new publications, and top-notch birding equipment.

All ABA members receive **Birding**, the official bimonthly magazine of the organization, and **Winging It,** the monthly newsletter. Both publications are chock-full of birdfinding advice, identification details, and up-to-date birding news. Members also receive discounts from ABA Sales on bird books, tapes, optical equipment, and accessories. ABA also publishes an invaluable Membership Directory, conducts sell-out biennial conventions and regional conferences, and sponsors bird-related tours of various durations to domestic and foreign birding hot-spots.

All persons interested in these aspects of bird study are invited to join. If you bird beyond your backyard, ABA membership will help you discover a whole new world of birding adventure and expertise. A membership form is included in this book.

American Birding Association
PO Box 6599
Colorado Springs, Colorado 80934-6599

This book is dedicated to Father Tom Pincelli, whose enthusiasm for the birds and the habitats of the Lower Rio Grande Valley has made that area a finer place for the birds and birders who visit and live there.

PREFACE

My first trip to the Rio Grande Valley of Texas was in 1957. I still remember my great expectations of finding new and exotic birds, and find them I did! I added 59 lifers to my list, and dozens of new mammals, reptiles, and plants. My trips to the Rio Grande are now annual events, but I still have the same great expectations, and I usually add a new bird every year. I hope that this guide will help you to add a few new species to your list.

So wrote Dr. James A. Lane (1926-87), a great lover of nature and a philanthropist who shared his knowledge of birds and nature with others through his writing of his Birder's Guide series.

I worked with Jim Lane and his books from 1972. Upon his death in 1987, I took over his books and am trying to continue the work he started. It has been an exciting experience.

While the first guide to the Valley, done in 1971, was a modest effort of 72 pages, the book has grown and expanded over the years.

Those who have helped Jim Lane and me in previous editions follow: Peter Alden, Richard Albert, John Arvin, Jon Barlow, Charles Bender, Steve Benn, Gene Blacklock, Mr. and Mrs. O. C. Bone, David Chelimer, J. J. Clancy, Irby Davis, Mrs. J. Claude Evans, Mrs. Jim Epsy, Sharon Hackleman, Wes Hetrick, Vona Holt, Ty and Julie Hotchkiss, Ned Hudson, Capt. and Mrs. Elgin Hurlbert, Dwight Ittner, Roy Johnson, Mary Belle Keefer, Mr. and Mrs. Jack Keisling, Ed Kutac, Ray and Terry Little, Cruz Martinez, Terry Maxwell, Lena McBee, Kay McCracken, Dan McGrew, Bill Mealy, Denny Moore, Andy O'Neill, John Orgain, Noble Proctor, John and Barbara Ribble, Luis Santaella, Wayne Shifflett, Lanell Skinner, Elmer Smalzried, Lynda Snyder, Jerry and Nancy Strickling, Tom Supple, Jolan Truan, Jim Tucker, John and Gloria Tveten, Gary Van Essen, George Venatta, Roland Wauer, Fred Webster, Frances Williams, Hugh Willoughby, John Winter, and Barry and Kevin Zimmer.

I wish to thank everyone who has suggested and submitted changes for this new edition. I particularly wish to thank the following people: Jon Andrew, Elden and Sharon Bennett, Robert Bowland, Allan H. Chaney, Joyce Davis, Charles "Red" and Louise Gambill, Santos Gonzales, Dick Heller, M.L. Hill Jr., Joe Ideker, Jack Ivy, Jane Kittleman, Mark Lockwood, Sherry Nelson, Roy and Linda Northrop, Father Tom Pincelli, Mary Anna Roosa, John Schmidt, Chuck Sexton, John Sproul, Sally Strong, Brent Wauer, Roland Wauer, Frances Williams, and Barry Zimmer. Artwork by Shawneen Finnegan, Charles H. Gambill, and Gail Diane Luckner is much appreciated, as are the cover photographs by Vernon Eugene Grove, Jr., and the other photographs by Paul J. Baicich, Ty and Julie Hotchkiss, John Sproul, and Ro Wauer. I am especially grateful to my editor, Paul J. Baicich, to Cindy Lippincott who made the maps and doubled in editing tasks, to Bob Berman for his technical skills, and to the entire staff of the American Birding Association.

Since this book will be revised in the future, I hope that you will advise me if you find errors or omissions.

Harold R. Holt
Denver, Colorado
November, 1991

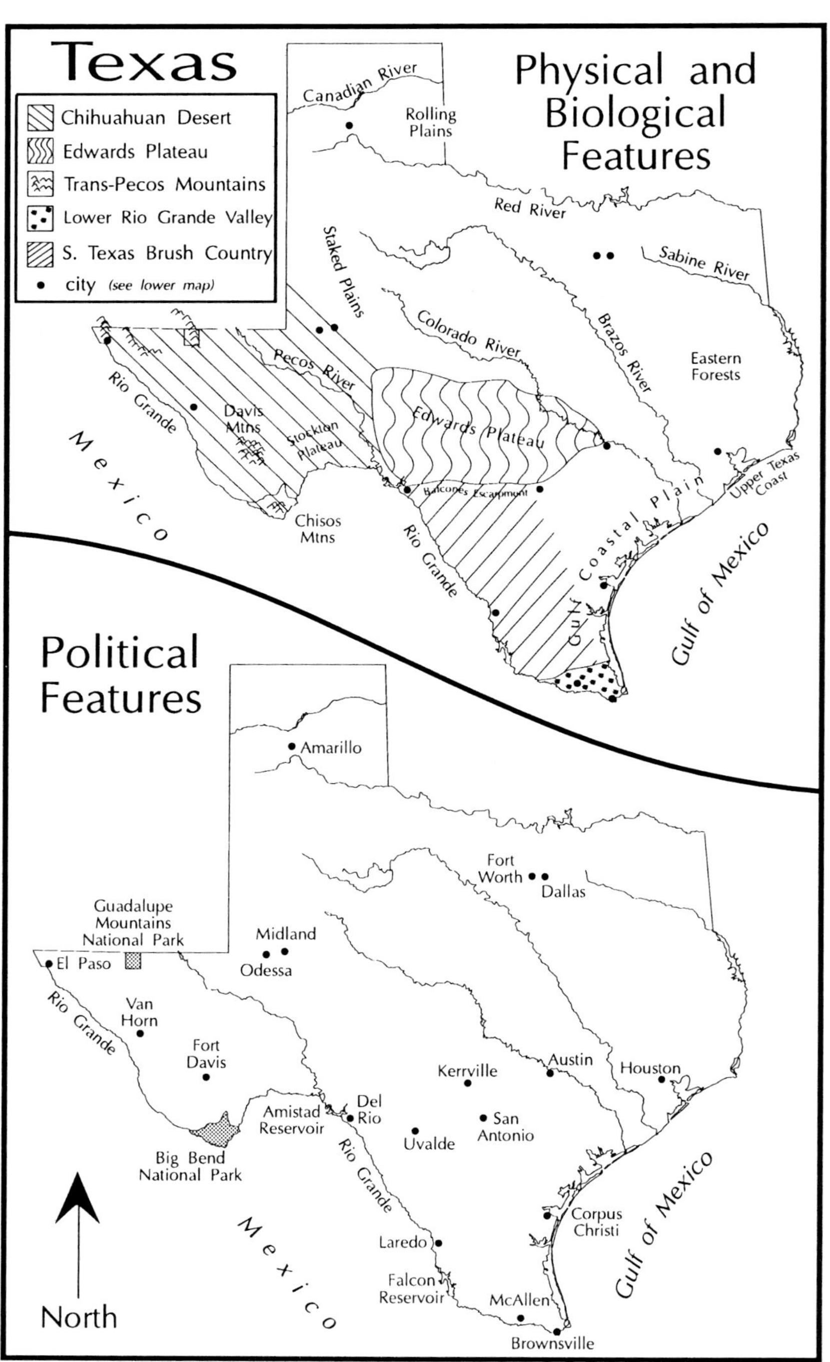
Texas
Physical and Biological Features
Chihuahuan Desert
Edwards Plateau
Trans-Pecos Mountains
Lower Rio Grande Valley
S. Texas Brush Country
city (see lower map)
Canadian River
Rolling Plains
Red River
Sabine River
Staked Plains
Colorado River
Brazos River
Eastern Forests
Pecos River
Davis Mtns
Stockton Plateau
Edwards Plateau
Balcones Escarpment
Rio Grande
Mexico
Chisos Mtns
Gulf Coastal Plain
Upper Texas Coast
Gulf of Mexico
Political Features
Amarillo
Fort Worth
Dallas
Guadalupe Mountains National Park
Midland
Odessa
El Paso
Van Horn
Fort Davis
Kerrville
Austin
Houston
Del Rio
Amistad Reservoir
San Antonio
Uvalde
Big Bend National Park
Corpus Christi
Laredo
Falcon Reservoir
McAllen
Brownsville
North

TABLE OF CONTENTS

Green Kingfisher
Gail Diane Luckner

INTRODUCTION

In that arid part of the United States known as the Southwest, water means life. Muddy ponds are ringed with crayfish castles, raccoon tracks, and cattle. Summer rains bring forth a burst of wildflowers, a horde of insects, and a chorus of toads. However, the greatest abundance of living things is normally found along the rivers, such as the Rio Grande.

This vital river begins in the snowfields of the San Juan Mountains of Colorado, but most of its 1885-mile course is through the barren deserts of New Mexico and Texas, where it is the life line of the land. Its precious waters irrigate the green valley, which stretches like an emerald necklace from the mountains to the sea.

The average tourist is likely to hurry across this arid portion of Texas and to lump it all as a monotonous desert and distant mountains, broken up only by occasional farms and cities. However, if the visitor takes time to stop and to look, he or she will find this valley to be a fascinating area of geological wonders and of biological surprises and a land with a fascinating history of Indians, Spanish settlers, cowboys, and pioneers.

The land may look deserted, but some 37 species of amphibians, 73 reptiles, 104 mammals, and 300 birds are found regularly along the Texas part of the river. Of the birds, about 120 are permanent residents, 60 are summer residents, 75 are winter visitors, and 50 appear only as migrants. Many others occur as accidentals or strays.

Even the birder might think of the Rio Grande as just another river if it were not the boundary between Texas and Mexico. Many exotic species are found in the United States only along this 1569-mile border, and who knows when another may occur in Texas? The river also crosses the 100th meridian of longitude, which is our mental dividing line between eastern and western species. El Paso is only 10 degrees of longitude or 500 miles west of Brownsville on the map, but the difference between their plants and animals is extreme.

Because of limited rainfall, much of the land along the Rio Grande has a superficial sameness of appearance. This parched look is further accentuated by the contrast between the irrigated fields and the natural vegetation of dry thorny brush, cactus, and short grass. Trees, for the most part, are restricted to stream valleys or mountain peaks. This sameness is deceptive. A closer inspection will reveal several distinct regions and a wide variety of habitats.

REGIONS OF TEXAS

For the sake of convenience, the Texas Ornithological Society separates the state into eight ecological regions. The area covered by this guide lies within three of these regions: South Texas, Edwards Plateau, and the Trans-Pecos. The extreme southern tip of South Texas is further separated as the Lower Rio Grande Valley. When a Texas says "The Valley", he means the area from Falcon Dam to the Gulf.

Texas is such a large state that it offers endless opportunities for good birding; however, the good spots are often many miles apart. The fabulous migrations, for the most part, take place along the coast. Most of the rare Mexican species are found only in the Lower Valley or in Big Bend. A few western species occur only at El Paso or in the Guadalupe Mountains, and at least two species are restricted to the Edwards Plateau.

WHEN TO COME

Many out-of-state birders plan to visit Texas in April to observe the spring migration along the coast. This is also a good time in the Lower Valley, but a little early for Big Bend, where many of the specialties do not arrive until May or late summer. If this is your first trip, it might be best to come in late April and early May.

A winter vacation in South Texas can be great. The days are usually warm and sunny, and the birds numerous. Several Christmas Bird Counts are taken in this area. To help on one or more can make your vacation more exciting and rewarding. This is also an excellent time for those Mexican rarities whose possible appearance thrills all birders.

For hardy birders, who do not mind daily temperatures of 100 degrees or more, midsummer can be exciting along the Rio Grande. The Lower Valley will be stifling, but the Chisos Mountains of Big Bend can be very pleasant.

The fall migration starts with shorebirds in mid-July and reaches its peak in September and October. Large concentrations of birds are not as common as in spring, but your chances of finding rare and out-of-place species are greater. There will also be fall-plumaged birds, which are so difficult to identify that with a little imagination you can make them into anything that you need for your list.

WHERE TO STAY

Nearly all of the towns along the river have motels, but in West Texas it may be hard to find a town. Under normal conditions it is not necessary to make reservations except near Big Bend and the Guadalupe Mountains. In the Lower Valley the best restaurants and motels are in Brownsville, Harlingen, and McAllen. Near Big Bend, Alpine is the largest city, and Whites City, New Mexico, has the only motels near the Guadalupe Mountains. The Edwards Plateau is an area where motels and campgrounds are numerous.

Two of the parks have lodges, and both are in excellent birding areas. The lodge at Big Bend (National Parks Concessions, Inc., Big Bend National Park, TX 79834; phone 915/477-2291) has fairly good food and accommodations. As in all national parks, the rates are steep. Indian Lodge in the Davis Mountains (Davis Mountains State Park, Fort Davis, TX 79734; phone 915/426-3254) is a beautiful spot to spend a vacation. Reservations are required at both.

Private trailer parks are plentiful in the Lower Valley and on the Edwards Plateau. Elsewhere your best bet is in the national and state parks.

A list of the state parks can be obtained from the Texas Parks and Wildlife Department, 4200 Smith School Road, Austin, TX 78744. Also ask for a checklist of birds for Bentsen, Falcon, Davis Mountains, and Hueco Tanks State Parks. Maps and other tourist information are available from the Texas Highway Department, Austin, Texas 78763, or the Tourism Division of the Texas Department of Commerce, Box 12728, Austin, TX 78711. Detailed county maps can be purchased for a small fee from Texas Highway Department, Planning Survey Division, Box 5051, Austin, TX 78763.

Two special permits are available for Texas State Parks. The *State Parklands Passport* exempts those 65 or older, or veterans with a 60 percent or greater Veterans' Administration disability, from park entrance fees. The Passport is available at most state parks; those eligible must apply in person with the proper identification or proof of disability.

The *Conservation Passport* is an annual state park entrance permit, which also provides holders with a small discount on camping fees and other items purchased in the park. The cost is $25 per year, from date of purchase. It is available at most state parks or by mail from: Texas Parks and Wildlife Department, 4200 Smith School Road, Austin, TX 78744 (send $25, driver's-license number, date of birth, and vehicle registration number). You will receive a sticker for your car and a wallet identification card for the times when you are not in your vehicle.

BIRDING BEHAVIOR

Years ago, especially when birding was not so popular a pastime as it is now, we did not dwell much on the appropriate behavior of birders in the field. But with increased popularity of our avocation come added responsibilities. On the inside back cover of this book is a copy of the "American Birding Association Code of Ethics." I encourage all who use this book to take the spirit and letter of the Code to heart. Generally, the code indicates that birders must:

1. Always act in ways that do not endanger the welfare of birds or other wildlife;
2. Always act in ways that do not harm the natural environment;
3. Always respect the rights of others;
4. Assume special responsibilities when birding in groups.

For the region covered in this book, I wish to emphasize two important aspects of birding ethics. First, birders should always, but especially in Texas, respect the private property of others. Trespassing in Texas is a major offense to many native Texans, and birders should be especially sensitive to this fact. It is better to err on the side of caution than to assume that it is fine to bird on someone else's property. The sites described in the book are usually public ones. For those which are not, the text usually indicates how to obtain permission to bird. Second, the use of tapes is becoming less and less acceptable. Using tapes to agitate owls, secretive species, and especially endangered birds is inappropriate. Spishing usually can do the job, anyway.

CAMPGROUNDS

Location	Name	Comment
Brownsville	Brazos Island State Recreation Area (23 miles east on SH-4)	No facilities; open Gulf Beach.
Mission	Bentsen-Rio Grande Valley State Park (7 miles southwest on P-43)	All facilities; excellent birding.
Falcon	Falcon State Park	All facilities; good birding.
Austin	Lake Austin City Park (12 miles northwest off FM-2222)	All facilities; excellent birding.

	McKinney Falls State Park (7 miles southeast off US 183)	All facilities; excellent birding.
Kerrville	Kerrville-Schreiner State Park (3 miles south on FM-173)	All facilities; good birding.
Johnson City	Pedernales Falls State Park (7 miles northeast on RM-3232)	All facilities; excellent birding.
Vanderpool	Lost Maples State Park (4.7 miles north on FM-187)	All facilities; excellent birding.
Uvalde	Garner State Park (39 miles north on US-83)	All facilities; good birding.
Del Rio	Amistad National Recreation Area (13 miles west on US-90)	Few facilities; fair birding.
	Seminole Canyon State Park (8 miles west of Comstock on US-90)	Facilities; few birds.
Big Bend National Park	Chisos Basin (5,400-feet elevation)	Showers available at the lodge.
	Rio Grande Village (2,100-feet elevation)	No showers; good birding.
Fort Davis	Davis Mountains State Park (4 miles west on SH-118)	All facilities; good birding.
Toyahvale	Lake Balmorhea State Park	All facilities; few birds.
El Paso	Hueco Tanks State Park (20 miles east off US-62)	All facilities; good birding.
Monahans	Monahans Sandhills State Park (3 miles east on I-20)	All facilities; few birds.

ORGANIZATIONS

Audubon Society chapters and independent Audubon Societies are active in Austin, San Antonio, El Paso (915/581-9470), and the Lower Valley, Frontera Audubon Society (512/565-6773).

The most active group in the state is the Texas Ornithological Society (c/o Jolene Boyd, 326 Live Oak, Ingram, TX 78025; $15.00 per year), which meets twice a year. Attending one of the spring or fall meetings is a fun way of meeting birders from all over the state.

For information about the American Birding Association (Box 6599, Colorado Springs, Colorado 80934; 800-634-7736; $30.00 per year), see page v.

Also be sure to use the Lower Rio Grande Rare Bird Alert—512/565-6773, the Austin Rare Bird Alert—512/483-0952, the San Antonio Rare Bird Alert—512/733-8306, and the statewide Rare Bird Alert—713/992-2757 for the most up-to-date information on the bird scene.

INSECTS

Only Alaskans have ever met a mosquito quite as large or as tough as those that harpoon you in Texas. Luckily, insect repellents are effective and sold widely. Liquid types are harder to apply, but they last longer, and the bugs do not find them quite so tasty.

The grassy areas of Texas can be loaded with vicious little critters known as chiggers. These tiny red mites raise welts, which itch like, well, like crazy. The welts may not appear for a day or so, but they last for weeks. Chiggers attack wherever clothes fit tightly, such as around the beltline and sock tops.

A major advance to repel mosquitoes, chiggers, or ticks is Permanone. It is available in most states as Permakill, Permanone, or Permethrin Arthropod Repellent. Before a trip it is sprayed on clothing and binds with the fabric, remaining effective through five launderings. Non-toxic to humans and other mammals, Permanone has tested as high as 99.9 percent effective in repelling insects when combined with DEET used on exposed skin.

Remedies for chigger bites are almost as abundant as the bugs themselves—they range from nail polish to meat tenderizer.

The best advice is not to get them in the first place. In Texas never lie down on the grass in spring. Try to avoid areas of grass and weeds, or walk rapidly when crossing them. Spray your sox and pant-legs with an insect repellent before going afield, and take a hot soapy bath upon returning.

As if chiggers were not enough, you must also watch out for ticks. Luckily, both seldom occur in the same area. Ticks prefer brushy places, and chiggers prefer grassy ones. Do not remove ticks by pulling. Their proboscis will break off and form a sore. Usually they can be made to let go by applying a hot instrument such as a recently burnt match. External applications of alcohol are also effective; however, internal applications may be more stimulating. Several species of ticks that are found in Texas carry Lyme and other diseases; take precautions to discourage bites. Check yourself often.

Africanized bees arrived in South Texas in 1990. The following year over 200 swarms were found in the Lower Rio Grande Valley, as far north as Corpus Christi, and as far west as Laredo. All indications are that they will continue to spread. Apparently, lawn-mowers and other machinery used near their swarms tend to agitate them. Stay away from bee swarms. The only known protection, when you are being attacked, is to out-run the bees.

HOW TO USE THIS BOOK

Since the main purpose of this guide is to help in finding the special birds of the region, at least three places are listed for each. If these places are outstanding birding spots, they are shown in **bold-faced type**. Most of the birds can be found by stopping only at these good sites.

Many of the places mentioned are followed by a number, thus: (11.6). This system indicates the mileage from the last spot so listed.

This guide is designed to be used on a trip from Brownsville upriver to El Paso, with detours to the Edwards Plateau and Guadalupe Mountains National Park. On your first trip to the area, you will probably find this direction to be the more productive. There are several reasons for this statement. First, many of the migrant birds return to the Lower Valley in late March and April, which is several weeks before they return to the higher elevations of Big Bend. Second, most of the unusual Mexican species are easiest to find in the Lower Valley between the Gulf and Falcon Dam. When approaching from the other direction, one has a tendency to waste a lot of time in the rather barren stretch between Big Bend and Falcon Dam, where the Mexican species are much harder to find.

If you have only a limited time to cover the land along the Rio Grande, it is suggested that you rush right down to the coast. From there you should bird at least one day at the Audubon Sabal Palm Grove Sanctuary and

Laguna Atascosa National Wildlife Refuge, one day at Santa Ana National Wildlife Refuge, one day at Bentsen-Rio Grande Valley State Park, one-half day at Falcon Dam, and a day or so on the Edwards Plateau. Just getting to Big Bend takes almost a day, and you will need at least two days to quickly cover the park. Except for the Gambel's Quail and the curious "Mexican" Mallard, you will probably not add anything by going to El Paso, unless it is on your way. The duck can be found almost as easily at Marfa, the Davis Mountains, or Lake Balmorhea. The Davis Mountains are fun to bird, and, although one seldom adds much to the list, this is the only place to see Montezuma Quail and nesting Common Black-Hawk.

CURRENT NAMES

The American Ornithologists Union (AOU) nomenclature committee has published a 38th Supplement (**Auk**, Vol. 108, No. 3, pp. 750-754, July 1991) to its **A.O.U. Check-list of North American Birds**. In the last few supplements several species have been "split" while some others have been "lumped". This list was compiled in an attempt to standardize the common names. Naturally, not everyone agrees. Many of the changes are simple ones, made by adding "Common", "American", or "Northern" to separate American species from those of other lands. Others were made to bring our names into compliance with those used in other English-speaking countries.

The bird names used herein basically follow the American Birding Association's **ABA Checklist: Birds of the Continental United States and Canada**, 4th edition, 1990. Listed below are some names which differ from those used in our older, standard field guides. Old names are in parentheses.

Clark's Grebe (split from Western Grebe)
Neotropic Cormorant (Olivaceous)
Anhinga (American Anhinga)
Tricolored Heron (Louisiana)
Green-backed Heron (Green)
Tundra Swan (Whistling)
Black-bellied Whistling-Duck (Black-bellied Tree Duck)
Fulvous Whistling-Duck (Fulvous Tree Duck)
(Mexican Duck: conspecific with Mallard)
Northern Pintail (Common)
Black-shouldered Kite (White-tailed)
Snail Kite (Everglade)
Common Black-Hawk (Lesser Black Hawk)
Harris's Hawk (Bay-winged)
Northern Bobwhite (Common)

Montezuma Quail (Harlequin)
Wild Turkey (Common)
Common Moorhen (Common Gallinule)
Northern Jacana (North American)
Red-necked Phalarope (Northern)
Common Ground-Dove (Ground Dove)
White-tipped Dove (White-fronted)
Eastern Screech-Owl (split from Common Screech Owl)
Western Screech-Owl (split from Common Screech Owl)
Flammulated Owl (Flammulated Screech Owl)
Northern Saw-whet Owl (Saw-whet Owl)
Common Poorwill (Poor-will)
Pauraque (Common Pauraque)
Magnificent Hummingbird (Rivoli's)
Elegant Trogon (Coppery-tailed)
Cordilleran Flycatcher (split from Western Flycatcher)
Couch's Kingbird (split from Tropical Kingbird)
Great Kiskadee (Greater)
Brown-crested Flycatcher (Wied's Crested)
Dusky-capped Flycatcher (Olivaceous)
Greater Pewee (Coues' Flycatcher)
Eastern Wood-Pewee (Eastern Pewee)
Western Wood-Pewee (Western Pewee)
Northern Beardless-Tyrannulet (Northern Beardless Flycatcher)
Northern Rough-winged Swallow (Rough-winged Swallow)
Gray-breasted Jay (Mexican)
Common Raven (Northern)
Chihuahuan Raven (White-necked)
American Dipper (North American Dipper)
Rufous-backed Robin (Rufous-backed Thrush)
Clay-colored Robin (Clay-colored Thrush)
American Pipit (Water Pipit)
Yellow-green Vireo (re-split from Red-eyed Vireo)
Northern Parula (Northern Parula Warbler)
Tropical Parula (Olive-backed Warbler)
Gray-crowned Yellowthroat (Ground Chat)
Canyon Towhee (split from Brown Towhee)
Altamira Oriole (Lichtenstein's)
Audubon's Oriole (Black-headed)
Northern Cardinal (Red)
Lesser Goldfinch (Dark-backed)
Dark-eyed Junco (Northern)
(Gray-headed Junco: conspecific with Dark-eyed Junco)
Yellow-eyed Junco (Mexican)

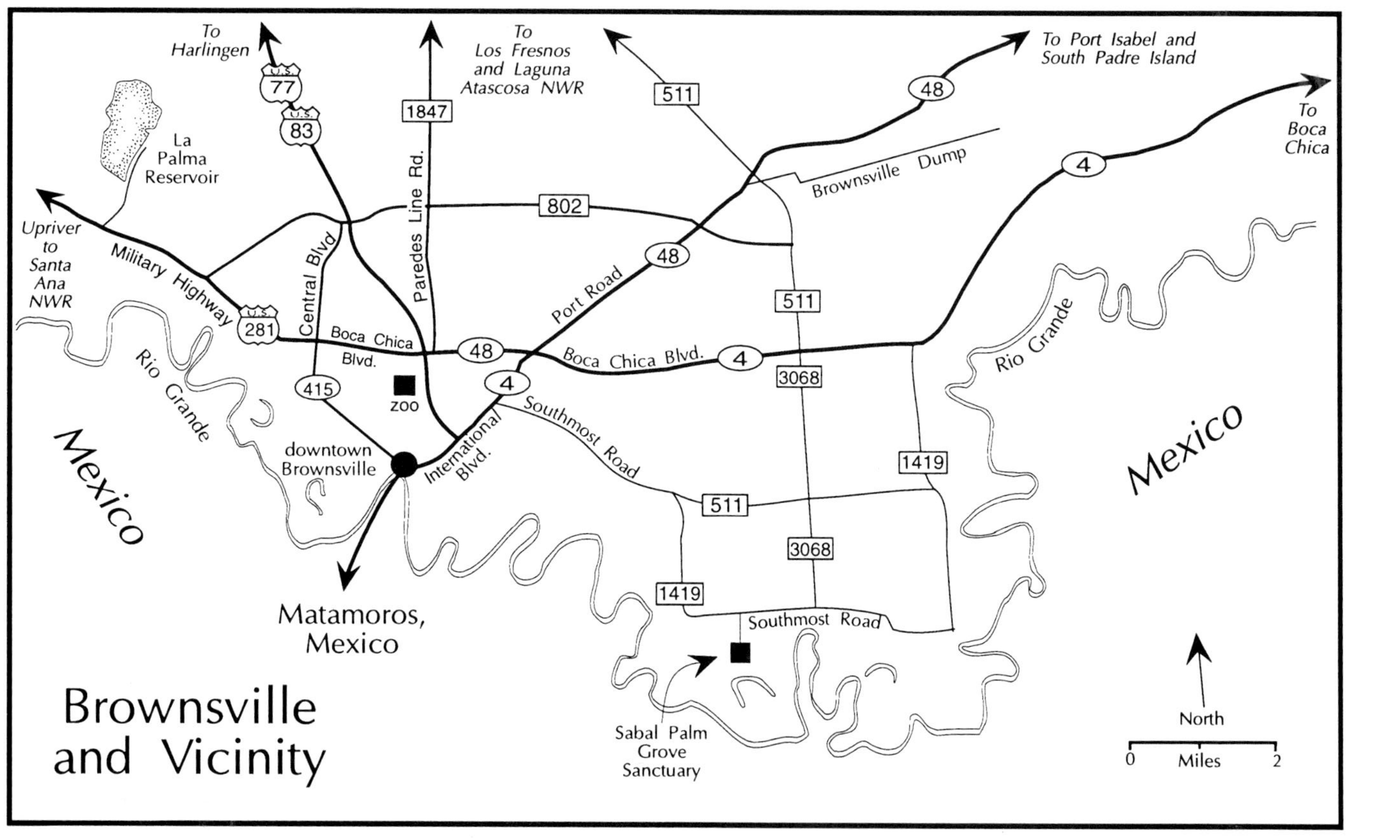

Brownsville and Vicinity
To Harlingen
U.S. 77
U.S. 83
To Los Fresnos and Laguna Atascosa NWR
1847
511
To Port Isabel and South Padre Island
48
To Boca Chica
4
La Palma Reservoir
Upriver to Santa Ana NWR
Military Highway
U.S. 281
Central Blvd
Paredes Line Rd.
802
Brownsville Dump
Port Road
Boca Chica Blvd.
415
zoo
downtown Brownsville
International Blvd.
Southmost Road
3068
1419
Rio Grande
Mexico
Matamoros, Mexico
Sabal Palm Grove Sanctuary
North
0
Miles
2

BROWNSVILLE AND VICINITY

When a Texas birder says "The Valley", he means the Lower Rio Grande Valley, or that area from Falcon Dam to the Gulf and northward to Raymondville. The local Chambers of Commerce call it "The Magic Valley". The visiting birder will call it an exotic wonderland, because many essentially Mexican species occur here and nowhere else in the United States. Though this book will take the birder much farther afield than the Lower Rio Grande Valley, this is where we begin.

The climate is subtropical with mild winters and hot, humid summers. Only about once a decade does it get cold enough to cause severe frost damage or dry enough to be considered a severe drought. The rainfall is generally moderate, but hurricanes occasionally deluge the area with devastating rains. However, these rains create numerous ponds, a situation which encourages the nesting of waterbirds.

Below Rio Grande City the river leaves the rolling hills and brushlands of the Texas Thorn Scrub and emerges onto the coastal plain. In the days before dams and levees, the river meandered widely across the area, creating a vast flood-plain. Heavy rains normally brought floods, and in their wake grew dense thickets and subtropical jungles. Today, these fertile plains are covered by citrus groves, vegetable farms, and growing cities. Only a few patches of the original thickets and forests remain.

The farmlands swarm with the usual Rock Doves and House Sparrows. European Starling, a species that within memory was infrequent in the Lower Valley, is becoming very common now. The more desirable species have been reduced by the loss of habitat and the heavy use of pesticides; however, there are still a few excellent spots with native vegetation and abundant wildlife. And efforts to expand the growing "Wildlife Corridor" will seek to secure more valuable land for wildlife within the four-county Lower Valley—Starr, Hidalgo, Cameron, and Willacy. The "Wildlife Corridor" Project is a public/private effort to set aside about 4 percent of the land area in the Valley for wildlife. Fragments of land with native vegetation and adjacent properties are being purchased to build the corridor. (The Lower Rio Grande Valley National Wildlife Refuge, when completed, may contain over 107,500 acres and stretch in individual segments from the mouth of the Rio Grande up to Falcon Dam, and north to Laguna Atascosa National Wildlife Refuge.) In travels throughout the Lower Valley birders will come across parcels of the growing corridor. While some are open to birding and hiking, others are not. Many refuge parcels are currently overgrown and impassable in any case, though some have public roads intersecting them, roads from which you can actively bird. We can only hope that the entire project continues to grow and that birders get increasing access to potential birding areas. In the meantime, do not trespass on the tracts so marked.

BROWNSVILLE

Our introduction to the Valley begins in Brownsville. The intersection of Highways 4, 77/83, and 415 at Elizabeth Street and International Boulevard in downtown Brownsville is the starting point for this tour.

Brownsville, which grew up around old Fort Brown after the Mexican War, is located at the foot of the International Bridge leading across the Rio Grande to Matamoros, Mexico. During the Civil War the Brownsville/Matamoros connection became "the back door to the Confederacy," the main exporter of cotton to Europe and a major import-site of materials and supplies for the South. Brownsville, now with 100,000 inhabitants, has outgrown its frontier character, yet is still connected economically and culturally with Matamoros, its sister city across the river. A very large percentage of the inhabitants of Brownsville are of Mexican descent, some tracing their lineage back several hundred years to the area's first non-native settlers.

If you wish to cross the border into Mexico, it is a simple matter. No passport, visa, or other papers are required by American citizens unless you plan to stay for more than 72 hours or to travel over 12 miles south of the border. On reentering the country, you will be checked by a customs officer, who will ask where you were born and what you are bringing back. If you have a foreign accent, it is wise to carry proof of citizenship. It might be wise to have a bill of sale for foreign-made cameras and binoculars, or you can register them with the customs office before crossing into Mexico.

At present $400 worth of goods (except for liquor) may be brought back duty-free. It is easy to spend $400 in Mexico, because the shops are filled with pottery, jewelry, leather goods, and stoneware.

If you have extra time in Brownsville, a visit to the **Gladys Porter Zoo** can be very rewarding. A variety of native birds is on display in their Audubon Aviary and Walk-through Aviary for easy viewing. On the grounds you may see wild birds such as Neotropic Cormorant, nesting Green-backed Heron, Great Kiskadee, and Common Moorhen. Buff-bellied Hummingbird may be resident. To reach the zoo, located at 500 Ringgold Road, just follow the signs from the 6th Street exit off Expressway 77/83.

Also in Brownsville, especially during the winter months, you will find small flocks of Red-crowned Parrots. Large flocks of Green Parakeets are often intermixed with the parrots. These birds are newcomers north of the Rio Grande within recent years. For a couple of winters there were a few Yellow-headed Parrots, too. How many of these are escapes and how many are legitimate wild birds from Mexico is open to speculation. The Red-crowned Parrots were found first, three birds in December 1982, and are now nesting. Their legitimacy seems most secure. They and the Green Parakeets are usually easy to find in the northwest section of the city in the area on both sides of Central Boulevard from Boca Chica Boulevard to and beyond Los Ebanos Boulevard.

Occasionally, a Clay-colored Robin or a Golden-crowned Warbler may show up in winter somewhere in the city.

Throughout the city watch for signs which designate an area to be a Wildlife Habitat Area, City of Brownsville. The sign, in color, depicts a nesting Hooded Oriole. These areas are being developed as monies allow, and should improve with age.

SABAL PALM GROVE SANCTUARY

The Rio Grande empties into the Gulf of Mexico some 20 miles east of Brownsville. To begin a birding tour of the area, the first place to stop is National Audubon's **Sabal Palm Grove Sanctuary**. To reach the Sanctuary go southeast from International Boulevard on Southmost Road (FM 1419) to the gravel entrance road on your right (5.6). The gate is 0.9 mile up the road by the old Rabb Plantation House. The Rabb Plantation, established in 1876, originally occupied more than 20,000 acres. The Sabal Palm Grove Sanctuary is a fee area. Hours are 8-5 November-April, Thursday-Monday, and May-October only on weekends. (phone: 512/541-8034; PO Box 5052, Brownsville, TX 78523.)

The 172-acre sanctuary was acquired by the National Audubon Society in 1971, and preserves the largest remaining stand of the native Texas Sabal Palm. Some 32 acres are palm forest (the rest of the sanctuary is old farm fields) and are home to many tropical plants and animals. This tract is about all that is left of the dense palm forest that inspired early Spanish explorers to call the lower Rio Grande "El Rio de las Palmas." The beautiful grove is a great place for finding several notable bird species, some of which barely

Headquarters and Museum at Sabal Palm Grove Sanctuary Paul J. Baicich

range north of the Rio Grande. Look for Plain Chachalaca, Pauraque, White-winged and White-tipped Doves, Common Ground-Dove, Groove-billed Ani, Buff-bellied Hummingbird, Brown-crested Flycatcher, Great Kiskadee, Green Jay, Tropical Parula, Olive Sparrow, and Altamira Oriole. Recent winter sightings of Crimson-collared Grosbeak and Gray-crowned Yellowthroat (both very rare) have been recorded. During migration, warblers are often common in early morning or late afternoon. Also watch for the very striking Zebra Longwing Butterfly.

BOCA CHICA

To reach Boca Chica from Brownsville, go northeast on International Boulevard (Highway 4), bear right with Highway 4 as it turns east on Boca Chica Boulevard, and proceed to the Gulf (22.0).

If you are coming from Sabal Palm Grove Sanctuary, continue east on 1419 to 3068 (0.7) and turn left (north) to Highway 4 (3.4), where you turn right (east) to the Gulf (18.0). In years of good rains, or after a hurricane, which the area gets from time to time, you will find numerous mudflats along the way to check for shorebirds. During migration check the Black

Mangrove and Ebony Trees for passerines. At the Gulf, you can drive on the **damp** sand at low tide for miles. Up the beach to the north is the undeveloped Brazos Island State Recreation Area. Brazos Island is not an island at all, but a peninsula beach. The jetties at Brazos Santiago Pass (about 5 miles north) are a good spot for Brown Pelican. Down the Boca Chica Beach to the south is the mouth of the Rio Grande (2.5). Here, just behind the sand dunes, is a good stand of Black Mangrove which has been great for migrants over the years. The beaches are good for shorebirds such as Ruddy Turnstone, Sanderling, Black-bellied, Snowy, and Piping Plovers, and gulls. In summer you may find Wilson's Plover, Least, Sandwich, Royal, and Caspian Terns. Migration time also brings a good flight of hawks including Broad-winged and Swainson's and a few Merlins and Peregrine Falcons which you may see sitting on top of the higher sand dunes. Out in the waves of the Gulf watch for Brown Pelican and perhaps a Northern Gannet.

BROWNSVILLE SANITARY LANDFILL

(Mexican Crow Sanctuary)

Another good spot is the City Dump. To reach it go northeast from downtown on Highway 4 (International Boulevard). At the intersection of International Boulevard and Boca Chica Boulevard, Highway 4 turns right, but you should continue straight ahead onto Highway 48 (Port Road). Pass FM 802 (2.9), and then bear right at the "Y" in the road (0.7) toward the Port of Brownsville. You will soon reach the Port guard-house (0.5), where you bear right. Continue past the water tower on the right until you see the landfill entrance. The ever-changing entrance to the dump is currently 1.2 miles past the guardhouse. At the check-station, hold up your binoculars and tell them you are looking for birds. (The dump is closed on Sundays.) Proceed to where the trucks are dumping their garbage. It may be as much as two miles from the check-station.

Like dumps everywhere, this one attracts numerous birds. Gulls are usually plentiful. Franklin's Gulls may be abundant during migration. However, the big thing to look for here is the Mexican Crow, which closely resembles a Fish Crow.

The Mexican Crow was first recorded in the United States in 1968, but it is now sometimes abundant at the dump November through January. There are even a few recorded nestings in the area. It frequents the dump whenever the garbage trucks arrive, usually between 9am and 4pm. Its numbers vary, but sometimes it is the most numerous crow-like bird at the

Browsnville Sanitary Landfill — Paul J. Baicich

dump. You should have little difficulty in finding it among the numerous Great-tailed Grackles and Chihuahuan Ravens. Check comparative sizes and tail lengths, and listen for the frog-like croak of the Mexican Crow.

LAGUNA ATASCOSA NATIONAL WILDLIFE REFUGE

The **Laguna Atascosa National Wildlife Refuge** (fee area; 45,190 acres) is covered in the Lane Guide entitled *A Birder's Guide to the Texas Coast,* but it is so close by and so productive that it merits repeated treatment here. It is reached from Brownsville by driving north on the Expressway 77/83 to Boca Chica Boulevard. Go east and quickly watch for a turn north on Paredes Line Road (FM 1847). Continue through the little town of Los Fresnos to Highway 106 and turn right (east) and make a left at the "T" into the refuge (PO Box 450, Rio Hondo, TX 78583; phone 512/748-3607), a total of some 27 miles.

Originally set aside as a wintering-ground for ducks and geese, the refuge is now managed for the rich biodiversity which it exhibits. A total of 389 species of birds have been recorded here, including the endangered Aplomado Falcon (first released here in 1985), Peregrine Falcon, Piping

Plover, (Southern) Bald Eagle, and Brown Pelican. Many other species found only in the Lower Rio Grande Valley will fill out your life list. In the fall, a half-million ducks descend on the refuge along with 10,000 Snow Geese, 2,000 Sandhill Cranes, and countless shorebirds and other winter migrants.

Spring migration begins in mid-April and can be a spectacular sight when a strong northern wind and rain farther up the coast keep the warblers grounded for a day. Migrant warblers filling the trees and Scissor-tailed Flycatchers lining the fencerows, combined with returning summer residents like the Brown-crested Flycatchers calling from tree tops and colorful Blue Grosbeaks and Painted and Indigo Buntings make a memorable sight.

The refuge lies along the inland side of placid Laguna Madre and is protected from the sometimes stormy Gulf by the sand dunes of Padre Island. Brushlands, prairies, salt-flats, mud-flats, beaches, bays, and freshwater ponds on the refuge all attract a variety of wildlife. Two road tours (open daily from sunrise to sunset) and four walking trails can bring you to all of these areas. (If you also wish to visit a remote part of the refuge not open to vehicles, you can join one of the monthly birding field trips in winter. Reservations are taken beginning the first of each month and fill up quickly.) *Use of tape recordings to attract wildlife is prohibited within the Refuge.*

Shortly after passing the first refuge sign (10 miles east of Rio Hondo) you will come to the first of four walking trails. **Whitetail Trail** (5-mile loop, parking area on right) is a primitive trail maintained on an irregular basis. It goes through an area of mesquite and grass that is most productive in early morning. Greater Roadrunners, Bewick's Wrens, Blue Grosbeaks, and Painted Buntings nest here. In winter you may find Say's Phoebe and numerous sparrows. Keep in mind that the refuge's brushy areas are renowned for their high population of Western Diamondback Rattlesnakes.

The Visitor Center, located 7 miles from the first refuge entry sign, is open from 10am to 4pm daily October-April, weekends only in September and May, and is closed June through August. Maps, checklists, books, and wildlife information are available here. Some of the best birding can be found in the area around the Center itself. Green Jay, Tufted (Black-crested) Titmouse, and Golden-fronted Woodpeckers flit from tree to tree in the parking lot and picnic area. White-tipped Doves and Buff-bellied Hummingbirds visit the feeders at the front of the building. Behind the building at the far end of the parking lot is a tree-lined ditch famous for its nesting Yellow-green Vireos. This is a good spot to check out Great Kiskadee, Couch's Kingbird, Brown-crested Flycatcher, and spring warblers.

Mesquite Trail (1.5-mile loop) begins at the west end of the parking lot. It will yield a good selection of birds. White-tailed Deer and Nine-banded Armadillos stroll along this path in early morning or late evening, and signs of Coyote are present at any time of day.

Bayside Drive begins to your right just before reaching the Visitor Center parking lot. This 15-mile paved road has many turnouts so you can stop to view the birds as you travel through various habitats. The first half-mile passes through dense thickets of thornbrush where Plain Chachalacas call out each morning. Greater Roadrunner, Pauraque, Golden-fronted and Ladder-backed Woodpeckers, Verdin, Bewick's and Cactus Wrens, White-eyed Vireo, Long-billed Thrasher, and Olive Sparrow prefer this dense thorny growth. You may want to leave your car in the Visitor Center parking lot and walk the first part to increase your chances

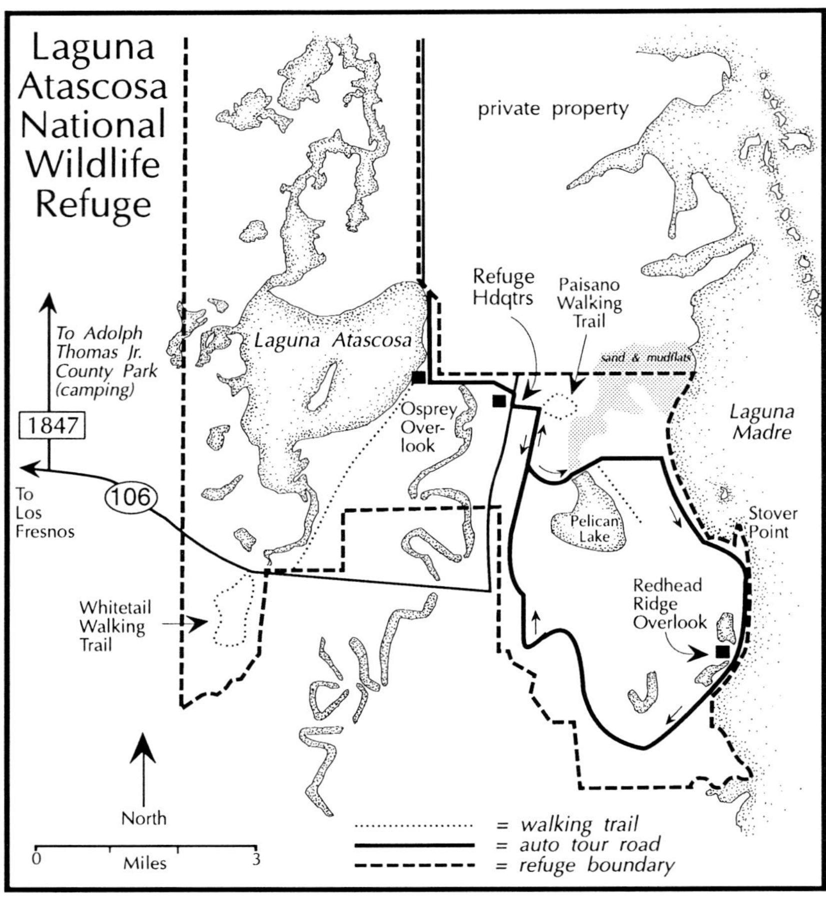

of seeing these birds in winter, or Groove-billed Ani, Yellow-billed Cuckoo, White-winged Dove, Couch's Kingbird, and Painted Bunting in spring and summer. Varied Buntings have nested here, but they are difficult to find. Collared Peccary or Javelina sometimes are seen as they nibble on the Prickly Pear Cactus pads along the roadside.

The parking area for **Paisano Trail** is on your left shortly after the road curves to the south. The short (1.5-mile) paved trail passes through thorny trees and shrubs once typical of South Texas. Huisache, Tepeguaje, Allthorn, Granjeño (Spiny Hackberry), and others provide food and shelter to wildlife in this part of the country where little native cover remains. Plain Chachalacas, doves, sparrows, Verdin, buntings, deer, and even Bobcat are frequently seen along this route. A side trail (5 miles) leads through the Granjeño Research Natural Area, a small wilderness area set aside for biological study.

To continue the tour, go south for a mile to the junction of the one-way loop. Turn left and watch the open prairie and surrounding trees for the Aplomado Falcon. They began to be released at the Refuge in 1985, and may yet establish themselves in the area. Look for other raptors here, too. A mile past the junction you will come to Pelican Lake, a fresh-water impoundment in wet years. In winter, various ducks and pelicans can be found, and in spring and summer, you can see Black-bellied Whistling-Ducks. Least Grebes are uncommon throughout the year, but may be more regular in summer. As you continue check the brush along the road for Curve-billed Thrasher, Cactus Wren, and Black-throated Sparrow. Grassy areas should have Savannah, Vesper, White-crowned, and possibly Le Conte's, Grasshopper, and Field Sparrows in winter, Clay-colored in April. Both Cassin's and Botteri's are permanent residents, but you will probably have to hear them singing to tell them apart.

When the road reaches the **Laguna Madre**, pull out to your left and check the area to the north with a scope carefully. All along the shore you are likely to find Great Blue, Little Blue, and Tricolored Herons, Great, Snowy, and Reddish Egrets, Roseate Spoonbill, Laughing Gull, Forster's, Royal, Sandwich, and Caspian Terns, and Black Skimmer. In winter or during migration there may be Common Loon, Eared Grebe, American White Pelicans in huge numbers, Wood Stork, Double-crested Cormorant, Piping, Semipalmated, and Black-bellied Plovers, Greater and Lesser Yellowlegs, Red Knot, Long-billed and Short-billed Dowitchers, Dunlin, Long-billed Curlew, Marbled Godwit, American Avocet, and Least, Stilt, Semipalmated, and Western Sandpipers. In summer look for Black-necked Stilt, Least Tern, and (less common) Neotropic Cormorant, and American Oystercatcher or rarer Magnificent Frigatebird or Mountain Plover.

Redhead Ridge Overlook is worth the short hike to top of the hill for a view of South Padre Island, the Laguna Madre, and the surrounding ponds. Local hunters recall a time when Redheads literally filled the bay. The ducks were easy targets from this high ridge.

After following the shoreline for some three miles, the road veers away and crosses several other habitats. First there is the *Spartina* marsh, where Clapper Rails and Seaside Sparrows live. In winter there may be King and Virginia Rails, Soras, and Sedge Wrens. The road then enters an arid grassland with scattered patches of mesquite and yucca that bloom in February. White-tailed Hawks and Crested Caracaras have nested here. In summer look for Common and Lesser Nighthawks, Blue Grosbeak, White-winged Dove, Couch's Kingbird, and Painted Bunting; in winter, Vermilion Flycatchers; and Cassin's and Botteri's Sparrows any time of year. The salt-flats are next. Wilson's Plovers nest here, and in migration Lesser Golden-Plovers and Upland and Buff-breasted Sandpipers use the area. The road swings north and crosses open areas where you can again look for hawks, sparrows, and Long-billed Curlews before returning to the beginning of the loop.

The 2-mile **Lakeside Drive** starts just past the Visitor Center. Turn left and follow the road a short distance to where it crosses a resaca (an old river bend, now maintained artificially). You may find Bufflehead, Northern Shoveler, or other ducks in winter, Roseate Spoonbill, egrets, herons, American Avocets, Black-necked Stilt, Least Grebe, and Caspian and Black (in migration) Terns at other times, depending on season and water levels.

Past the resaca, check every bird that looks like a grackle to be sure it isn't a Groove-billed Ani. Eastern Meadowlarks sing from the surrounding fields in winter and Dickcissels in spring. An area on your left was planted with seedlings by volunteers in 1989. The refuge is converting many old fields in this area to native vegetation that will provide additional food and shelter to the birds, Ocelots, and other wildlife that depend on brushland. The road dead-ends at the parking area for **Osprey Overlook** on the east shore of Laguna Atascosa. The lake is filled with ducks and geese during the winter months. Eighty percent of the entire North American population of Redheads winters here. Shorebirds and waders use the shoreline, in case you missed them elsewhere. The surrounding fields to the north or south hold large flocks of wintering Sandhill Cranes and Snow, Canada, Ross's, and Greater White-fronted Geese. You may walk along the service roads behind the barriers. In winter you may be able to find a Sprague's Pipit or a Le Conte's Sparrow. A short walking-trail follows the shoreline to the north. It can be very good for buntings, grosbeaks, and other migrants in spring and for Greater Roadrunners, Groove-billed Anis, and other residents in summer. A side road to the north just before you reach the parking area follows the lake for approximately one mile to a locked gate. You may park here and walk in along the service roads that surround the lake; however, they are not marked, and there is no shade. A short distance from the gate is a pond on private property to the right (please stay on the road side of the fence). Yellow-crowned and Black-crowned Night-Herons perch on the overhanging limbs.

As you leave the refuge, check the entrance road for any of the birds that you may have missed. Harris's Hawks, Crested Caracaras, and vultures will perch in large trees or on the telephone poles.

Nearby camping facilities are available at the north end of the Refuge in Adolph Thomas Jr. County Park on FM 1847 (phone: 512/748-2044) or at Isla Blanca Park on South Padre Island (phone: 512/761-5493) for those wishing to get an early start.

Great Kiskadee
Shawneen Finnegan

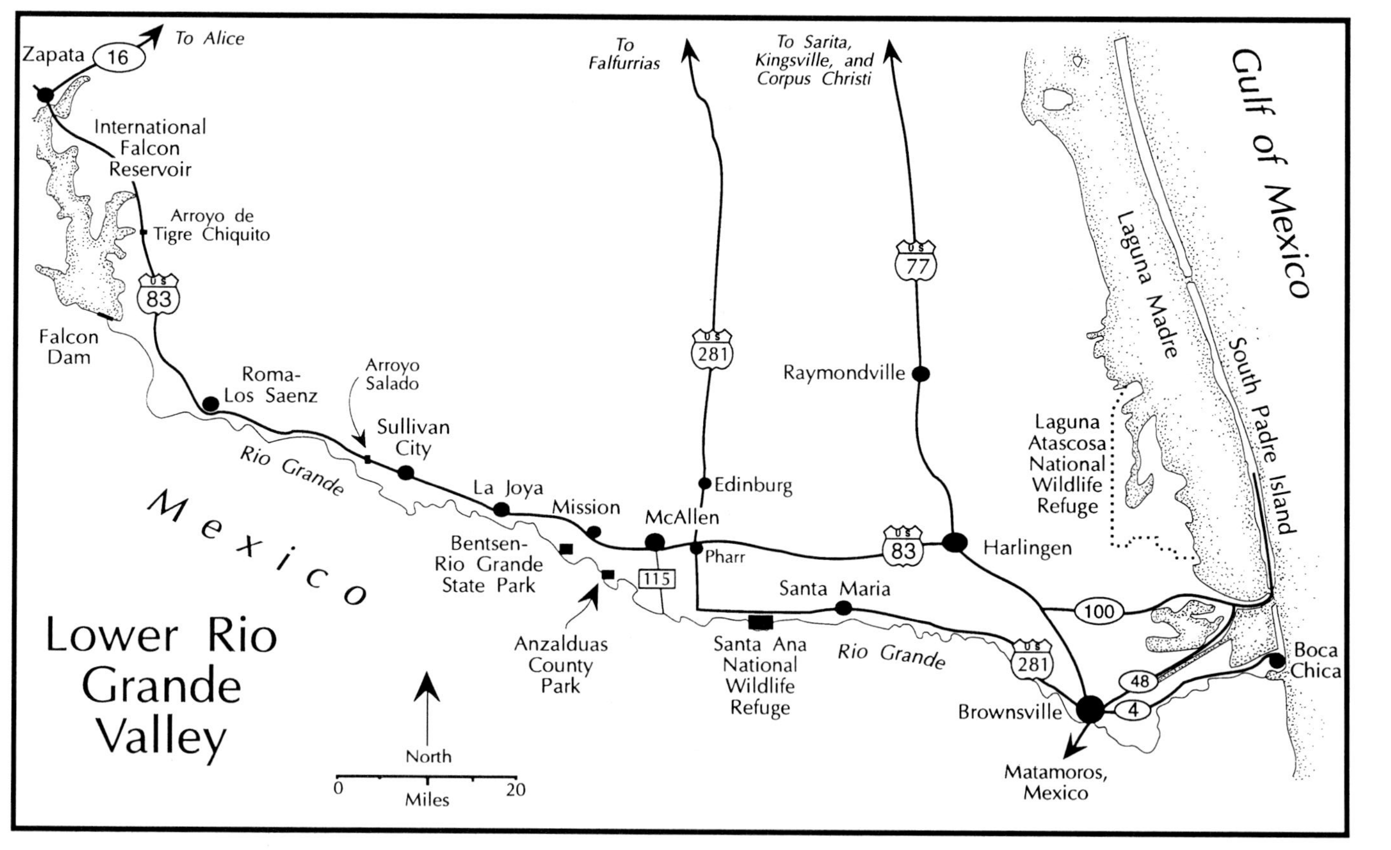
Lower Rio Grande Valley
Zapata
16
To Alice
International Falcon Reservoir
Arroyo de Tigre Chiquito
US 83
Falcon Dam
Roma-Los Saenz
Arroyo Salado
Sullivan City
Rio Grande
La Joya
Mission
McAllen
Mexico
Bentsen-Rio Grande State Park
115
Anzalduas County Park
To Falfurrias
US 281
Edinburg
Pharr
To Sarita, Kingsville, and Corpus Christi
US 77
Raymondville
US 83
Harlingen
Santa Maria
Santa Ana National Wildlife Refuge
Rio Grande
US 281
Brownsville
Matamoros, Mexico
100
48
4
Boca Chica
Laguna Atascosa National Wildlife Refuge
Laguna Madre
South Padre Island
Gulf of Mexico
North
0
20
Miles

Upriver: Brownsville to Falcon Dam

From Brownsville west to Rio Grande City, the fertile flood-plain of the Rio Grande was once covered by dense thickets and subtropical woodlands. Most of these have been replaced by cities, farms, and citrus groves, which are great for cars, vegetables, and grapefruit, but not for native birds. Great-tailed Grackles, House Sparrows, and Brown-headed and Bronzed Cowbirds are abundant on the farms, but the more desirable species are restricted to the remaining patches of natural vegetation. Several of the preserves for native flora and fauna are located along Highway 281, locally following the Military Highway some 50 miles upriver before turning north through Pharr. The Military Highway continues west, zigzagging its way along smaller roads, and ending at Rio Grande City.

Since most of the cities and towns with their congestion of cars and people are located on Highway 83 a few miles north of the Military Highway, this highway is a good route for birding. You will find it easy to stop along the way. (On the Military Highway you will bypass Harlingen, one of the two cities in the Lower Valley with an active airport. The other airport is in McAllen. Harlingen and many of the other towns along Highway 83 abound in motels, restaurants, and gas stations.)

Most of the fields along the Military Highway are planted for winter vegetables, cotton, red milo, or sugar cane. In this mild climate, up to three crops a year can be raised on irrigated land. Farming is a major industry in the Valley.

You will not go far before becoming aware of some tall graceful palms lining the roads. While a few recent wintertime freezes did in many of the palms, a number remain. The very tall, skinny palms are Mexican Fan Palms. Occasionally, you will find shorter, stockier fan palms. These are either California Fan Palms or Texas Sabal Palms. Some yards will have large robust Canary Island Date Palms, which have long fronds with many leaflets. Barn Owls roost in many of the taller palms, and you might see one by driving this road at night. Watch also for Northern Yellow Bats and Brazilian Free-tailed Bats.

To reach the beginning of the Military Highway in Brownsville, go west on Boca Chica Boulevard from International Boulevard (Highway 4). Pass under the freeway (Highway 77/83) (1.5) and cross Highway 77 Business (1.3) (Central Boulevard). Beyond this point Boca Chica Boulevard becomes the Military Highway. Start watching for an irrigation canal (3.6) that crosses the highway. If it has not recently rained, you can turn right onto the dirt road along the west bank. This will take you to the La Palma Reservoir (0.7), which can be good for ducks in winter, shorebirds in migration, and Neotropic Cormorants at any time of year.

Some of the best birding spots are the little ponds along the highway. At any season, and especially after some rain, they may yield Least and Pied-billed Grebes and whistling-ducks. In migration shorebirds may be common. Look for Solitary, Pectoral, White-rumped, Least, Western, Semipalmated, and Stilt Sandpipers, Greater and Lesser Yellowlegs, Long-billed Dowitchers, American Avocet, Black-necked Stilt, and Wilson's Phalarope. In winter there should be ducks, including Green-winged, Blue-winged, and Cinnamon Teals.

The abundance of Least Grebes in the area is very unpredictable. Some years they are fairly common, but normally they are hard to find. In those years when they are scarce everywhere, they can usually be found on the Old Cannon Pond. To reach it continue up the highway, watching on the right for a roadside rest area with a cannon (17.4). Just beyond, a dirt road on the right leads to the pond (1.4). Look for signs of recent travel. This road can be almost impassable in wet weather.

The pond is on the Resaca del Rancho Viejo tract of the Lower Rio Grande Valley National Wildlife Refuge. The tract is not open, so do not leave the road to cross the fence here. Because of the thick vegetation around the pond, you may have to wait a while before the grebes appear, but your time will not be wasted. A number of good things have been turned up here. In addition to the migrating land-birds in the bushes, you may find Neotropic Cormorant, Black-bellied Whistling-Duck, and shorebirds.

Continuing west on Military Highway, you will soon come to Farm Road 2556 (4.3), which is the main crossroad in the little settlement of Santa Maria. Beyond the town, the highway runs close to the levee. Where the road makes a bend, watch on the left for the Cameron/Hidalgo County marker post (0.8). Next to it, a dirt road leads to the top of the levee, from which you can look over the Santa Maria Section of the Lower Rio Grande Valley National Wildlife Refuge (closed to visitors). Shortly after entering Hidalgo County, you will come to a low area (0.4) with ponds on both sides of the road. The ponds in this area are very good for shorebirds, grebes, and in spring for both Fulvous and Black-bellied Whistling-Ducks. These ponds are in an old bend of the Rio Grande.

SANTA ANA NATIONAL WILDLIFE REFUGE

Continuing west, you will come to Farm Road 493 (11.8). Start watching for the flying-goose sign that marks the turnoff to the Santa Ana National Wildlife Refuge (4.7). The visitor center is a short way down on the right. Stop in for maps of the refuge's trail system, a bird checklist, and to take a look at the recent sightings in the log book. The refuge drive is open for car traffic from 9am to 4:30pm daily, from late April to mid-June and again from late August to late November. From late November to mid-January you can use the drive on Tuesdays and Wednesdays. From mid-January to mid-April it is closed to automobile traffic altogether. From mid-June to late August the drive is open every day except Sunday. On days the refuge drive is closed, you must walk or take the tram (fee), which is operated by the Frontera Audubon Society (Weslaco) and runs every 2 hours.

Some birders have been known to utilize their bicycles on the refuge drive when it has been closed to automobiles. The refuge drive is currently open to bicycles *any time of year* from 9am to 4:30pm. (Keep bicycles off the walking trails, park them off the refuge drive, and do not travel the wrong way on the one-way refuge drive.)

These confusing Wildlife Drive openings may change from year to year, so be sure to check at the headquarters for the current schedule. Here, however, is a refuge schedule for other than the drive:

Visitor Center Open: 8am to 4:30pm weekdays; 9am to 4:30pm weekends and most holidays

Visitor Center Closed: Thanksgiving, Christmas, New Year's Day.

Walk-in access to the refuge: dawn to dusk daily.

Over 300 species of birds have been recorded in this unique refuge, but only about half that number occur at any one time. However, you will probably be happy with the ones which you find. Soon after you step from your car, you will realize that this is a birder's paradise.

The refuge, which nestles in bends of the Rio Grande, is covered by a tangle of brush and subtropical trees similar to those found in northeastern Mexico. This native vegetation harbors many unusual plants, mammals, reptiles, birds, and insects. A few of the plants around the headquarters are labeled. The rest of the flora and fauna offers a real challenge in identification.

Some of the best Santa Ana birding is available by short walks from the parking lot and headquarters building. Just past the headquarters Visitor

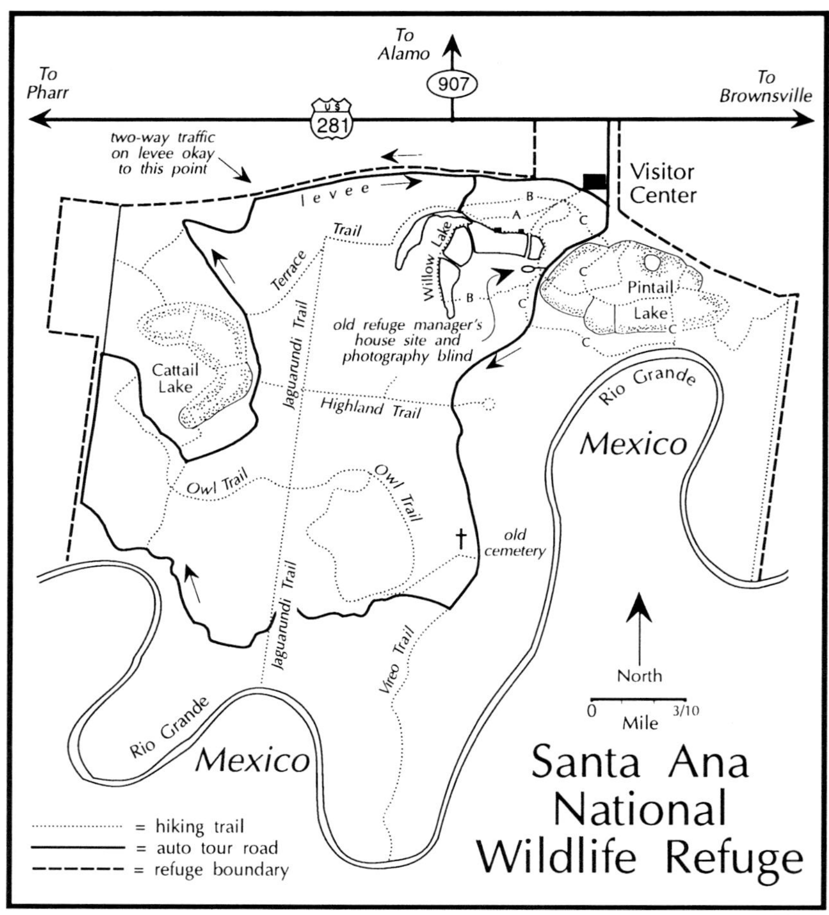

Center entrance is a trail across a bridge and irrigation ditch, past two ponds (good for Least Grebe and Least Bitterns in spring), to a trailhead. Here you can choose which trail to take. If time is short, try *Trail A* first. This leads directly to Willow Lake. Least Grebes, Green and Ringed Kingfishers, Neotropic Cormorant, and other birds are found here. In winter there is a possibility of Anhinga and a sprinkling of ducks, including Cinnamon Teal. In summer the nesting-boxes are filled with Black-bellied Whistling-Ducks, and the cattails may harbor Least Bitterns. Watch the overhanging brush around the lake for flycatchers and warblers. Listen for an Olive Sparrow as it scratches through the leaf litter on the ground. By now you should have spotted a Great Kiskadee and heard its raucous calling.

As you walk left along the lakeshore, you will come to two observation points. You will probably notice a Golden-fronted Woodpecker scolding from the top of a tree at the Couch's Kingbirds and Brown-crested Flycatchers. Then you may see a White-tipped Dove strolling across the clearing. A flash of yellow may announce the arrival of a Green Jay. A burst of orange proclaims the presence of an Altamira or a Hooded Oriole. So much for the first fifteen minutes in the refuge. Now you will have to start working for your lifers.

Each of the two lake observation points will provide excellent views of the water and the shoreline. A short walk past the second observation point, a blind, *Trail A* turns away from the lake and returns to the trailhead, but you will notice an unimproved trail to the right. This connects with *Trails B and C,* past two reedy sections of Willow Lake with undependable water levels. As you approach a small pond on the left, look sharply. You will be approaching the old manager's house site.

The old manager's house has been torn down, together with related buildings, but the old parking lot will probably remain. The red-flowering Shrimp Plants at the site will often draw Buff-bellied Hummingbirds. The area around the old parking lot can be good for several other birds. For several years Groove-billed Anis nested (late April) in a Texas Ebony tree at the east end of the parking area. Even the rare Clay-colored Robin is found here nearly every spring. Long ago, Tropical Parulas nested in the moss-draped Ebony trees or elms in the yard. They still appear in the vicinity from time to time, but most of the recent sightings have been at the rest areas up Highway 77 on the King Ranch and beyond the scope of this book. [See *A Birder's Guide to the Texas Coast*.]

This short route from the Visitor Center parking lot to the old manager's house site will have lead you through a selection of fine birding areas. If time allows, you should attempt walking all of *Trails A and B*.

On days when you can enter into the refuge by car via the Wildlife Drive, you can continue past the Visitor Center, over the levee, and through the third gate, where you will reach the old manager's house site and parking lot on the right.

From this lot take the trail on the left behind to reach the photography blind. The birds are quite visible from this blind, and *if it is not being used by photographers*, you will want to linger there to observe the birds that come to feeders usually kept full during winter months. These feeders will draw Plain Chachalacas, White-tipped Doves, Green Jays, Long-billed Thrashers, Altamira Orioles, Olive Sparrows, and other birds.

Pintail Lake is found directly across the road. Follow *Trail C* in winter and you can find an assortment of ducks and shorebirds about the lake. Look for Green Kingfisher here, too.

After spring and summer rains, frogs and toads may be abundant about the lakes. Most will be Rio Grande Leopard Frogs; however, you may find Great Plains Narrowmouth Toad, Sheep Frog, Giant and Gulf Coast Toads, and Mexican Tree Frog.

The most common turtle in this area is the Red-eared Slider Turtle of mud-bottomed ponds and sluggish streams. It can be identified by a bright red stripe behind the eye, which is easily seen because these large turtles often crawl out on rocks and logs to bask. However, the red stripe fades in older individuals. The Red-eared has a rounded lower jaw, a feature that is easily observed if the turtle is chewing on your finger.

There are two other turtles here. The Yellow Mud Turtle is uncommon in ponds, canals, and streams with mud bottoms, but it may just be missed because it is mainly nocturnal and it does not crawl out of the water to bask. It is a small (5"), dull, unmarked turtle with a strong musky odor. If its head is sticking out of the water, you may note that it has a yellow throat

Trail A to Willow Lake at Santa Ana National Wildlife Refuge — Paul J. Baicich

but no stripes. The large (females 14"), pancakelike Spiny Softshell may be found in refuge lakes and along the Rio Grande.

You may also find the Texas Tortoise, which was once fairly common throughout the dry, brushy areas of South Texas. It has club feet and a yellow square in the center of each large scute.

To explore the refuge you should drive its one-way, 7-mile road at least once. Of course, each trip usually produces something new. The area along the road beyond the fenced-in pump station (0.2) can be good for White-tipped Dove, Green Jay, Long-billed Thrasher, and Olive Sparrow.

There are many places to stop along the road, and nearly all of them are worthwhile. For at least three years a pair of Rose-throated Becards nested in a large tree on the circle at the end of the foot trail which starts directly across the road from the Highland Trail (0.3). The cactus patch behind the Old Spanish Cemetery (0.5) hides a pair of Cactus Wrens and sometimes a Greater Roadrunner. For several years becards tried to nest near the big tree across the road. You may not find the becards, but you will see the remains of what was once the largest Ebony tree in the United States.

Much of the area is covered by jungle-like thickets, which can be hard to bird from the car. To really get a feel for the refuge, try hiking some of the trails, such as the Vireo Trail (0.2).

A very productive, 2-mile hike to view the Rio Grande can be started from the second parking area (0.7) on the left at the Jaguarundi Trail. Go south (left) on this trail for 0.3 mile.

Cattail Lake (2.0) is always worth a look. Most of the birds sneaking in and out of the reeds will be Pied-billed Grebes, American Coots, and Common Moorhens, but the lake can produce Least Grebe, Sora, and in summer Least Bittern and Purple Gallinule. Such uncommon species as Masked Duck and Hook-billed Kite have also been seen here.

Also check the area around the lake. Pauraques can sometimes be flushed out of the shaded thickets on the south corner of the pond, where you may also see a Giant Toad. Greater Roadrunners and Cactus Wrens like the dry area of mesquite and cactus along the Terrace Trail.

One of the hardest to find of the permanent residents is the Northern Beardless-Tyrannulet. With a fancy name like that, one would hardly expect it to be a nondescript little bird, but it is. Even when the bird is stumbled upon, one is never quite sure of what it is. It does not always act like a flycatcher. It has been found in thickets all over the refuge, such as along the Vireo Trail, the Owl Trail, the Highland Trail, and near the house site. You will probably find this bird by chance, but if you set out to find

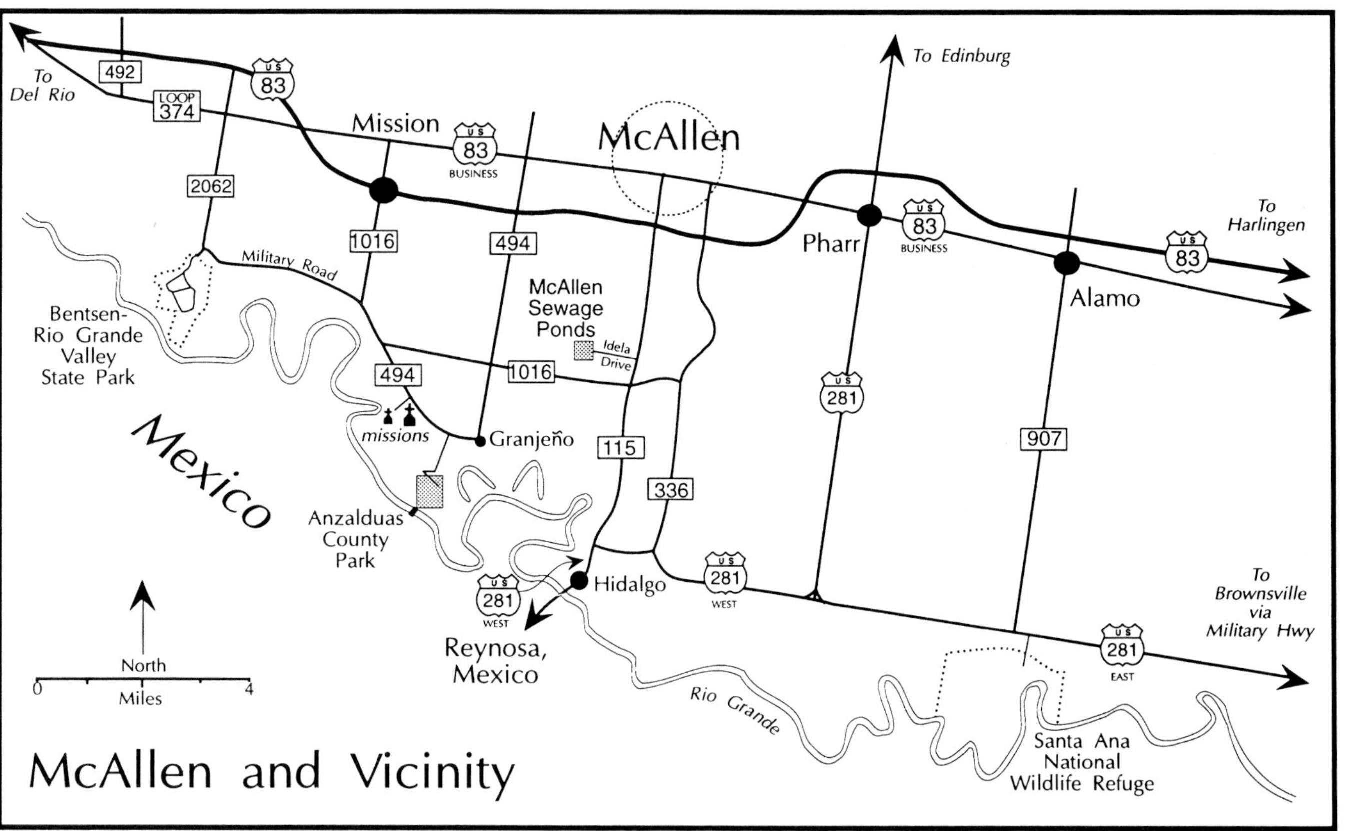

To Del Rio
492
LOOP 374
US 83
2062
Mission
US 83 BUSINESS
McAllen
To Edinburg
Pharr
US 83 BUSINESS
To Harlingen
US 83
Alamo
1016
494
Military Road
Bentsen-Rio Grande Valley State Park
McAllen Sewage Ponds
Idela Drive
494
1016
missions
Granjeño
115
336
US 281
907
Mexico
Anzalduas County Park
Hidalgo
US 281 WEST
US 281 WEST
Reynosa, Mexico
To Brownsville via Military Hwy
US 281 EAST
North
0
4
Miles
Rio Grande
Santa Ana National Wildlife Refuge
McAllen and Vicinity

one, go early. It is easier to locate by song (*ee, ee, ee, ee*) than by sight, and it normally sings early in the morning.

White-tipped Doves will usually walk across the road rather than fly. On the other hand, a Red-billed Pigeon flashes across at tree-top level like a dark falcon. Only occasionally does one perch where you can get a good look, but some satisfying sightings may occur when the bird comes to the ground to drink.

When you reach the levee (1.3), start watching for raptors. A common permanent resident is the Harris's Hawk, but the Black-shouldered Kite is sometimes seen over open areas like Pintail Lake or the fields along the northern and western boundaries. In fall and winter, you may see Sharp-shinned, Cooper's, and Red-tailed Hawks, Northern Harrier, and even Red-shouldered and Gray Hawks, or Common Black-Hawks. During the fall of 1975, many lucky birders saw up to five Hook-billed Kites from this levee. Watch for this raptor, especially during the late winter months, on top of dead-tree snags.

The big show of hawks, however, comes in March and April when the Broad-winged Hawks migrate. They often come by the thousands to rest and roost in the trees. From the levee in the morning or the evening, you can often see huge kettles forming. On March 27, 1976, an estimated 100,000 Broad-winged Hawks passed over the refuge!

Such exciting rarities from Mexico as Crane Hawk and Yellow-faced Grassquit have also appeared at Santa Ana in the winter. And Golden-crowned Warbler and Ruddy Ground-Dove have been found on a few occasions. It is always wise to be particularly alert at Santa Ana—almost anything can show up.

MCALLEN

Continuing west on Highway 281 from the refuge, you will soon cross Farm Road 907 (Alamo Road) (0.5). Where Highway 281 turns north (3.5) toward Pharr, go straight ahead on Highway 281 West toward Hidalgo and Reynosa. Go past Highway 336 (3.2) to the end of the road (1.2) in Hidalgo. Turn right onto Highway 115. (If you turn left, you will go to Reynosa, Mexico.) For the McAllen Sewer Ponds go past Farm Road 1016 (3.0) and turn left at the first signal (1.0) onto Idela Drive. The McAllen Sewer Ponds begin at S. 37th, where you will find water-filled impoundments off the dikes on the left. Drive onto the levee and circle the pond. (Avoid driving the levee for three days after any heavy rains.) Although there are some additional low wet areas, only one pond remains as of this writing. The pond(s) can be quite good at times for ducks, ibises, shorebirds, and Least Grebes, especially in winter and migration. How long the area will be a good birding site is in question, after an expansion of the industrial area to the south, and with the city of McAllen unsure of the sewer pond site's future use.

Many birders use McAllen, the biggest town in Hidalgo county, as a trip headquarters. This city of 80,000 is named after John McAllen, who was born in Scotland in 1826 and arrived in the Valley in the early 1850s. The town itself was not founded until 1909, a few years after the arrival of the Missouri-Pacific Railroad. At that time commerce began to grow around citrus and vegetable crops. Today McAllen has an airport, plenty of motels and restaurants, and is a quick drive from either Santa Ana or Bentsen-Rio Grande Valley State Park.

(To get to Santa Ana National Wildlife Refuge from McAllen, drive east on Highway 83 for about 10 miles to the Route 907 exit in Alamo. Go south on Highway 907 for about 8 miles to where the road ends at Highway 281—the Military Highway—and go left for 0.3 miles to the sign on the right to Santa Ana National Wildlife Refuge. For Bentsen-Rio Grande Valley State Park, start from the intersection of 10th street and Highway 83, go west on Highway 83, and exit in 7.8 miles to Loop 374. Continue west on Loop 374 following the signs for about 1.5 miles. Turn left—south—onto FM 2062 [Bentsen-Palm Drive] and for 2.7 miles to the park entrance.)

Like Brownsville, McAllen is another place for parrot roost sites. Practically every winter there are Red-crowned Parrots and Green Parakeets roosting somewhere in McAllen. Some recent sites have been on the east end of Dallas Avenue (in the vicinity of Mockingbird Street) and on the north side of town on Wisteria Avenue just west of 10th Street. Some birders have driven up and down N. Main Street, north from LaVista, with their car windows open for one hour after sunrise or one hour before sunset to listen for flocks of roosting parrots. However, sites do change from year to year, and it is usually best to check with the Lower Rio Grande Rare Bird Alert for the current locations.

ANZALDUAS COUNTY PARK

From the McAllen Sewage Ponds return to Farm Road 1016 and continue west. At Farm Road 494 (2.6) turn left toward Granjeño. As the road turns right (1.4), continue past the Granjeño cemetery and turn left at the sign (1.6) for Anzalduas County Park. (Fee on Saturdays and Sundays.)

(Anzalduas County Park can also be approached from Highway 83 by exiting at Farm Road 494 and going south to where the signs will direct you to the park.)

The picnic grounds can be crowded on weekends, but otherwise are good for Common Ground-Dove and Inca Dove, Golden-fronted

Woodpecker, Couch's Kingbird, Brown-crested Flycatcher, Tufted (Black-crested) Titmouse, Altamira and Hooded Orioles, Summer Tanager, and migrants.

At the stop sign (0.2) turn left and go over the levee to the area below the dam (0.7). In this section of the park some lucky birders have found Northern Beardless-Tyrannulet. The clear water below the dam at the end of the road may be attractive to any of the three kingfishers, Belted, Green, or Ringed. The wooded area along the fence is the Gabrielson Tract of the Lower Rio Grande Valley National Wildlife Refuge. It is not currently open to the public.

If you go back to the park entrance and walk left (west) down the levee, you will soon come to another section of the refuge, the Madero tract. This area is not open either, but you can scan it from the road. Return to Farm Road 494 and turn left. As soon as you pass the big Oblate Monastery (0.8), go over the tracks and turn left onto the first road over the levee (0.2) to the tiny La Lomita Mission, founded in 1865 and rebuilt in 1899. It abuts the west end of the refuge tract and has a pleasant little picnic ground.

BENTSEN-RIO GRANDE VALLEY STATE PARK

Continue on Farm Roads 494 and 1016 (also signed as Military Road) west to the curve (0.8). Instead of going right with 1016, take the unmarked road straight ahead as you cross the railroad tracks. You might check the little pond (1.7) on the left at the stop-sign for Least Grebes. Continue on to the next stop sign (1.6) at Farm Road 2062 (Bentsen-Palm Drive). Turn left and drive directly into Bentsen-Rio Grande Valley State Park (0.2), the best birding spot in the Lower Valley. ($3.00 per day, plus fee for camping and hot showers.) (PO Box 988, Mission, TX 78572; phone: 512/585-1107) Given its long, hyphenated name, most birders just call the park "Bentsen."

Before entering the park you can turn right and drive along the levee if you wish. This is a fine area from which to watch hawks, and the first half-mile has sometimes been a good spot to look for Hook-billed Kites and Red-billed Pigeons.

The 587-acre park itself is one of the finest in the state park system. It is on land donated in 1944 to the state by Senator Lloyd Bentsen's parents. Much of the original subtropical vegetation has been preserved, and it abounds with birds. This is a delightful spot to camp, although it is very crowded on weekends, particularly in winter. Recently, it has also been packed with visitors and campers during Eastertime.

The birds here are about the same as those at Santa Ana Refuge (over 275 species have been found here), but you can always seem to find a few more than at Santa Ana. Around the picnic area and the campground, the

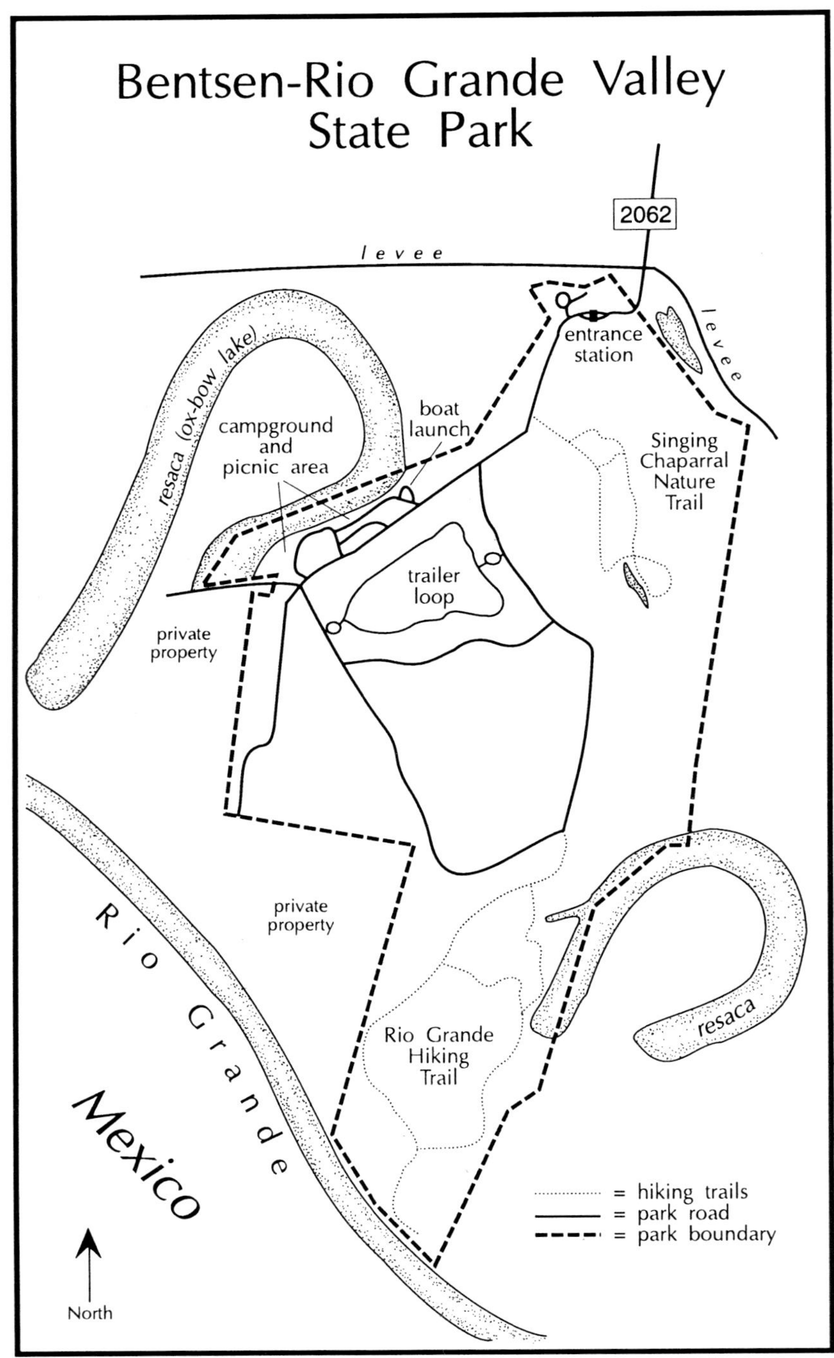
Bentsen-Rio Grande Valley
State Park
2062
levee
levee
entrance
station
resaca (ox-bow lake)
boat
launch
campground
and
picnic area
Singing
Chaparral
Nature
Trail
trailer
loop
private
property
private
property
Rio Grande
Mexico
resaca
Rio Grande
Hiking
Trail
= hiking trails
= park road
= park boundary
North

birds are quite tame. The inner road loop consists of trailer sites and picnic tables where many "winter Texans" will feed the birds. There you can get close looks at Plain Chachalaca, White-tipped Dove, Golden-fronted and Ladder-backed Woodpeckers, Green Jay, Altamira Oriole, and Tufted (Black-crested) Titmouse. The shyer birds such as Harris's Hawk, Red-billed Pigeon, Groove-billed Ani, Brown-crested and Ash-throated Flycatchers, and Long-billed Thrashers can often be found on the Singing Chaparral Nature Trail or along the Rio Grande Hiking Trail to the river. A few ducks and shorebirds can be found on the resacas at each end of the park, but these lakes are privately owned and hunted. Along the river you should see Great Kiskadee and one or more of the three kingfishers.

Another chief attraction here is the night birds. Pauraque, Common Nighthawk, Eastern Screech-Owl, and Great Horned, Barn, and Elf Owls can be found. During migration, you might find Chuck-will's-widow, Whip-poor-will, Common Poorwill, and Lesser Nighthawk. Ferruginous Pygmy-Owl has been recorded here, but do not expect to see it.

For years a pair of Elf Owls nested in a telephone pole across the road from the picnic area. Today try the trailer loop for the Elf Owls. They come out as soon as it starts to get dark, and return to their roost holes at dawn.

Pauraques come out to sit on the roadways as soon as darkness falls. The glow of their bright orange eyeshine is easy to pick out if you drive the back roads slowly. On very dark nights they may quit feeding after a very short time, but they start again just before dawn, a good time to see them.

Owls may frequent the roadways, too, but they stick to the trees. The Eastern Screech-Owl often sits around the lights of the restrooms to catch bugs. The Great Horned likes the open areas along the river or at the edge of the farmlands.

The park continues to be the best spot in the United States for finding Hook-billed Kites, though they may favor one or another location in the park from year to year. There may be Clay-colored Robins in the park in winter, often around the trailer loop. And many other rarities have appeared within the park—Roadside Hawk, Crimson-collared Grosbeak, Masked Tityra, Ruddy Ground-Dove, and Blue Bunting, to name a few tantalizing species.

Like the vegetation, many of the insects are subtropical varieties. Bug-watchers will have a field day. Be sure to look inside the toll booth at the excellent display of butterflies, which were collected by W. W. McGuire and Mike Richard.

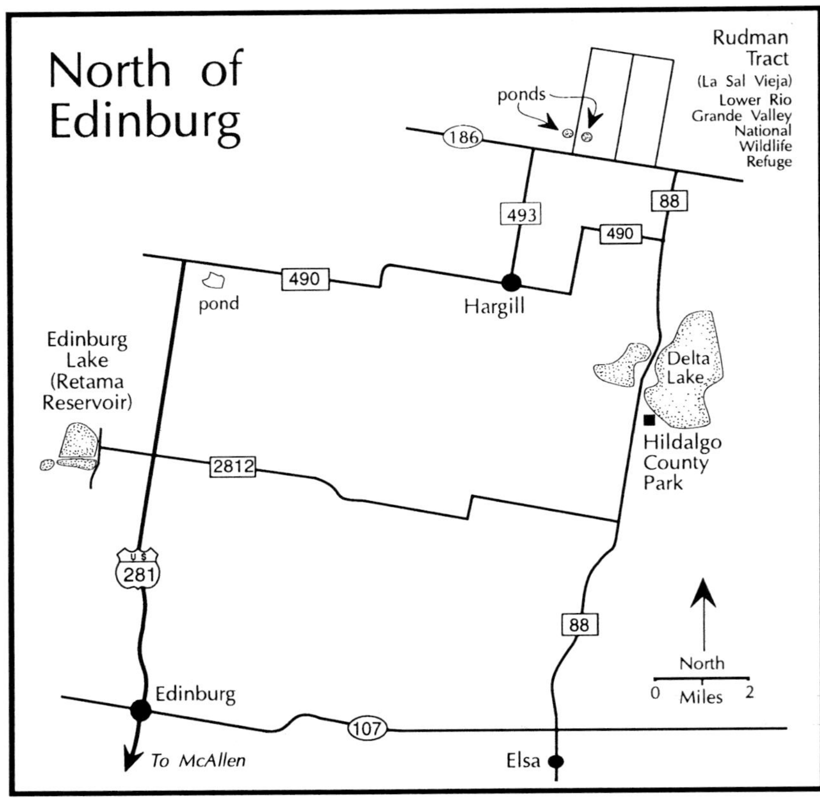

EDINBURG

For those with extra time to spend, a trip to the farmlands north and east of Edinburg may produce a list of different birds. In winter there may be many ducks, geese, and Sandhill Cranes.

From Highway 107 in Edinburg, go north on Highway 281. Opposite Farm Road 2812 (6.3) you can get to Edinburg Lake (Retama Reservoir) by turning left on a road which soon (0.3) turns to gravel and leads to a "T" (1.0). Turn left and go up the bank on the right (0.3). This lake is at its best in winter, when you may find ducks and shorebirds. Despite the signs, birders can walk the dikes during daylight hours. Alternately, you can continue on the road as it swings right to a parking lot at the road's end (0.2). From here you can walk up onto the dike and view the lake.

A Northern Jacana was found along the road to the right at the "T" (north) from mid-November to late December 1981. The cattail-lined slough here is spring-fed. Masked Ducks have been found here occasionally. Check these areas for Green Kingfishers also.

Continuing up Highway 281, at Farm Road 490 (4.3) turn right toward Hargill. The patches of mesquite can offer Vermilion and Ash-throated Flycatchers, Curve-billed Thrasher, Pyrrhuloxia, and, in summer, Painted Bunting. A few little ponds in this area are good for shorebirds and have even produced Masked Duck.

Follow Farm Road 490 as it zigzags across the area, watching for ponds. At Hargill (8.0) turn left onto FM 493 until it reaches Highway 186. Turn right here until you see a dirt road on the left (1.0) where you turn. Bird the pasture on the left to the small pond (0.5); another pond is just across the road. Both are very good for ducks and Vermilion Flycatcher in winter; Crested Caracara frequent the fields nearby. Continue a total of three miles; turn right and continue a mile. You are now birding the Rudman Tract of the Lower Rio Grande Valley National Wildlife Refuge. There are three country roads here, each three miles long and a mile apart, with a county road along the north, and Highway 186 along the south. The Rudman Tract is excellent for hawks and winter sparrows of all kinds. Among raptors, look for White-tailed Hawk, Harris's Hawk, and Crested Caracara. The easternmost road in this complex is just a half mile west of Highway 88. Turn right at Highway 88, and proceed to Delta Lake (4.5). The lake can be good for ducks and shorebirds. Continuing 0.4 mile turn left into Hidalgo County Park, open dawn to dusk, for more ducks and migrant passerines. An Elegant Trogon was observed here for a week in January 1990.

At Farm Road 2812 (3.7) turn right (west) and check more fields and ponds. At Highway 281 (11.5) turn left to return to Edinburg (6.0).

Crested Caracara
Charles H. Gambill

LA JOYA

Return to Highway 83 and continue west into the drier parts of South Texas. By the time you reach La Joya (a town which is 11 miles from Mission, and a well-known "speed-trap"), you will have left much of the subtropical vegetation behind and started to enter the arid, hilly brushlands or chaparral country, which covers much of the coastal plains below the Edwards Plateau. For over 200 miles to the north and west, you will encounter a land that is poor, alkaline, and marginal in productivity. This was formerly a grassland. Previously overgrazed, the area has more recently been converted to birdless "improved" pastures and irrigated fields.

For those people who are not going farther west than the McAllen/Mission area, it is possible to see some of the desert birds fairly close at hand. Take Highway 83 to La Joya. As you leave town, the road curves to the left and goes down a slight grade. In the middle of the curve, FM 2221 goes north. This road turns right after 6 miles. Continue straight ahead for about two miles while watching intermittently on your left in the thickets of mesquite, acacia, and cactus where many desert birds such as Black-throated Sparrow, Lark Bunting, dozens of Pyrrhuloxias, and an occasional Black-tailed Gnatcatcher can be seen, as well as Scaled Quail, Verdin, and Cactus Wren. Birding here is probably best in early morning. In warm seasons rattlesnakes may be encountered if you decide to wander into the brush.

Farther west on Highway 83 is the small town of Sullivan City. The four-lane road currently ends at the west edge of town. Some 3.4 miles beyond the beginning of the two-lane road (or 9.6 miles from the FM 2221 turnoff), watch for a roadside sign for a wash called Arroyo Salado. Cave Swallows nest under the culvert here. They can be seen in the area at almost any time of year. (A severe winter freeze may push the swallows out, however.)

Many of the cities along the highway west of Mission look as if they had seen better days, and indeed some have—Rio Grande City and Roma-Los Saenz were once busy steamboat ports. You will find only a few motels available for use as your upriver birding headquarters in Rio Grande City.

As you continue west into Starr County, you will notice an increase in the number of ravens and hawks. American Crows do not occur in this area, so any crow-sized bird should be a Chihuahuan Raven—although you may have to look at a lot of them before the wind ruffles their neck feathers enough to expose the white below. Harris's Hawk is the common buteo for most of the year, but you may see a Red-tailed. The latter is far more abundant in winter, when Rough-legged and Ferruginous are possible, too. During the spring and fall, you may expect anything. This area is on the main migration route for Broad-winged and Swainson's Hawks and Mississippi Kites.

Broad-winged Hawks roost in trees or thickets, but Swainson's Hawks roost on the ground. They prefer newly-plowed fields before the lumps have been broken by the disc. If you arrive in the area in the morning before the thermals rise, you may find thousands of Swainson's Hawks sitting around on the fields.

Belted, Ringed, and Green Kingfishers have been found at various places along the river. The key to their abundance is clear water for fishing. Because of erosion and pollution, most of the water in the Rio Grande is cloudy. About the only areas where clear water can be found are below the dams, which slow the water and allow suspended particles to settle. One of the clearest places is the 15-mile stretch below Falcon Dam, and kingfishers are common here.

There are several places where you can gain access to the river below the dam. One is just beyond Roma-Los Saenz (46 miles west of Mission). Go west on Highway 83 and turn left onto Farm Road 650 (1.0 west of town) toward Frontón. The Roma-Los Saenz city dump (2.5) on the right attracts Chihuahuan Ravens, and the fields are good for Sage (winter) and Curve-billed Thrashers and winter sparrows. Frontón is itself 2.5 miles farther down the road. As you enter the town, keep left at the "Y", go 1 block, and turn left onto a road a half-mile to the river. There is not much birding in this area, but you may find something. Altamira and Audubon's Orioles are resident. If you're very lucky you may see a Muscovy Duck on the river. Here the Rio Grande follows a much more southerly direction on its way from Del Rio.

SANTA MARGARITA RANCH

Until recently, the hottest birding spot on the river was the Santa Margarita Ranch. It can be reached by going west on Highway 83 from the Frontón Road (FM 650) and watching on the right for a sign about an approaching roadside rest area. Just beyond the sign the highway curves right, but you should bear left with the old highway (5.7). After crossing a little bridge (where you may want to pause to look over the swallows), turn left onto an unmarked dirt road (0.7). Follow this as it bends right and tops a hill overlooking the ranch buildings on the left. Turn left at the entrance road (1.1) and proceed to the first or second house on the left. (After heavy rains, the road to the ranch house is soft and slick. Please park along the main road and walk in, but do not block the road.)

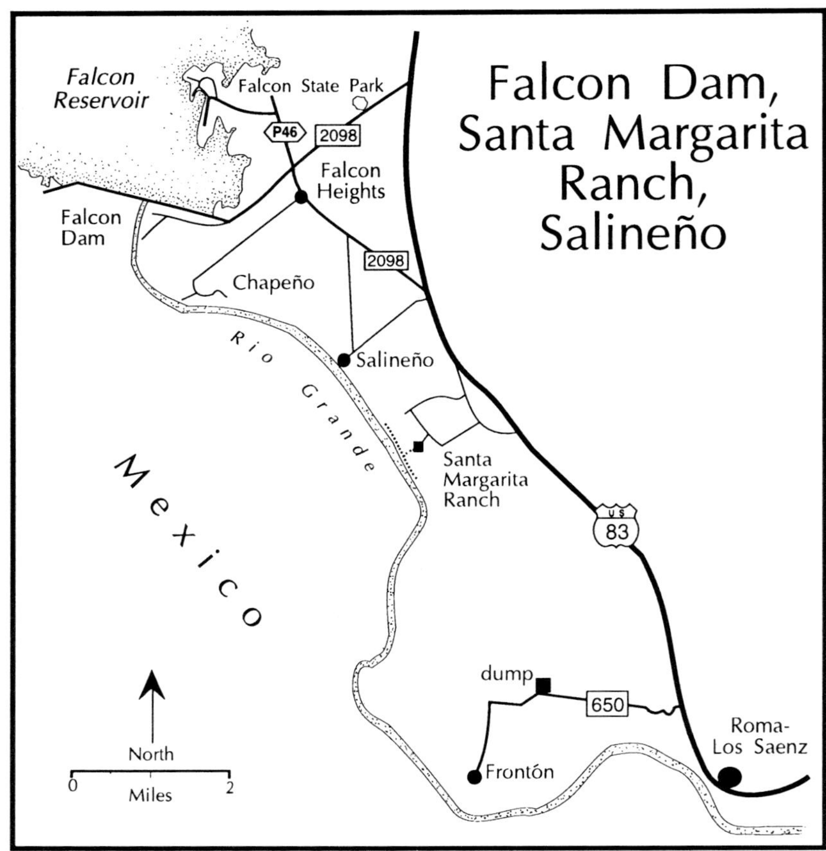

Because of the dogs stay in your car and beep your horn. Someone will come out. In wet weather park just beyond the houses at the top of the hill. Do not try to drive down to the river. You will never make it back up the hill.

The ranch was deeded to the Gonzalez family in an old Spanish Land Grant. It is not public property. A charge ($1.00 per person) is made for the privilege of birding here, and it is a dollar well spent. The residents, however, want to make sure that they will not be liable for any injury or accident on the property, and that visitors understand that they bird at their own risk.

In June of 1974 a flock of Brown Jays, (and later a nest), was discovered on the ranch. This brought a rush of birders and set in motion the "Patagonia Picnic Table Effect." (This is the phenomenon, named after the famous roadside rest area in Arizona, wherein the news of one good bird brings in many observers. They in turn discover more rarities, which in turn attract more observers, ad infinitum.) A few of the rarities found here have been Zone-tailed Hawk and Common Black-Hawk, Sulphur-bellied Flycatcher, Clay-colored and Rufous-backed Robins, and Golden-crowned Warbler.

If you are not one of those blasé listers who are interested only in the unusual, you will find the Santa Margarita Ranch good for such mundane species as Muscovy Duck, Plain Chachalaca, Red-billed Pigeon, White-winged and White-tipped Doves, Greater Roadrunner, Groove-billed Ani, Pauraque, Ringed and Green Kingfishers (best with low water), Golden-fronted and Ladder-backed Woodpeckers, Couch's Kingbird, Great Kiskadee, Brown-crested and Ash-throated Flycatchers, Northern Beardless-Tyrannulet (summer; rare), Green Jay, Cactus Wren, Long-billed and Curve-billed Thrashers, Audubon's and Altamira Orioles, Pyrrhuloxia, Blue Grosbeak, Painted Bunting, and Olive Sparrow.

Normally, the easiest way to find Ringed and Green Kingfishers and Brown Jay is to walk straight down the half-mile trail from the parking area to the river and watch for them to fly across the water. Be sure that they are on the American side before you count them on your ABA list. However, the jays may be feeding in the mesquite thickets either up or down the river. Since these large birds are rather noisy, you can usually locate them without much difficulty if they are around, but they are shy and hard to see.

You may find Green Kingfisher out in the open near the middle of the river, but it is more likely to be hidden among the willows along the shore.

Red-billed Pigeon
Charles H. Gambill

The way to find this secretive little bird is to walk quietly along the trail downriver and check all of the branches overhanging the water. This small kingfisher needs shallow water for fishing and prefers the isolated pools that are left when the river is low. The depth of the river fluctuates greatly depending upon the daily release of water from the dam; however, the lowest water usually occurs early in the morning.

If you do not find the kingfishers at the ranch, try some of the other places farther upriver such as Salineño (Sah-le-NAYN-yo), Chapeño (Chah-PAYN-yo), or below Falcon Dam. As you leave the ranch, turn left (west) onto the graveled road. Follow it around until it returns to the old highway (1.6). Here you can turn left to reach Highway 83 (0.4). Along the way check the arid brushlands for Ash-throated and Vermilion Flycatchers, Cactus and Rock Wrens, Pyrrhuloxia, and Cassin's and Black-throated Sparrows.

SALINEÑO

Go west on Highway 83 until you can turn left (1.2) toward Salineño (1.7). One thing that you are sure to notice is the cemetery. The Mexican custom of placing brightly-colored wreaths on the headstones makes this a lively-looking graveyard. As the road forks, bear right and watch for three speed-bumps before the town square; they can be traumatic! Continue past the town square and straight through to the river. There is not much

Altimira Oriole
Shawneen Finnegan

area for birding, but when the river is low, or normal, all three kingfishers (Belted, Ringed, and Green) are often to be found. Muscovy Ducks have become more plentiful in recent years and sometimes are easily seen as they fly back and forth across the river.

About 60 yards back from the river is a fenced-in area of mobile homes with a long rolling gate, the entrance to the area where several "Winter Texans" deploy many bird feeders. Birders are welcome inside the Salineño Birder Colony to observe the many birds which come to the varied feeders. The residents welcome the opportunity of helping visiting birders look for specialties, and are happy to give out information about the birds and other birding areas in the vicinity. Most of the residents are here from November to April.

For visiting groups of eight or more birders, it is necessary to call in advance. Phone: 512/848-5753 or 848-5451. This will help assure that someone is prepared to host your group.

Many birds are attracted to the numerous feeders and plants around the colony, such as Inca and White-tipped Doves, Black-chinned Hummingbird, Great Kiskadee, Golden-fronted and Ladder-backed Woodpeckers, Green and Brown Jays, Bewick's Wren, Long-billed and Curve-billed Thrashers, Tufted (Black-crested) Titmouse, Orange-crowned and Yellow-rumped Warblers, Olive and Lincoln's Sparrows, Altamira and Audubon's Orioles, Lesser and American Goldfinches, and others. Studying Brown Jays up close at the feeders is a particular treat.

At the Water Treatment Pond next to the dirt road look for Sora, Common Moorhen, Green Kingfisher, and warblers.

As you leave the trailer area, you may want to try the Salineño dump road. Turn left at the first opportunity (0.2). The road is hard-topped for 0.4 mile but turns into dirt thereafter. This road (which can be very slick and not passable after a rain) goes by the Salineño dump and continues on to FM 2098. Here you can find Red-tailed and Harris's Hawks, Scaled Quail, Golden-fronted and Ladder-backed Woodpeckers, Chihuahuan Raven, Verdin, Cactus Wren, Long-billed and Curve-billed Thrashers, Pyrrhuloxia, Olive Sparrow, and other interesting birds.

CHAPEÑO

To reach the former settlement of Chapeño go a quarter-mile beyond the Salineño Road on Highway 83 and turn left onto Farm Road 2098, which leads to Falcon Dam. As you enter the town of Falcon Heights, watch on the left for a graveled road (2.8) opposite the Catholic Church. (If you took the Salineño dump road detour through to 2098, that intersection would leave you about 1.5 miles from the turnoff by the church.) Turn left onto the graveled road and go southwest until the road bends left (2.5 miles). As you drive watch for Verdin, Black-throated Sparrow, and Pyrrhuloxia. You will notice several small dirt roads going off to the right. The third dirt road (0.3) leads to a clearing on the water.

All three kingfishers can be found along this broad sweep of the river, although the Belted and Green are normally here only in fall and winter. The Ringed has nested in the banks of the gullies that are back from the river, and Barn Owls can often be found in the old holes. Look for Audubon's Orioles here, too. Muscovy Ducks may be seen perching in trees overhanging the water, swimming in the river, or flying across the water.

At the western edge of Falcon Heights, there is a major intersection (0.5). From this point, Farm Road 2098 goes northeast for 2.5 miles to rejoin Highway 83. Drive east on this road and you will find a lake on the north side (1.7) which in winter may have Greater White-fronted Geese, Hooded Merganser, and Ruddy Duck. Park Road 46 goes north 1.0 miles into Falcon State Park (formerly called Falcon State Recreation Area), and Spur Road 2098 goes west for 2.0 miles to the dam. On both sides of this road is Starr County Park (limited facilities on the right—north—side). It is good for Cactus Wren, Curve-billed Thrasher, Northern Mockingbird, Pyrrhuloxia, and wintering sparrows.

FALCON STATE PARK

Falcon State Park (573 acres) does not have much vegetation, but it does have a good collection of birds and reptiles. If you are camping, this is a good spot from which to work ($3.00 per day plus a fee for camping, hot showers, hook-ups, screened shelters.)

In the thorny brushlands along the road into the park and around the campgrounds, you should see Harris's Hawk, Common Ground-Dove, Greater Roadrunner, Great Horned Owl, Golden-fronted and Ladder-backed Woodpeckers, Bewick's and Cactus Wrens, Northern Mockingbird, Curve-billed Thrasher, Brown-headed and Bronzed Cowbirds, Pyrrhuloxia, Northern Cardinal, and Lark and Cassin's Sparrows. In summer you may see Ash-throated Flycatcher, Blue Grosbeak, Painted Bunting, and Dickcissel. In winter look for American Kestrel, Say's Phoebe, Sage Thrasher, Eastern Bluebird (Western and Mountain are possible), Loggerhead Shrike, Brewer's Blackbird, Lesser Goldfinch, Lark Bunting, and Savannah, Grasshopper, Vesper, Clay-colored, Field, and White-crowned Sparrows.

Hooded Oriole can usually be found in summer around the office. One year it nested in the light-standard right next to the bulb. Altamira and

Hooded Orioles are found occasionally in the camping areas if someone has put out sugar-water feeders.

The best area for feeders is in the trailer section. Scaled Quail, Northern Bobwhite, Greater Roadrunner, and sparrows are often common about the trailers, particularly in winter. Check down the hill for Black-throated Sparrow. You may find Verdin and Bell's Vireo in the taller patch of mesquite along the bottom of the wash.

As a rule the lakeshore is not too productive because of the numerous boats and fishermen, but you may see a few coots, ducks, and American White Pelicans. Occasionally, there are large flocks of cormorants, mostly Double-crested in winter with a few Neotropical in summer. There is one little sheltered bay full of dead snags that can be good for Green Kingfisher, Spotted Sandpiper, and American Pipit. To reach it go to the far end of the loop in the area of screened shelters. Here, you will find a path leading to the beach, where you should turn left and follow the shore until you come to the bay.

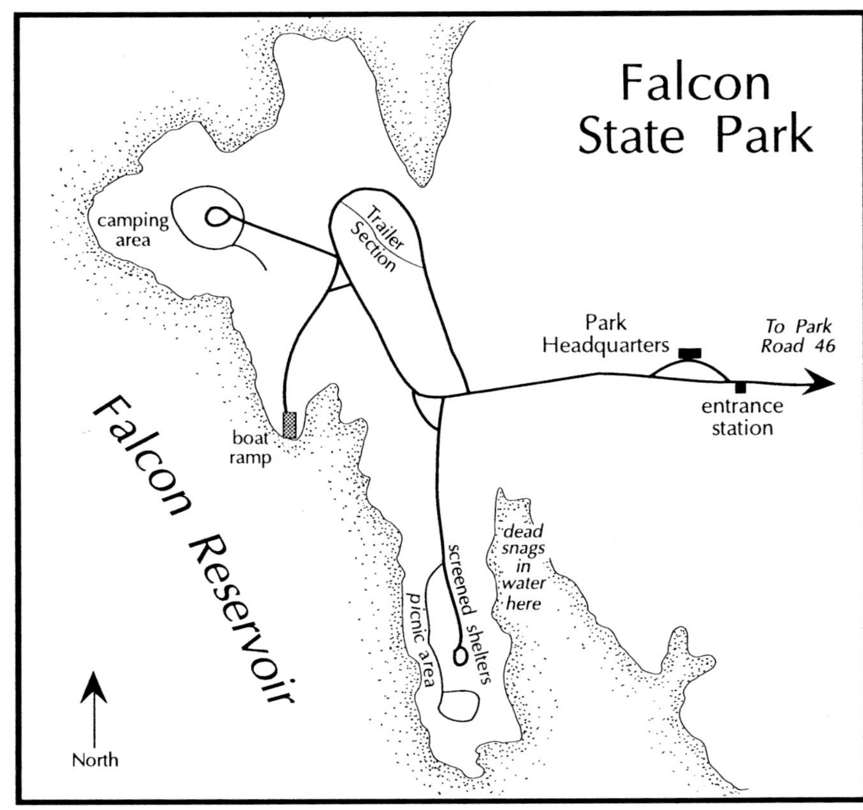

Since the lake has been established, the number of frogs and toads has increased considerably. They may be abundant after heavy rains in the spring and summer. The Rio Grande Leopard Frog and Gulf Coast Toad are usually the most common, but you may find others such as Blanchard's Cricket Frog, Mexican Burrowing Toad, and Sheep Frog.

With the abundance of food, snakes have increased, also. By driving the back roads at night, you may find Checkered Garter Snake, Western Ribbon Snake, Mexican Hognose Snake, Western Coachwhip, Schott's Whipsnake, Western Rough Green Snake, Texas Indigo Snake, Texas Patchnose Snake, Great Plains Rat Snake, Texas Glossy Snake, Bull Snake, Desert Kingsnake, Texas Longnose Snake, South Texas Ground Snake, Western Hooknose Snake, Texas Night Snake, Northern Cat-eyed Snake, Flathead Snake, Texas Blackhead Snake, Massasauga, and Western Diamondback Rattlesnake. However, on most nights you will not be lucky enough to find a single snake.

Falcon Dam spillway from the overlook parking lot — Paul J. Baicich

FALCON DAM

From a view-point near the middle of the dam, you can scan the lake for ducks, cormorants, gulls, and terns. However, you must pass through customs on the way back, and that can be a real inconvenience if your car is packed with gear. It's easiest if you just ask if you can park at customs and walk out on the dam road.

The area below the dam is much better. To reach it, go west on Spur Road 2098 for 1.0 mile and veer left onto a small, paved road. (This road is reached well before you come abreast of the customs-station.) Drive on to the spillway parking area (1.8). (A new gate near customs, however, is locked from 6pm to 6am, and all day on holidays.) From the top of the wall you can scan the concrete floor below. When there is a trickle of water, shorebirds may be common, particularly during migration. Most will be Least Sandpipers, but this is a good spot for Baird's. With luck, you may find Green and Ringed Kingfishers, and, in summer, Red-billed Pigeon. A number of dabbling ducks winter in the river below the spillway. And, in summer, Cliff Swallows will nest on the dam face.

Park at the end of the spillway and walk past the gate on the dirt road leading downriver. In about three-quarters of a mile you will reach the old "hobo" camp and clothesline pole in a grove of Ebony trees. (Alternately, you may choose to follow a trail of sorts, which starts just beyond the pile of big rocks and follows the edge of the river bank.) The grove attracts about the same birds as are to be found at the Santa Margarita Ranch or Salineño, but some lucky people have seen such things as Gray and Zone-tailed Hawks, Ferruginous Pygmy-Owl, Elegant Trogon, Varied Bunting, and White-collared Seedeater.

At the west end of the abandoned campsite, by the old clothesline pole, there is an access to the river. This is an excellent spot from which to watch for Osprey, Red-billed Pigeon, and Ringed Kingfisher as they fly up and down the river. A Green Kingfisher can often be found by wading upstream a short way when the water is low. Of course, you may just want to sit here and watch the river go by.

The Green Kingfisher perches very close to the water on a rock or low overhanging limb. It flies so low and sits so still that most birders, expecting behavior like that of the flamboyant Belted Kingfisher, miss it. Usually, it is heard before it is seen. Its *click-click-click* call can be easily imitated by knocking stones together quickly. Sometimes it will answer!

A Ringed Kingfisher perches up high like a Belted. It flies higher and is even noisier. In the early morning, if there is one around, you will probably not miss it.

All three kingfishers are more active when the water is low, exposing the rocks and concentrating the fish. The river is normally low in the morning before water is released from the dam. By noon the water is often too high for the birds to feed.

You may explore the area further by one of two routes which wind up at the same place, an old Girl Scout campground farther downriver. If you take the road to the left, the distance is approximately three-quarters of a mile to where it meets the river. A "trail" through the woods, paralleling the river, is shorter by a quarter-mile and may yield Brown Jays, Audubon's Oriole, or Ferruginous Pygmy-Owl.

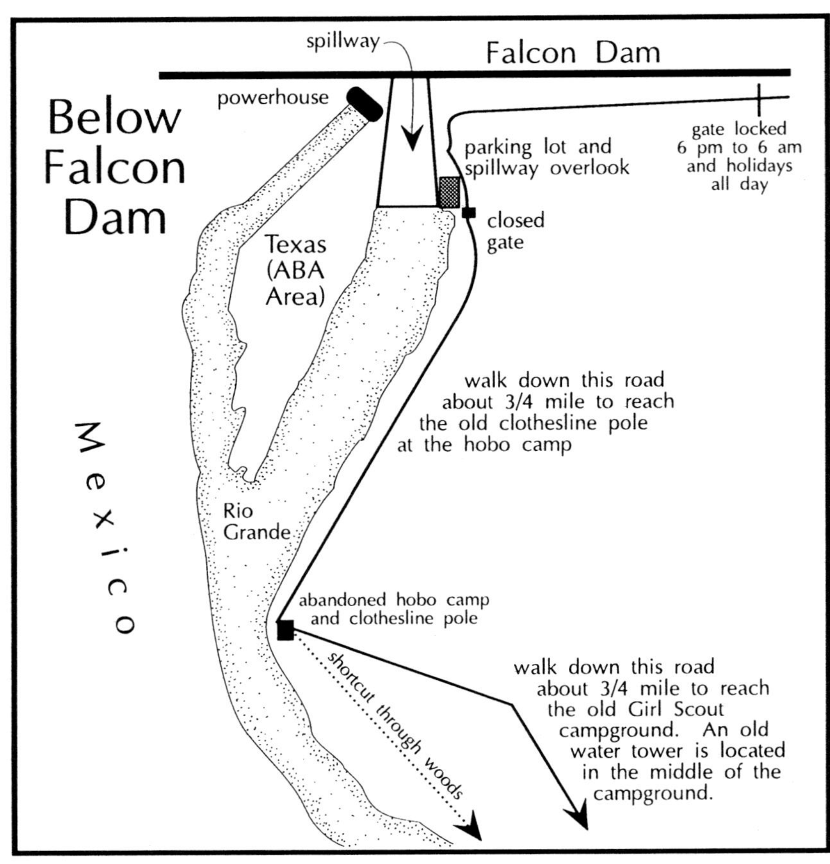

It may be advisable not to bird remote areas around here alone because of the proximity of known routes used by drug-runners in the vicinity of Falcon Dam and other parts of Starr County.

Rio Grande just below Falcon Dam — Paul J. Baicich

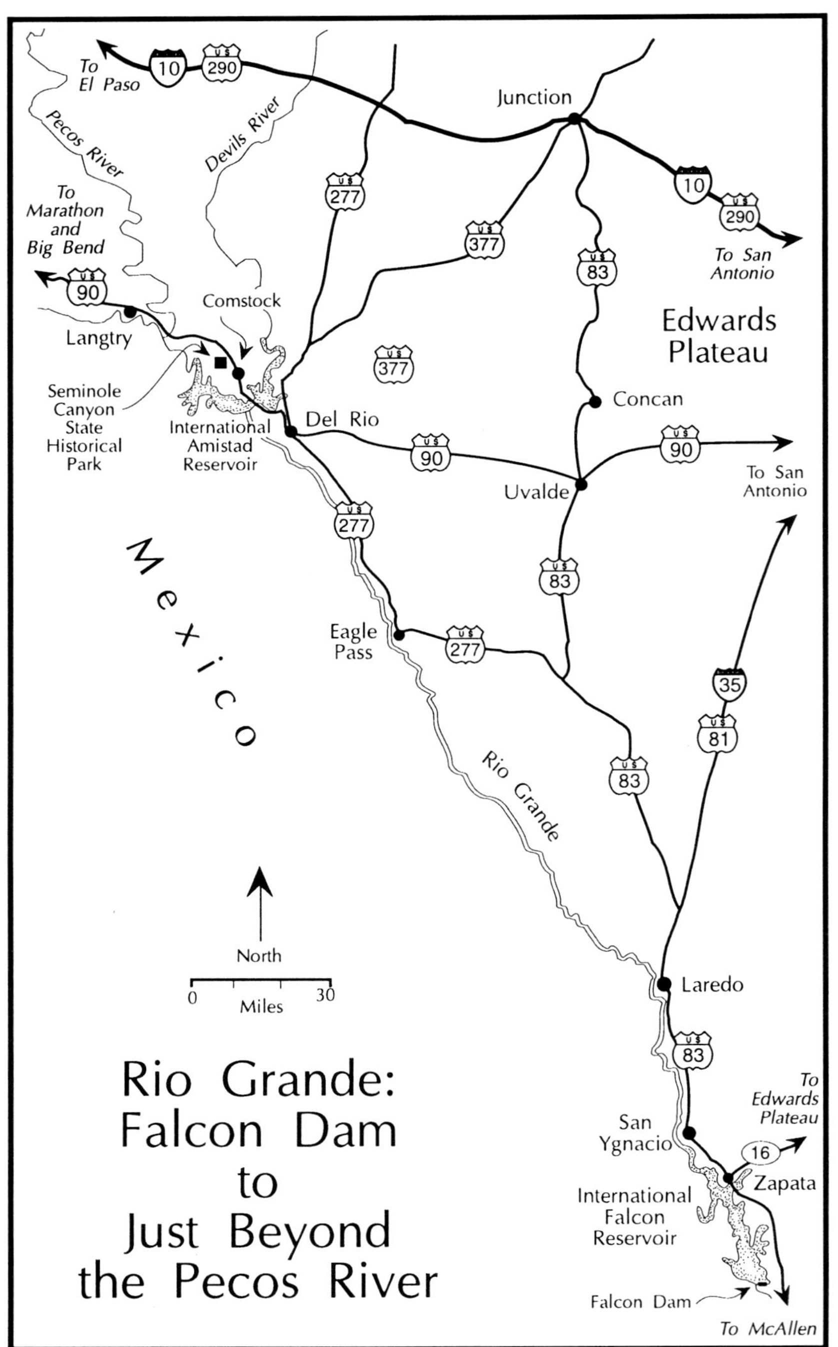

To El Paso
10
290
Junction
Pecos River
Devils River
To Marathon and Big Bend
277
377
10
290
To San Antonio
83
90
Comstock
Langtry
377
Edwards Plateau
Seminole Canyon State Historical Park
International Amistad Reservoir
Concan
Del Rio
90
90
To San Antonio
Uvalde
277
Mexico
83
Eagle Pass
277
35
81
Rio Grande
83
North
0
30
Miles
Laredo
83
Rio Grande: Falcon Dam to Just Beyond the Pecos River
To Edwards Plateau
San Ygnacio
16
Zapata
International Falcon Reservoir
Falcon Dam
To McAllen

FROM FALCON DAM TO JUST BEYOND THE PECOS

Between Falcon Dam and Big Bend, the land is arid, thinly vegetated, and rather unproductive. There are still a few good places to stop, however. Some 7.3 miles from the intersection of Highway 83 and Route 2098 you may want to check a culvert area over a creek called Tigre Chiquito for Cave Swallows, especially if you missed them at Arroyo Salado, covered in the last chapter. If a lot of water is backed up from Falcon Dam, look for water-birds and ducks here. Also be on the alert for Crested Caracaras on this stretch of road.

Recently, within the last few years, a small flock of White-collared Seedeaters has been found at the City Park in Zapata (27.0) upriver from Falcon Dam (from Highway 83 and Spur Road 2098). The park is two blocks west on 9th Avenue from Highway 83. Check the area behind the pond. If they are not found there, continue upriver on Highway 83 to San Ygnacio (14.0). They have been found regularly here for over 13 years. They have been found behind the post office and elsewhere, such as behind the cemetery, which can be reached by following Hidalgo Street to where it becomes a dirt road out of town. (The bank of the river nearby is also an excellent vantage point for observing Red-billed Pigeons from mid-March through August.) Currently the best area for White-collared Seedeaters is at the end of Washington Avenue behind the old houses. Also try the end of Treviño Street, but be aware that some recent "improvements" have reduced the weedy and seedeater-attractive areas in the town.

While you're there, check the resaca with surrounding picnic tables on Agua Avenue off Uribe Avenue. Depending on the season and the height of the water, you may look down and see egrets, puddle ducks, or even a Muscovy Duck.

Rather than continuing on Highway 83 to Laredo and later to Highway 277 to Del Rio, you might make better use of your time by going north from

Zapata on Highway 16 to San Antonio for a spring or summer visit to the Edwards Plateau at Austin or Kerrville, or you can save time by using Interstate 35 from Laredo to San Antonio (155 miles). Then you can later go west to Del Rio and follow the text below. But even in Del Rio you will not find much. Laredo to Del Rio is 181 miles.

DEL RIO

Informal Del Rio is a green oasis amid the South Texas plains at the southern edge of the Edwards Plateau. It is also located on the Rio Grande and the eastern edge of the Chihuahuan Desert. Within the city, to aid in the oasis effect, is Texas's third-largest springs, San Felipe Springs, which feeds 90 million gallons of pure water each day into San Felipe Creek. The creek winds its way through the municipal golf course and through the several city parks. Complementing the birdlife of the area in winter and during migration is the Amistad Reservoir, completed in 1969 by damming the Rio Grande twelve miles upstream from Del Rio.

When you enter Del Rio (32.0) on Highway 90, watch on the right for San Felipe Springs Road at the east side of the golf course. Turn right, drive to the end, and turn left at the gate (open from 7am to 5:30pm) and on to the spring house. Park and you can bird along the spring. Back at the fork, walk across the bridge and bird along the west side of the creek. Birds found here year-round include Green Kingfisher, Great Kiskadee, Black Phoebe, Vermilion Flycatcher, and Lesser Goldfinch. In winter look for Marsh Wren (rare), Brewer's Sparrow (rare), Sprague's and American Pipits (rare), and Horned Lark.

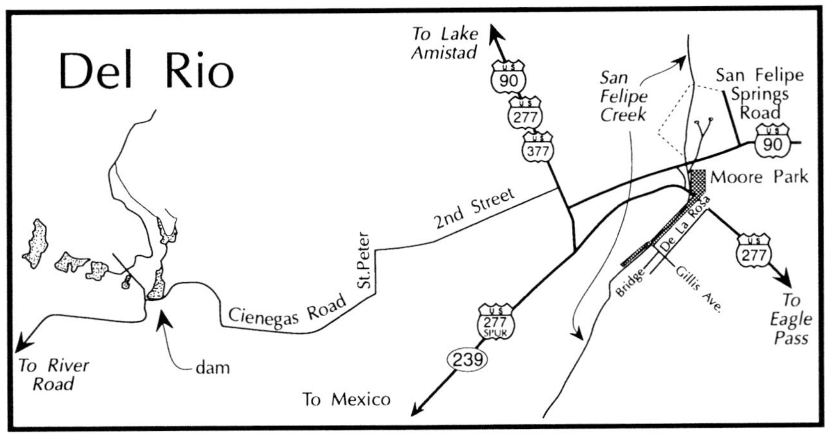

Return to Highway 90 and turn right. Almost immediately you will see the beginning of **Moore Park** on your left. Many birders have had their first look at a Green Kingfisher here. This elusive bird is usually found near the railroad bridge or on down near the park's swimming-pool. Because of its small size and secretive habits, this bird is easy to overlook. At least you should see some of the abundant Mexican Ground Squirrels.

To check the rest of the park system along the creek on the south side of Highway 277, continue west on Highway 90 and turn left (south) onto Highway 277 (0.25) to De La Rosa (0.3), turn right (southwest) two blocks, and park at the Ampihtheater Center. There is a paved trail following the creek which continues through the park for another half mile. Or continue to drive southwest on De La Rosa three blocks and turn right one block onto Gillis Avenue and left on Bridge to the creek, pond, and picnic area. The whole park is also good for spring and fall migrants such as Hermit Thrush, Nashville, Orange-crowned, Yellow, and Yellow-rumped Warblers, and Rufous-sided Towhee.

Another good area is the roadside thickets between the Rio Grande and the railroad just west of the city. It is an avian meeting-spot for East and West, with a touch of the Lower Rio Grande. Here you should find Northern Bobwhite and Scaled Quail, Eastern, Black, and Say's Phoebe's, Great Crested, Ash-throated, and Brown-crested Flycatchers, Carolina, Canyon, and Cactus Wrens, Northern Cardinal and Pyrrhuloxia, Clay-colored and Rufous-crowned Sparrows, and Orchard, Northern, and Hooded Orioles. Golden-fronted and Ladder-backed Woodpeckers are common. Bronzed and Brown-headed Cowbirds are common in summer, but much less so in winter. Olive Sparrows, although difficult to find, are actually present in good numbers.

To reach this area of thickets and other habitats from the downtown starting point of Highway 90 (Gibbs Street) and Highway 277/377 (Avenue F), go two blocks north and turn left (west) onto 2nd Street. Drive to the end (1.2) at the cemetery and turn left onto St. Peter and right onto Cienegas Road (0.2) to a farm pond and dam (1.7). Look over the ducks (some are domestic) and the cormorants. Neotropic Cormorants can be common here, especially in summer. At the corner turn left under the railroad and check the ponds and thickets along the way to River Road, where you turn right (2.0). Summer residents include Black-bellied Whistling-Duck and Groove-billed Ani, along with many of the above. The road follows along the river north to a locked gate (5.0). You can park here and walk farther up the road along the railroad tracks. Additional birds such as Great Kiskadee, Black Phoebe, Vermilion Flycatcher, and Couch's Kingbird may be found.

AMISTAD NATIONAL RECREATION AREA

The creation of Lake Amistad just northwest of Del Rio with the building of Amistad Dam in 1969 has attracted shorebirds and waterfowl usually associated with coastal areas and has encouraged extensions in range of such basically tropical species as Great Kiskadee, Black-bellied Whistling-Duck, and Ringed Kingfisher. The reservoir, administered by both Mexico and the United States, has 64,860 acres at conservation pool level of 1,117 feet above sea level, storing 3,505,439 acre-feet of water. The United States' shoreline is 851 miles long, while Mexico has 304 miles. The recreation area provides boating, fishing, swimming, hunting, and camping. (There are five small primitive camping areas—free—with picnic tables under shelters, and chemical toilets.) Birding opportunities are numerous on the water and along the shore and also in the dry scrub of higher ground, composed of Blackbrush, guajillo, ceniza, yucca, Sotol, mesquite, Creosote Bush, leatherplant, and various cacti.

To reach the recreation area, drive north from Del Rio on Highways 90/277/377 to the National Park Service Headquarters on the right about four miles. Here you can pick up information, brochures, and books. A quarter-mile beyond, Highway 90 swings left (west). (Highways 277/377 continue north to and across the east arm of the reservoir [6.0] where a small campground may produce Curve-billed Thrasher and Black-throated Sparrow year-round. Cinnamon Teal and Lark Bunting have been recorded here in winter. Scissor-tailed Flycatcher is common in spring and summer.) But our route goes west with Highway 90 to Spur Road 454 (2.4) and follows signs to San Pedro Flats Campground, one of the better areas for birds. Here you should find such resident birds as Green Kingfisher, Cactus, Rock, and Canyon Wrens, Scaled Quail, Harris's Hawk, Chihuahuan Raven, Blue-gray Gnatcatcher (Black-tailed has been recorded), Verdin, and Pyrrhuloxia. In summer look for Pied-billed Grebe, Black-necked Stilt, Snowy Egret (rare), Black-capped Vireo (rare), Common and Lesser Nighthawks, and Hooded Oriole. In winter watch for Say's Phoebe, Sage Thrasher, and Green-tailed and Canyon Towhees. In migration look for American White Pelican, White-faced Ibis, Black-shouldered and Mississippi Kites, Snowy Plover (very rare), Long-billed Curlew (rare), Least, Pectoral, Solitary, Spotted, Upland, and Western Sandpipers (all rather rare), and Forster's Tern. Bald and Golden Eagles may occasionally be seen. Many species of sparrows are also found in migration and winter.

Continue west on Highway 90 to Road 349 (5.2) and turn left (south) to the Visitor Center on the dam (2.5). Turn around and go back to the

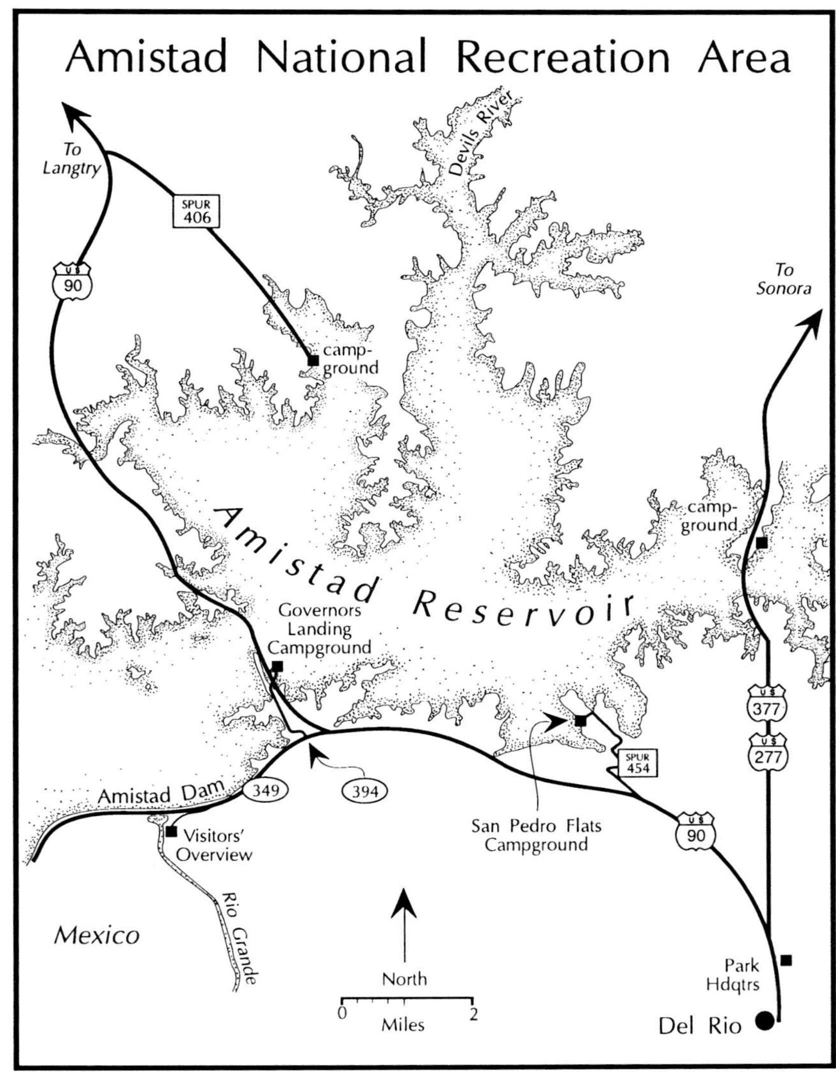

road (0.4) that leads to the Visitors' Overview, a short trail giving a good view of the river below the dam, and the down-river face of the dam. Green Kingfishers like the clear, shallow water below dams.

Return north on Road 349 to Road 394, just north of the railroad, and turn left to Governors Landing Campground (1.2). Check for passerines along this road, and look in the small ponds for Least and Pied-billed Grebes and ducks. It is not too unusual to find Canyon Wrens nesting in the roof supports of the picnic-table shelters.

Continue on Highway 90 west over the long bridge over the Devils River arm of Amistad Reservoir to Spur Road 406 (10.1) and turn right to the campground at the end (4.7). This good birding area has most of the same species as San Pedro Flats, but it has many more larger bushes and trees.

The barren land all around Amistad Reservoir may not be the greatest for birds, but it is excellent for reptiles. The common lizards in this rocky, thorny area of limestone between Del Rio and Big Bend are Texas Banded Gecko (nocturnal); Collared Lizard (the Reticulate Collared Lizard is found, for the most part, below the escarpment); Greater Earless Lizard; Crevice Spiny and Texas Spiny Lizards; Fence, Canyon, Tree, Desert Side-blotched, Texas Horned and Round-tailed Horned Lizards; Texas Spotted Whiptail; and Texas Alligator Lizard. The common snakes are Western Hognose Snake, Western Coachwhip, whipsnake, Mountain Patchnose Snake, Great Plains and Trans-Pecos Rat Snakes, Sonoran Gopher Snake, Gray-banded and Desert Kingsnakes, Texas Longnose Snake, Western Hooknose Snake (rare), Texas Night Snake, and Blacktail and Western Diamondback Rattlesnakes. Along the river and in other moist areas, look for Texas and Trans-Pecos Blind Snakes, Blotched Water Snake, Checkered and Black-necked Garter Snakes, Western Ribbon, Flat-headed, Plains and Southwestern Black-headed Snakes, Copperhead, and even the very rare Devil's River Black-headed Snake.

SEMINOLE CANYON STATE HISTORICAL PARK

Seminole Canyon State Historical Park (P.O. Box 820, Comstock TX 78837; phone 512/292-4464) on US 90, 9 miles west of Comstock, west of Amistad Reservoir. The popular attraction of the 2,173-acre park (entrance fee $3.00) is the Indian rock art (pictographs) found in massive rocky overhangs that provided shelter for early pre-Columbian cultures using the deep Cretaceous-limestone canyons. Seminole Canyon is one of the most spectacular, since its pictographs are believeds to be North America's oldest, thought to have been painted as long as 8,000 years ago. Fate Bell Shelter is accessible only by guided tour. The Visitor Center contains exhibits depicting the lifestyle of early man based upon artifacts and rock art. While at the Visitor Center, pick up brochures and a bird checklist.

Windmill Trail starts from the Visitor Center and leads half a mile to Seminole Spring in a draw near Main Canyon. This is a fairly easy hike. Birds to look for here and along the way are Zone-tailed Hawk, Green Kingfisher, Black Phoebe, Hooded Oriole, and the elusive Varied Bunting.

The **Rio Grande Trail** (6-mile round-trip) leads from near the campground to a scenic overlook on the Rio Grande shores of Amistad Reservoir. About halfway is a cutoff trail to the Pressa Canyon overlook. On this upland area watch for Scaled Quail, Verdin, Pyrrhuloxia, and Black-throated Sparrow. In winter Lark Buntings are rather common along with other wintering sparrows. During migration, spring and fall, watch for waterfowl and shorebirds at the river, and flycatchers and warblers along the trail. White-throated Swifts nest on the canyon walls along with Canyon Wrens and possibly Black and Turkey Vultures, and Chihuahuan and Common Ravens.

On leaving the park, continue west on US 90 to the first road on the left (1.5) and turn left (south) to the National Park Service's Pecos River District Headquarters (1.3). The scenic view of the mouth of the Pecos River at the Rio Grande is great. What you see today has looked much the same for thousands of years. The water level, however, is now 50 feet deeper because of backwater from Amistad Dam. From the self-guiding, quarter-mile **Nature Trail** and overlook you also can see the US 90 automobile bridge built in 1959.

LANGTRY

The Judge Roy Bean Museum is one mile west of the highway at Langtry (17.0). Bean was a justice of the peace, and the Jersey Lily Saloon was his courtroom. His colorful manner and unorthodox justice earned him the title of "The Law West of the Pecos". The Texas Highway Department has built a big, modern information-station, which is completely out of place in this setting. They have hidden the poor judge's saloon out back.

In the fall of 1976, a Rufous-backed Robin spent a week in the cactus garden at the information-station. The beautiful garden has a large variety of plants, all labeled, including 34 cacti, yuccas, and agaves, 19 species of trees, and 44 species of shrubs and others. Resident birds include Black-chinned Hummingbird, Scaled Quail, Cactus and Rock Wrens, Curve-billed Thrasher, Pyrrhuloxia, Black-throated Sparrow, Hooded Oriole, House Finch, and others.

Opposite the station a road leads down to the river. Here, you can look at the canyon of the Rio Grande. On the Mexican shore you may be able to pick out the old eagle's nest, which was over 6 feet high. It was used for years, but the birds were finally shot by some trigger-happy hunter.

Supplies and lodging are available at Sanderson (60.0). This town, like most of the others along the highway, was founded about 1881 as a watering-stop on the Texas-New Orleans Railroad. Today, tourists are the main source of revenue.

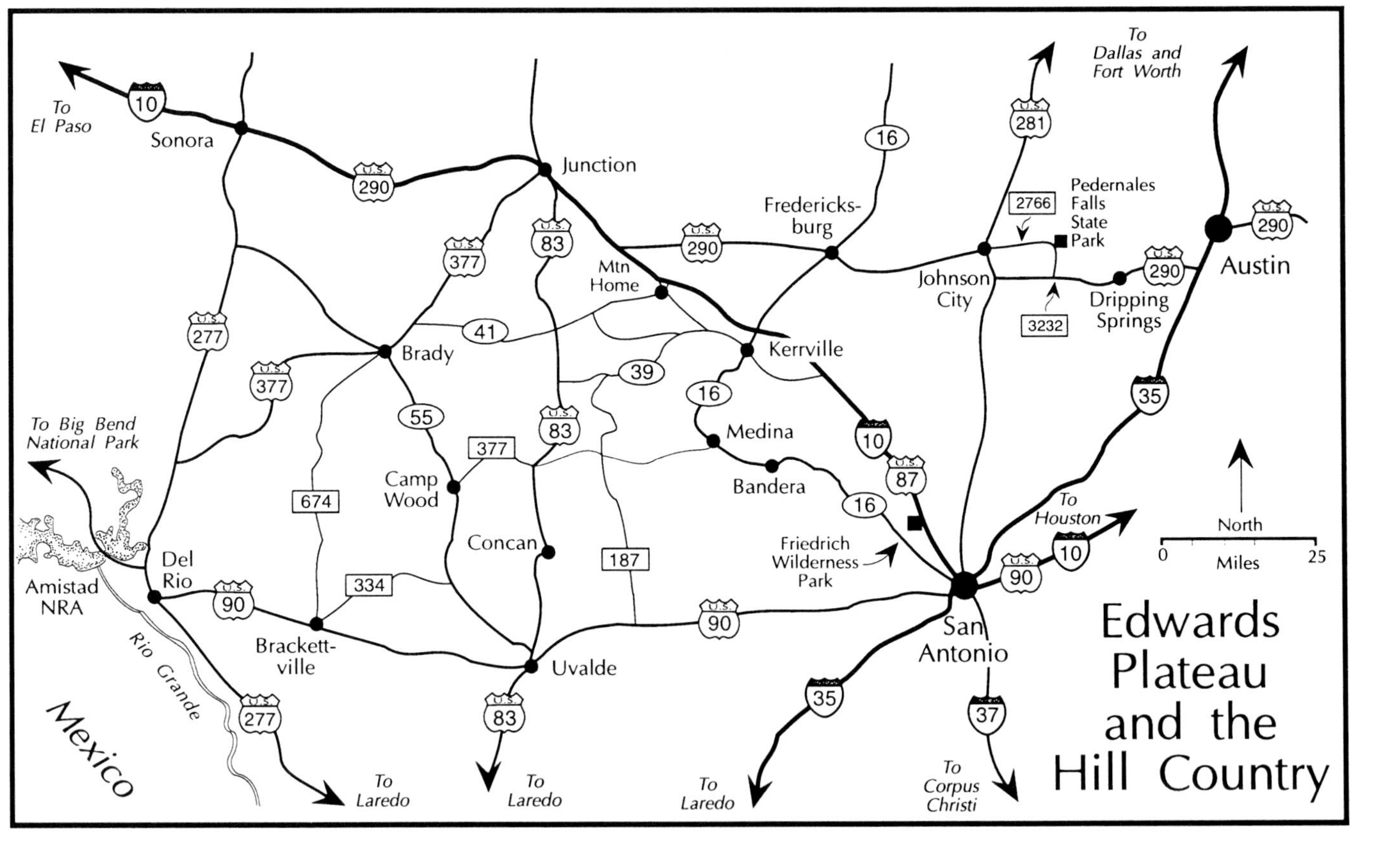
Edwards Plateau and the Hill Country
North
0
Miles
25
To El Paso
To Dallas and Fort Worth
To Big Bend National Park
To Houston
To Corpus Christi
To Laredo
To Laredo
To Laredo
To Laredo
Sonora
Junction
Fredericks-burg
Johnson City
Pedernales Falls State Park
Dripping Springs
Austin
Mtn Home
Kerrville
Brady
Medina
Bandera
Camp Wood
Concan
Friedrich Wilderness Park
Del Rio
Amistad NRA
Brackett-ville
Uvalde
San Antonio
Rio Grande
Mexico
10
290
377
83
290
16
281
2766
3232
290
277
41
377
39
16
35
55
83
377
10
87
674
16
334
187
10
90
90
90
35
37
277
83
290

THE EDWARDS PLATEAU

If you are generally following the route in this book, you might want to reach the Edwards Plateau by leaving the Rio Grande Valley at Laredo and traveling northward on Interstate 35. As an alternate, you might go as far north as Del Rio and travel eastward on US 90. Conversely, you might just want to start your trip to the Rio Grande Valley with a spring or early summer trip to the Edwards Plateau and then travel south to the Lower Valley. It all depends on your personal schedule, birding priorities, and the time of year.

The Edwards Plateau is a well-defined formation extending from the Pecos River, at an elevation of some 3,000 feet, to Austin at 550 feet. Its surface is a single massive block of limestone 600 to 800 feet thick, 100 miles wide, and 200 miles long. The top of the block has been dissected by streams into a rolling terrain which is honeycombed with caves and sinkholes. To the north the plateau merges rather smoothly with the Staked Plains, but on the south it is bounded by the Balcones Escarpment (Ball-CO-nes, Spanish for "balconies"). The western edge is marked by the deep canyons of the Rio Grande and Pecos River. Beyond these rivers the limestone block extends westward as the Stockton Plateau.

The arid western end of the plateau (annual rainfall of 12 inches) still retains some of its original shortgrass prairies, but many of them have been converted by overgrazing into rocky wastelands. The wetter eastern end, which Texans call the "Hill Country" (annual rainfall of 33 inches), is a delightful land of wooded hills, valleys, and clear sparkling streams.

Much of the plateau is occupied by sheep and goat ranches of limited economic value, although some of the land is set aside for recreation sites such as parks, guest-ranches, and hunting-preserves. However, the most important function of the plateau is that of an aquifer.

The limestone block collects vast amounts of water, which is slowly released along its innumerable springs. Some of the springs have enormous capacities. For example, San Solomon Springs at Balmorhea flow at a rate of 26 million gallons per day, and San Felipe Springs at Del Rio flow at a rate of 90 million. Both of these springs flowed at double these rates in the days before the plateau was overgrazed.

Because this is an overlap area for eastern and western species, the plateau is an excellent birding area. Many western species reach the eastern limits of their range here, and many eastern species reach their western limits. However, most birders plan to visit the Edwards Plateau to add three birds to their lifelist: Golden-cheeked Warbler, Black-capped Vireo, and Cave Swallow.

GOLDEN-CHEEKED WARBLER

Although highly colored, the now-endangered Golden-cheeked Warbler is not easy to find. You must be in just the right spot at just the right time. The birds arrive in early March and return to southern Mexico and Guatemala in late July. The best time to find one is from mid-March to late June, when the males are singing. Luckily, they sing from the treetops. But you should get out early in the morning.

Because the female Golden-cheeked always lines her nest with strips of bark from mature Ashe Junipers (locally called "cedars"), the nesting sites are restricted to areas of *cedar breaks*. The nest may be placed in any type

Golden-cheeked Warbler
Shawneen Finnegan

of tree, but there are always mature junipers nearby. It is because of this important requirement, and the fact that much of its habitat is being cleared for agriculture and urbanization, that the species could easily be headed for extinction. Nesting sites may range from the valley floor to the hilltops, but the preferred sites seem to be near the upper margins of canyons or on rough hillsides covered with oaks and junipers.

You should have no trouble locating a Golden-cheeked Warbler without using a tape. As with the endangered Black-capped Vireo, below, use of tapes to arouse and attract this species is completely inappropriate.

BLACK-CAPPED VIREO

The endangered Black-capped Vireo is even harder to see than the Golden-cheeked Warbler. Although widespread, this is not a common bird, and it is very shy. Trying to lure one out into the open for a good look is almost a hopeless task. It responds well to pishing and squeaking, but will often stay hidden in the middle of a bush. (Though the species will respond to taped calls, this technique may now be used only under a valid U.S. Fish & Wildlife Service research permit. *Do not use tapes.*) The best way to see this bird is to drive along slowly in the early morning until you hear one calling. Then, stop and wait for it to come out. Most of the colonies—particularly in the Austin area—are either in preserves with strict access control or on private property. Trespassing on any of these sites without permission can be a *very serious* transgression because of the controversy over endangered species in recent years. Please pay special attention to directions and warnings given on sites for this species in the following pages.

This vireo prefers ungrazed oak thickets that have a low, thick understory. The thickets may be on the flats, in the canyons, or on the hillsides. Its range is from Austin to Big Bend and northward to Oklahoma, but there are few places where the oaks have not been highlined by sheep or goats. (For its range in Texas, see the map on the next page.)

This bird arrives several weeks later than the Golden-cheeked Warbler, coming in late March and departing in August. The best time to see one is from about the second week of April to the end of May.

CAVE SWALLOW

The Cave Swallow historically nested in some 16 limestone caves and sinkholes ranging from Kerrville to New Mexico's Carlsbad Caverns. Recently, it has taken to nesting under highway bridges. This practice seems to be entending its range east to Kingsville, south to the Falcon Dam

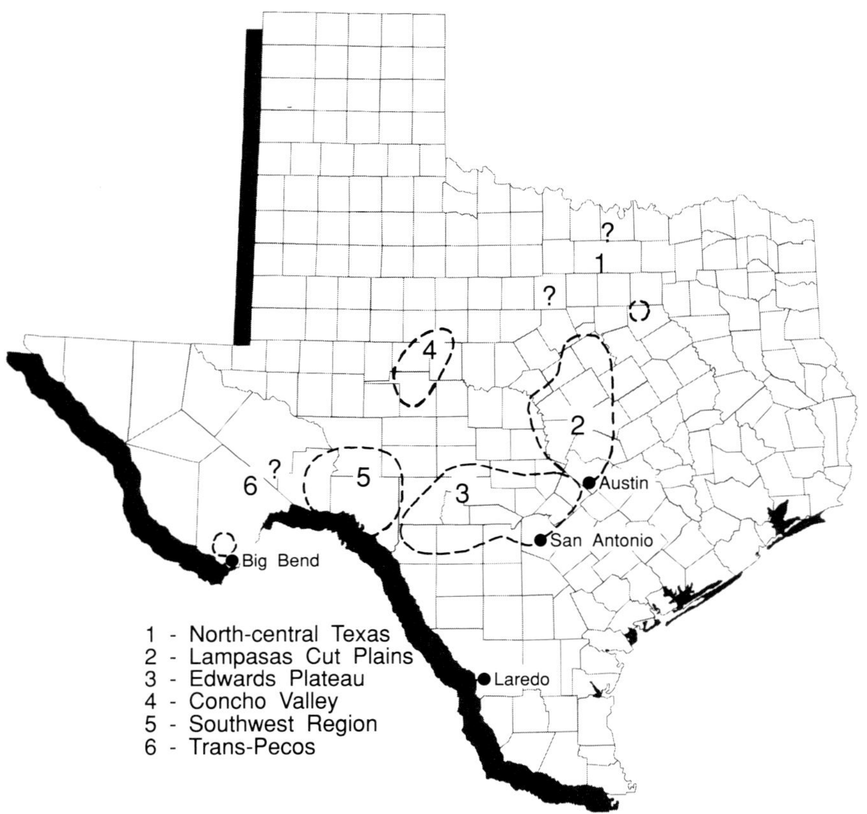

Texas distribution of Black-capped Vireo from 1980 to 1990.

area, and west practically to El Paso. Still, the Edwards Plateau is a prime area for finding the Cave Swallow. The Cave Swallow seems to be tolerated by the Barn Swallow in its nesting area but not necessarily by the Cliff (or vice versa).

Cave Swallows may arrive very early at nest sites, even by March. Most have arrived by the first of April and leave in late August or early September. (Locally in South Texas, more and more Cave Swallows seem to be staying in small numbers throughout the year.) When present, they are active and fairly easy to see if you are in the right spot.

The tour outlined below will give you a chance of finding all three of these specialties plus many other species. It will also show you some of the most beautiful scenery in Texas. The ideal starting points are San Antonio and Austin.

SAN ANTONIO

San Antonio is a delightful city in which to spend a day or so. In addition to the Alamo, the zoo, and the River Walk, you may also enjoy birding some of the city parks, especially **Friedrich Wilderness Park**.

To reach these 232 acres of typical Hill Country habitat preserved by the San Antonio Department of Parks and Recreation, go west on Interstate 10 for about 10 miles beyond Loop 410. Exit onto Camp Bullis Road, cross under the freeway, and drive north on the left frontage road for 1.2 miles. Turn left (west) at the *Friedrich Wilderness Park* sign, and drive one-half mile to the park entrance. The park (free) is open 9-5 Wednesday through Sunday, with no admittance after 4pm.

Golden-cheeked Warblers can be found from March 15 to the first of July in the coolest part of the park on the north-facing slopes of the central ravine. The habitat is mature cedars (junipers) mixed with Texas Oak, Black Cherry, and Cedar Elm. After the singing stops in June, the warblers can be harder to find.

Black-capped Vireos are found from early April to mid-July in the hottest part of the park along the southwest-facing rim of the ravine. The habitat is low, shrubby live oak, Evergreen Sumac, Agarita, and other shrubs. Other nesting species include Northern Bobwhite, Greater Roadrunner, Black-chinned Hummingbird, Golden-fronted and Ladder-backed Woodpeckers, Ash-throated Flycatcher, Verdin, Bewick's Wren, White-eyed and Bell's Vireos, Yellow-breasted Chat, Painted Bunting, Orchard and Northern Orioles, House Finch, and Lesser Goldfinch.

If you are going to Kerrville from San Antonio, take Highway 16 through Bandera, a very pretty drive. About 12 miles north of Medina, you will come to Johnson Canyon. Park near the highway sign marked "Hill" and walk down the slope. Black-capped Vireos and Golden-cheeked Warblers have been found in this area.

AUSTIN

Not only is Austin the capital of Texas, but it is also one of the most attractive and livable cities in the state. Named after Stephen F. Austin, colonizer of the first American settlement in Texas, the city of 400,000 contains cultural, educational, and commercial features aplenty. Situated in the wooded hills at the eastern edge of the Edwards Plateau, the city overlooks the Colorado River. Unlike most cities, which line their rivers with concrete and fill them with sewage, Austin has landscaped the Colorado with beautiful parks and paths. Many outdoor recreational

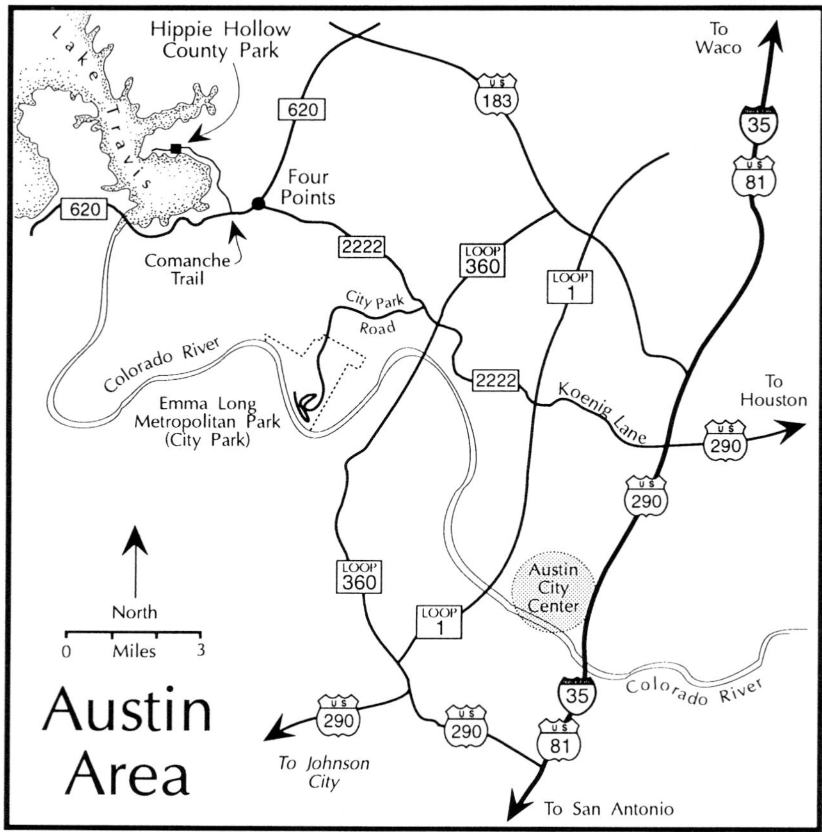

activities also revolve around the nearby Highland Lakes, and even in the midst of the large urban population there are such novelties as the colony of Brazilian Free-tailed Bats which resides beneath the Congress Avenue Bridge.

EMMA LONG METROPOLITAN PARK (CITY PARK)

Known simply as "City Park" to the locals, Emma Long Metropolitan Park is currently the spot most recommended by local birders for finding Golden-cheeked Warbler. To reach the park go north on Interstate 35 from downtown Austin and take the exit for Highway 290 (4.0), which goes east to Houston, but turn west on Farm Road 2222 (Koenig Lane). Go under Loop 1 Road (3.3) and proceed to Loop 360 Road (4.0). After passing this, start watching for the small signs marking City Park Road (0.5), which is on the left. *(Another 5 miles on Road 2222 will bring you to Road*

620. *Black-capped Vireos have been found along Road 620 to the left.)* Turn left and go to the top of the hill. From here to the end of the road (6.0), you will see much prime habitat for the warbler. Unfortunately, the first five miles of this road traverse private property, and developments are consuming more of the habitat each year. Warblers are still frequently heard and seen at the several dirt pullouts as the road skirts the hillside. Perhaps the best location in the park for finding the warbler is near the little rock bridge at the only creek-crossing on the road (4.5). Small foot-paths leading upstream and downstream from this bridge traverse prime warbler habitat.

COMANCHE TRAIL

The newest and most accessible "hot spot" for seeing the Black-capped Vireo west of Austin is along Comanche Trail and at Hippie Hollow County Park. From Four Points, turn south (left) onto RR 620 toward Mansfield Dam. Turn right onto Comanche Trail (1.2). Both the vireo and warbler can be found along the first mile of the road, primarily at the first sharp curve to the right (0.5). Bird only from the roadside here; do not enter the adjacent private property. If you miss the vireo here, proceed on to Hippie Hollow County Park (1.2). One to several pairs of Black-capped Vireos have nested around the edges of the park's large parking lot in recent years, and thus are among the most convenient to approach anywhere in the state. (*Do not play tapes here or anywhere around Black-capped Vireos.*) Also be advised that this is Austin's most popular "clothing optional" bathing-area. The beach is screened from view by the same brush occupied by the vireos. The sunbathers are used to birdwatchers, but if you wander down toward the beach you may get an eyeful of more than just vireos!

AUDUBON SANCTUARY

Travis Audubon Society owns and manages a 600-plus-acre wildlife sanctuary, located about twenty miles northwest of Austin, where Golden-cheeked Warblers nest in fairly good numbers. But during the nesting season (mid-March to late June) access is allowed **only by scheduled guided tours**, even to their own members. Regular tours on Saturdays in spring and summer to see Black-capped Vireos have been organized in recent years. You may call the Austin Area Audubon Alert (phone: 512/346-2055) which maintains a recording with the capacity for callers to leave messages. Anyone wanting to visit the sanctuary would either be given a name and number to call on the tape or could leave a message requesting further information.

PEDERNALES FALLS STATE PARK

Starting from Austin, go west on Highway 290 toward Fredricksburg. After passing Dripping Springs (24.0), start watching on the right for Farm Road 3232 (8.0), which leads to **Pedernales Falls State Park** (6.3) (entrance fee of $3.00 weekdays and $5.00 weekends, plus fee for camping or hot showers) with 4,800 acres stretching along both banks of the Pedernales River. Bald Cypresses and sycamores line the riverbanks while Ashe Juniper (cedar) and oaks cover the uplands.

The Golden-cheeked Warbler has been found along the upper part of the nature trail that starts next to campsite #291. In fact, the warbler is often seen right behind the sign for the trail. The warblers are also regular in the woods along the short trail to the "upper falls".

Other birds to be found include Golden-fronted and Ladder-backed Woodpeckers, Western Kingbird, Great Crested and Ash-throated Flycatchers, Eastern Phoebe, Cliff Swallow, Carolina Chickadee, Tufted (Black-crested) Titmouse, Verdin, Bushtit, Bewick's and Canyon Wrens, White-eyed Vireo, Summer Tanager, Blue Grosbeak, Painted Bunting, Canyon Towhee, Rufous-crowned and Black-throated Sparrows, and Lesser Goldfinch. Green Kingfishers are also seen occasionally along the Pedernales River in the park.

As you leave the park, turn right onto Farm Road 2766. At Johnson City (9.0) continue west on Highway 290 until you reach Ranch Road 1 (10.9), which leads to the LBJ Ranch. To visit the ranch, park at the state park on the south side of the road and board one of the tour busses, which will take you to the birthplace, the cemetery, and for a short tour of the ranch. The main ranch house is not open to the public because Lady Bird Johnson still lives there.

At Fredericksburg (14.0), which is famous for its German-style cooking, you can turn left onto Highway 16 toward Kerrville (24.0).

KERRVILLE

Kerrville (population 15,276, elevation 1,645 feet) is the hub of the vacation area for the Hill Country. Motels, guest ranches, and campgrounds are numerous in the vicinity. After seeing this pretty little town on the beautiful Guadalupe River, you may not want to go any farther. Birding can be good almost anywhere in the area.

Louise Hayes Park, which is just across the river from the downtown area, has some tall trees that can be good for warblers and other migrants.

Kerrville-Schreiner State Park (517 acres, entrance fee of $3.00 weekdays and $4.00 weekends, camping, hot showers), is just south of town. Take Highway 16 to Highway 173 (0.5) and turn left to the park (2.5). The best birding spot is usually on the hillside above the camping area. Wild Turkeys may be found here among the oaks. Some common resident species include Inca Dove, Greater Roadrunner, Belted Kingfisher, Golden-fronted and Ladder-backed Woodpeckers, Eastern Phoebe, Scrub

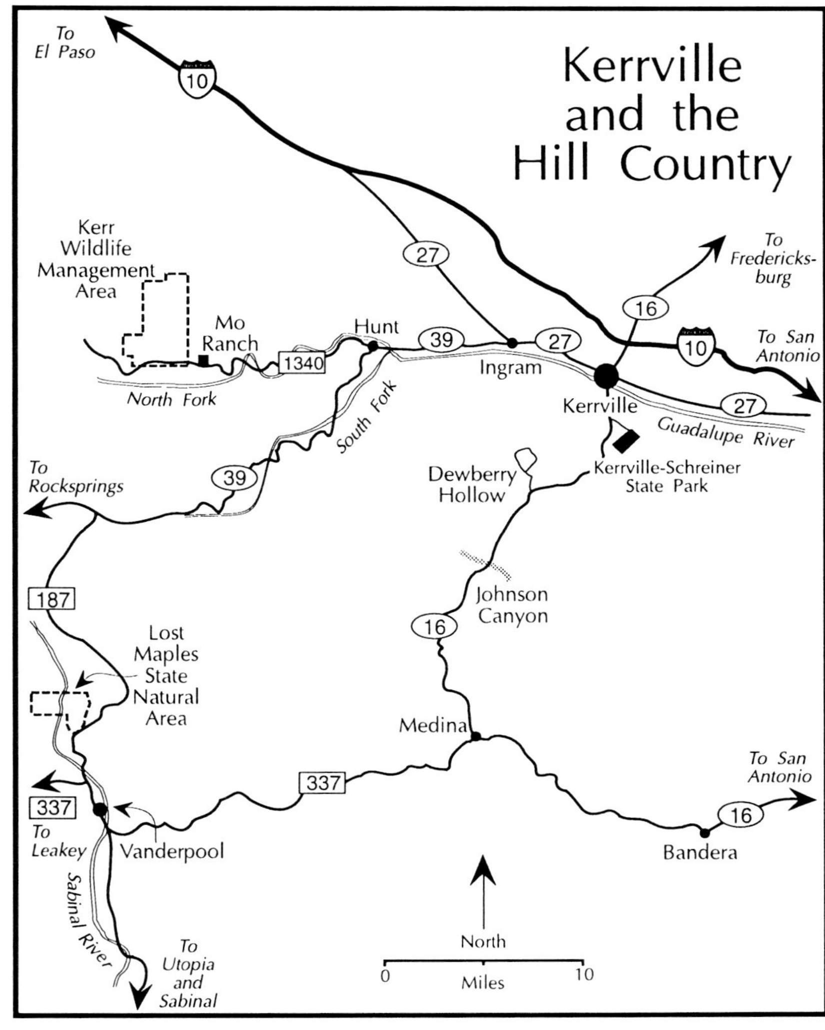

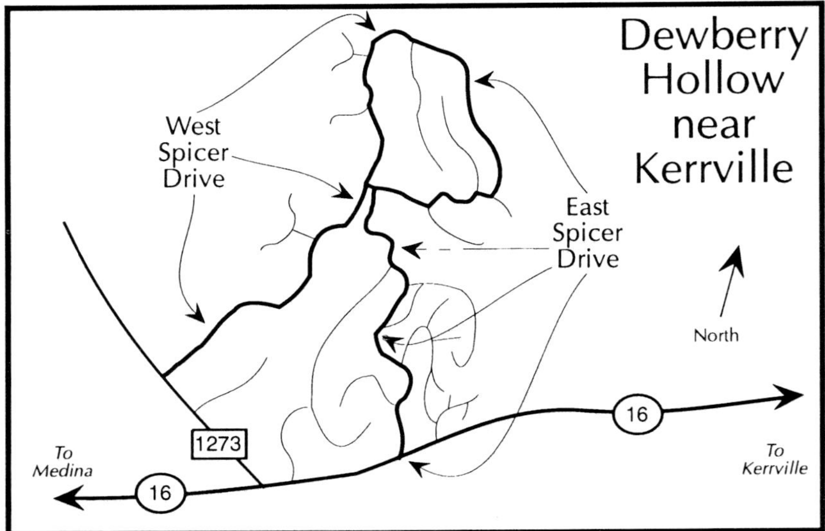

Jay, Carolina Chickadee, Tufted (Black-crested) Titmouse, Carolina and Bewick's Wrens, Eastern Bluebird, Northern Mockingbird, Northern Cardinal, Brown-headed Cowbird, and House Finch. Other summer nesters include Green-backed Heron, Yellow-billed Cuckoo, Chimney Swift, Cliff and Barn Swallows, White-eyed Vireo, Summer Tanager, and Bronzed Cowbird. Yellow-throated Warbler is an uncommon nester.

Johnson Canyon is good for Golden-cheeked Warbler. The canyon is along Highway 16 some 12 miles south of Kerrville or 12 miles north of Medina. Park near the highway sign which reads "Hill" and walk down the highway. The birds may be found anywhere in the stands of scrub oak. Of course, they are most active early in the morning.

A good spot for Black-capped Vireo close to town is Dewberry Hollow, located off Highway 16. Turn right onto East Spicer (7.3 miles from south side of the Guadalupe River). Jog right onto West Spicer (1.5). The vireo is all along this road. Either follow West Spicer around the loop to return to Highway 16, or retrace your route.

THE HILL COUNTRY

To reach the very heart of the Hill Country, go northwest from Kerrville on Highway 27 to Ingram (7.0). Turn west onto Highway 39, which runs along the Guadalupe River. At Hunt turn right onto Ranch Road 1340 to explore a beautiful stretch of the **North Fork of the Guadalupe River**. After a couple of blocks, watch on the left for a house with feeders, which swarm with Black-chinned Hummingbirds in summer.

The area along the river is great for Wood Duck, Cliff Swallow, Eastern Phoebe, Yellow-throated Vireo, Canyon Wren, and many other species. Green Kingfisher can be found here in summer if you look hard enough. This small, shy bird is easily overlooked because it perches close to the water on rocks or low overhanging limbs. Your best bet is to stop as often as possible and scan the river.

The Mo Ranch Church Camp (10.7) on the right is a delightful place to bird. Accommodations can be had during off seasons. On the Kerr Wildlife Management Area (2.0) (6,439 acres), Golden-cheeked Warblers nest annually within 100 feet of the spring in Spring Pasture, in one area of 400 acres of mature Ashe Juniper "cedar". Some 20 pairs of the endangered warbler nest within this area each year. Any employee can direct you to the spring.

Some 40 pairs of Black-capped Vireos nest within the Wildlife Management Area, with reports from management that they are doing well and increasing in numbers. Their preferred habitat is live-oak thickets that have a low, thick understory. Office hours are 8am to 5pm weekdays. If no one is around, drive the 4-mile interpretive driving tour. Pick up a copy of the guide at the registration booth. Northern Bobwhite and Wild Turkey are rather common here.

Beyond this point the road leaves the river and crosses open ranchland. Turn around, go back to Hunt, and continue west on Highway 39, which follows the **South Fork of the Guadalupe River**. This is just as pretty and birdy as the North Fork.

Eventually, the road leaves the river and crosses grasslands dotted with Shin Oak. Any Shin Oak thickets without a browse line might harbor Black-capped Vireos. Watch also for Wild Turkey, Greater Roadrunner, Great Horned Owl, Golden-fronted Woodpecker, Scrub Jay, Common Raven, Carolina Chickadee, Tufted (Black-crested) Titmouse, Verdin, Bushtit, Bewick's, Carolina, Canyon, and Rock Wrens, Brown Thrasher, Eastern Bluebird, Eastern Meadowlark, House Finch, Lesser Goldfinch, Canyon Towhee, and Lark, Rufous-crowned, Cassin's, Black-throated, Chipping, and Field Sparrows. In summer look for Common Poorwill, Chuck-will's-widow, Common and Lesser (rare) Nighthawks, Western Kingbird, Scissor-tailed, Great-crested, Ash-throated, and Vermilion Flycatchers, Eastern Phoebe, White-eyed, Bell's, and Red-eyed Vireos, Orchard and Scott's Orioles, Blue Grosbeak, Painted Bunting, and Grasshopper Sparrow. In migration you may see large concentrations of Mississippi Kites and Broad-winged and Swainson's Hawks, and in winter Lark Buntings and Savannah, Vesper, Clay-colored, White-crowned,

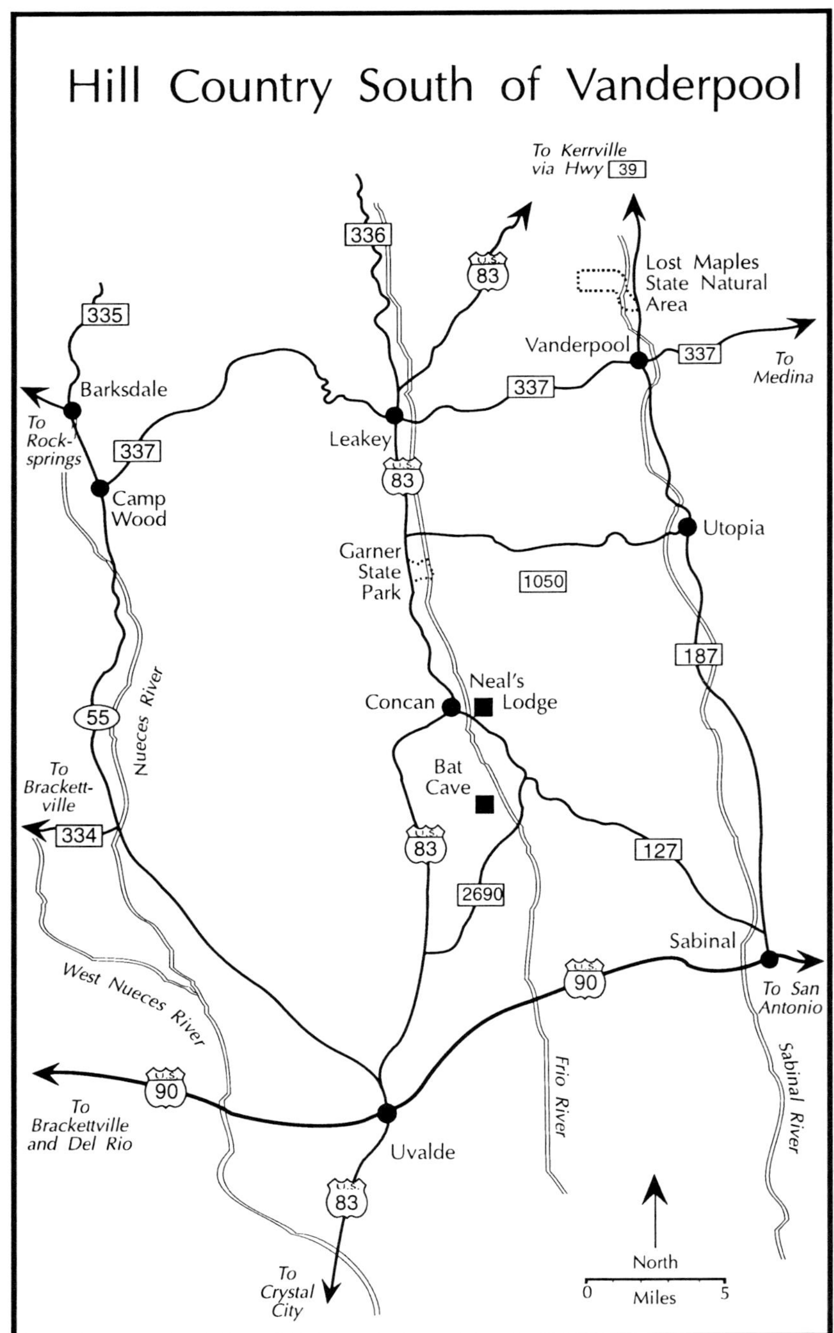
Hill Country South of Vanderpool
To Kerrville
via Hwy 39
336
U.S. 83
Lost Maples
State Natural
Area
335
Vanderpool
337
To
Medina
Barksdale
337
To
Rock-
springs
337
Leakey
U.S. 83
Camp
Wood
Utopia
Garner
State
Park
1050
187
Nueces River
Neal's
Lodge
Concan
55
Bat
Cave
To
Brackett-
ville
334
U.S. 83
127
2690
Sabinal
To San
Antonio
West Nueces River
U.S. 90
U.S. 90
Frio River
Sabinal River
To
Brackettville
and Del Rio
Uvalde
U.S. 83
To
Crystal
City
North
0
Miles
5

White-throated, Fox, and Lincoln's Sparrows. Also keep an eye out for the black race of the Rock Squirrel.

At Farm Road 187 (20.0) turn left. For the next few miles watch the telephone wires for Cave Swallows, particularly in late afternoon. South on the right, there is a windmill with a water trough (1.5), where the swallows often come to drink. If you do not see them here, check the utility wires between the buildings of the former Bonnie Hills Ranch (2.8) on the right.

LOST MAPLES STATE NATURAL AREA

One of the favorite spots of Texans for viewing fall colors is Sabinal Canyon, where an isolated stand of Big-toothed Maples turns a brilliant red. This remote area is in Lost Maples State Natural Area (9.8) (entrance fee of $3.00 weekdays and $4.00 weekends, camping, hot showers). Not only is this a very scenic spot, but it is also a good birding area. Both Golden-cheeked Warbler and Black-capped Vireo are regular here. One area for these much-sought-after birds is along the trail to the pond. With a bit of luck you may also see an Acorn Woodpecker or even a Zone-tailed Hawk. The hawk has nested in the upper part of the canyon for many years and can sometimes be seen flying up and down the stream or over the surrounding hills. Other nesting species include Greater Roadrunner, Green Kingfisher, Ladder-backed Woodpecker, Black Phoebe, Ash-throated Flycatcher, Common Raven, Scrub Jay, Bushtit, Pyrrhuloxia (rare), Painted Bunting, Canyon Towhee, Orchard Oriole, and Lesser Goldfinch.

GARNER STATE PARK

Continue south on Farm Road 187 through Vanderpool (4.7) to Utopia (10.5). Turn right (west) onto RR 1050 to US Highway 83 (15.0). Turn left after about a mile to **Garner State Park** (630 acres; entrance fee of $3.00 from September through May and $5.00 from June through August, camping, hot showers). Birding is often good in the park with its six miles of hiking-trails. The clear, spring-fed Frio River has large Bald Cypress trees lining its banks. Resident birds include Green Kingfisher, Black Phoebe, Scrub Jay, Common Raven, Verdin, Bushtit, Cactus, Rock, Canyon, Carolina, and Bewick's Wrens, Pyrrhuloxia, Canyon Towhee, and Rufous-crowned Sparrow. Additional nesting species may include White-winged Dove, Groove-billed Ani, Vermilion Flycatcher, Yellow-throated Warbler, and Hooded and Scott's Orioles.

One of the better and more remote parts of the park is along the road to the dump. This area can be reached by hiking a trail which begins just past the Shady Meadows Camping Area.

NEAL'S LODGE

Continuing south on Highway 83, turn left onto Highway 127 at Concan (7.3). **Neal's Lodge** (0.6) (PO Box 165, Concan 78838; phone 512/232-6118) is on the left on the beautiful Frio River. This attractive vacation spot, operating since 1927, has rooms and many housekeeping cabins available year-round. The cafe serves refreshing home-cooked meals every day from Memorial Day to Labor Day, and weekends only from Easter to Memorial Day and Labor Day through December. During January, February, and March arrangements can be made for large groups. A grocery store is available on the property.

Birds are abundant about the 300-acre grounds. Carolina, Canyon, and Bewick's Wrens, White-winged and Inca Doves, Eastern Phoebe, Hooded Oriole, and Rufous-crowned Sparrow can be found right around the buildings. At night you may hear Common Nighthawk, Common Poorwill, and Chuck-will's-widow. By walking up the road and across the cattle-guard behind the store, you can reach a dry hillside covered with cacti and thorny brush. This is the area in which to find Curve-billed Thrasher, Cactus Wren, Vermilion and Ash-throated Flycatchers, Say's Phoebe, Pyrrhuloxia, Canyon Towhee, Verdin, and Black-throated Sparrow. Unless there are lots of campers, a hike along the river will produce Black Phoebe and possibly a Green Kingfisher or a Yellow-throated Warbler. There is even a chance for Black-capped Vireo on the hill behind the store. The trail going up starts behind cabin #15, or take the road behind the store. If this area is crowded, try the trail on the other side of the river. It can be reached from the highway. Ask at the office for directions.

CONCAN BAT CAVE

If you are staying at Neal's Lodge, or are in the area in late evening, you may want to see bats. Drive east on Highway 127 to Farm Road 2690 (4.4). Turn right and start checking the swallows, especially at the low-water crossing on the Frio River (0.1). In the hills off to the right, there is a cave that harbors some 500 to 600 Cave Swallows and about 17,000,000 Brazilian Free-tailed Bats. The cave is not open to the public, but the swallows can usually be seen flying around, particularly in the evening. If you set up a scope at the wooden gate (1.6) on the right, you can see the bats come swirling up like a stream of smoke just at dark.

CAMP WOOD ROAD

Return to Highway 83 and drive north past Garner State Park and continue to the little town of Leakey (17.0 miles from Concan), where you will find restaurants, stores, and cabins. Turn left in the heart of town onto the Camp Wood Road (Ranch Road 337), which runs along a ridge through stands of scrub oak. Although birds are fairly common here, most birders ignore the little ones and concentrate on the numerous Turkey Vultures. Over the years, this has been one of the better spots for Zone-tailed Hawks, and the only way to find one is to check all of the vultures. In flight, even at close range, the Zone-tailed looks almost identical to the vulture. The hawk's black and white tail-bands can be seen only with the aid of binoculars. By looking at enough Turkey Vultures, you will find, sooner or later, a Zone-tailed Hawk.

At Camp Wood (20.7) you have a choice of routes. The shortest one is to turn south onto Highway 55 toward Uvalde, and the birding can be good. At the Nueces River (3.6) check the area below the dam for Green Kingfishers. For several years a pair nested on the east side of the road in a small bank on the north side of the stream. Cave Swallows have attempted to nest in the road culverts (12.0), but the nests are usually wiped out by high water. At Farm Road 334 (2.5) turn right toward Brackettville (30.0) to continue your trip up the Rio Grande.

A longer but more productive route is to turn north at Camp Wood onto Highway 55 toward Rocksprings (29.0), where you may find Cave Swallows. They can usually be found in summer northeast of town along Highway 41 about a mile east of Highway 377. They nest in the Devil's Sinkhole, which is about a mile south of Highway 41 at this point.

From Rocksprings go south on Highway 674, a very scenic road along the West Nueces River. This road will again take you through prime habitat for Golden-cheeked Warbler and Black-capped Vireo. Beginning about 16 miles south of town, stop and listen each time the road passes through good habitat—mature junipers for the warbler and scrub oaks for the vireo. If you are here before 10am or on a cloudy day, both species will probably be heard and seen. The vireo can often be enticed right out into the open by pishing. (*No tapes, please.*)

The highway ends at Brackettville (58.0), where you can turn west to Del Rio. This stretch of road is much drier. Although you may find more western species, it may be a great let-down after the lush vegetation and clear streams of the Hill Country.

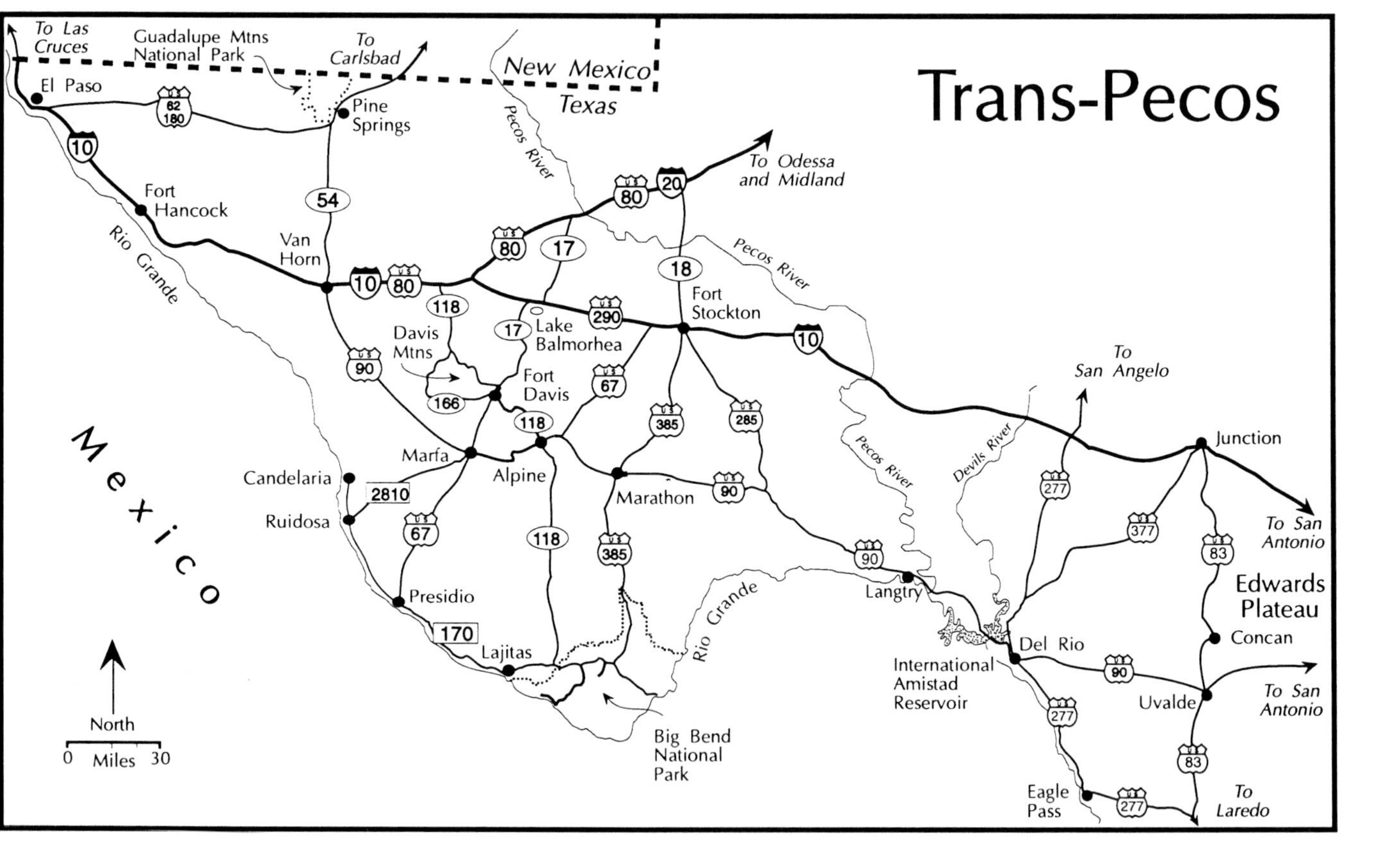
Trans-Pecos
To Las Cruces
Guadalupe Mtns National Park
To Carlsbad
New Mexico
Texas
El Paso
Pine Springs
Pecos River
To Odessa and Midland
Fort Hancock
Van Horn
Rio Grande
Fort Stockton
Lake Balmorhea
Davis Mtns
Fort Davis
To San Angelo
Junction
Marfa
Alpine
Candelaria
Ruidosa
Marathon
Devils River
To San Antonio
Edwards Plateau
Concan
Mexico
Presidio
Lajitas
Langtry
Del Rio
International Amistad Reservoir
Uvalde
Big Bend National Park
Eagle Pass
To Laredo
North
0 Miles 30
10
62
180
54
80
20
17
18
118
290
90
166
67
385
285
277
377
83
2810
170

FROM JUST BEYOND THE PECOS TO THE BIG BEND AREA

Most of the Trans-Pecos—that is, Texas west of the Pecos River—is a part of the northern Chihuahuan Desert, a sparse region of thorny brush, cacti, and seasonal grasses. Much of the terrain is composed of rocky slopes, barren hills, and open plains filled with Creosote Bushes. Its climate is normally dry and temperate, although the area may be raked by blizzards, cloudbursts, and heat waves.

From the foregoing description, you might think that West Texas would be the last spot on earth to visit, but it has a brighter side. In great contrast to the desert, there is a series of elevated plateaus and mountains running down the center of the Trans-Pecos. The towering peaks, rugged canyons, and park-like plains of the higher mountains offer some of the most exciting scenery in Texas, and the high-mountain air has a tantalizing crispness.

The Trans-Pecos has many bird species that nest nowhere else in Texas: Peregrine Falcon, Montezuma and Gambel's Quails, Band-tailed Pigeon, Flammulated Owl, Whip-poor-will, White-throated Swift, Blue-throated, Lucifer, and Broad-tailed Hummingbirds, Western Wood-Pewee, Cordilleran Flycatcher, Cassin's Kingbird, Violet-green Swallow, Steller's and Gray-breasted Jays, Mountain Chickadee, Pygmy Nuthatch, Black-tailed Gnatcatcher, Western Bluebird, Hermit Thrush, Crissal Thrasher, Phainopepla, Hutton's Vireo, Orange-crowned, Virginia's, Colima, Lucy's, and Grace's Warblers, Painted Redstart, Hepatic and Western Tanagers, Black-headed Grosbeak, Rufous-sided Towhee, Black-chinned Sparrow, Dark-eyed (Gray-headed) Junco, and Pine Siskin. A few other species that are not unique to the area, but nest there, include Scaled Quail, Greater Roadrunner, Black-chinned Hummingbird, Scrub Jay, Cactus and Rock Wrens, Curve-billed Thrasher, Pyrrhuloxia, and Black-throated Sparrow.

MARATHON

With the end of the Indian uprisings in West Texas in the 1880s came the settlers with their cattle. And with the arrival of the railroads, a booming cattle industry sprang up. By that time, the Marathon community was well-established as a rail stop, and all Big Bend cattle passed through its stockyards. One big cattle baron, Alfred Gage, built the Gage Hotel in 1927 as his headquarters for his 600-section ranch, the largest landholding in Texas. It is said that over a million head of cattle were bought and sold in the lobby of the Gage hotel. Today, the restored hotel offers a welcome rest and West Texas dining for visitors arriving in or departing from the Big Bend area.

To visit a small county park, turn south on the paved road 0.5 mile west of the intersection of Highways 90 and 385 to the entrance (5.0). (Pavement gives way to dirt after about four miles.) Before reaching the park, the road crosses a creek. This area has been somewhat productive in winter for Sora, Ring-necked Duck, and Eastern Phoebe. Inside the park the creek is dammed to form a small pond. Also in the park are numerous cottonwood trees as well as an open, grassy area. Birds to be found here are Golden-fronted Woodpecker, Yellow-bellied and Red-naped Sapsuckers, Vermilion Flycatcher, Black Phoebe, Marsh and Cactus Wrens, Brown Creeper, and, in winter, numerous sparrows.

Before leaving Marathon for Big Bend, make sure that you have plenty of gasoline. The park entrance at Persimmon Gap is 42 miles south on US 385. The Visitor Center (park headquarters) at Panther Junction is another 26 miles.

BIG BEND NATIONAL PARK

Halfway between El Paso and Laredo, the Rio Grande swings deeply into Mexico to form a huge 107-mile bend. The southernmost part of the bend is now enclosed in Big Bend National Park. This great desert preserve, established in 1944, covers some 775,243 acres or about 1,200 square miles.

Traveling about the park, you are not likely to forget that this is a part of the Chihuahuan Desert. The land is extremely harsh and dry for much of the year. But it is usually lush and green in the late summer and fall after the rainy season starts. Nearly every plant has thorns, and water is usually very scarce.

Despite the harshness, or maybe because of it, this vast park is enticing and magnificent. Its rocky plains stretch in endless panoramas to the distant hills. Its majestic mountains stand etched against a brilliant sky, and the river drifts through towering canyons. A closer look will reveal even more fascinating things. The plants are new and different. The birds and mammals are strange, and even the reptiles are exotic. This is a whole new world to explore.

One of your first stops should be at the Visitor Center (open 8am-5pm), where you can look over the exhibits and books. The naturalist on duty can be very helpful in getting you oriented. You may want to buy a few books, road and trail guides, topographic maps, and checklists of the reptiles, mammals, and birds. Look for Ro Wauer's *Field Guide to Birds of the Big Bend*. (Wauer was a Park Naturalist at Big Bend for years, and helped greatly with this chapter.)

Gasoline can be a problem. Service stations are few and far between, and they do not open very early or stay open very late. Be sure to fill up before leaving Alpine or Marathon. There are gas stations just outside the park at Study Butte. There are only two service stations in the park—one at Panther Junction; the other, at Rio Grande Village. There are campgrounds at Rio Grande Village, the Basin, and at Castolon, as well as small stores. For non-campers, there is a modern lodge, dining room, and stone cottages in the Basin. Advance reservations are strongly recommended; phone 915/477-2291.

Although the good birding spots are widely scattered in this vast park, over 435 species of birds have been found along with 78 species of mammals and 65 species of reptiles and amphibians. You will be lucky to find half that many. Before rushing off in all directions, get yourself a map and circle the best areas. There are dozens of little springs and canyons that may yield good birds. Some of the better places are listed below.

Rio Grande Village This is usually the best year-round birding area in the park. There are several sections to the Village, and the best place to start is at the little store. Park here and walk into the cottonwood grove behind the store. Be sure to check the pond and the boat ramp at the river. This is also a group campsite area.

Among the trees you may find White-winged Doves, Common Ground-Doves, Eastern (rare) and Western Screech-Owls (night), Great Horned Owl, Golden-fronted and Ladder-backed Woodpeckers, Vermilion Flycatcher, Northern Mockingbird, Great-tailed Grackle, Brown-headed Cowbird, House Finch, and Lesser Goldfinch. In summer look for Harris's Hawk, Inca Dove, Yellow-billed Cuckoo, Elf Owl (night), Black-chinned Hummingbird, Western and Cassin's (rare) Kingbirds, Orchard Oriole, Bronzed Cowbird, Summer Tanager, Blue Grosbeak, and Painted Bunting. In winter watch for Northern Flicker (Red-shafted),

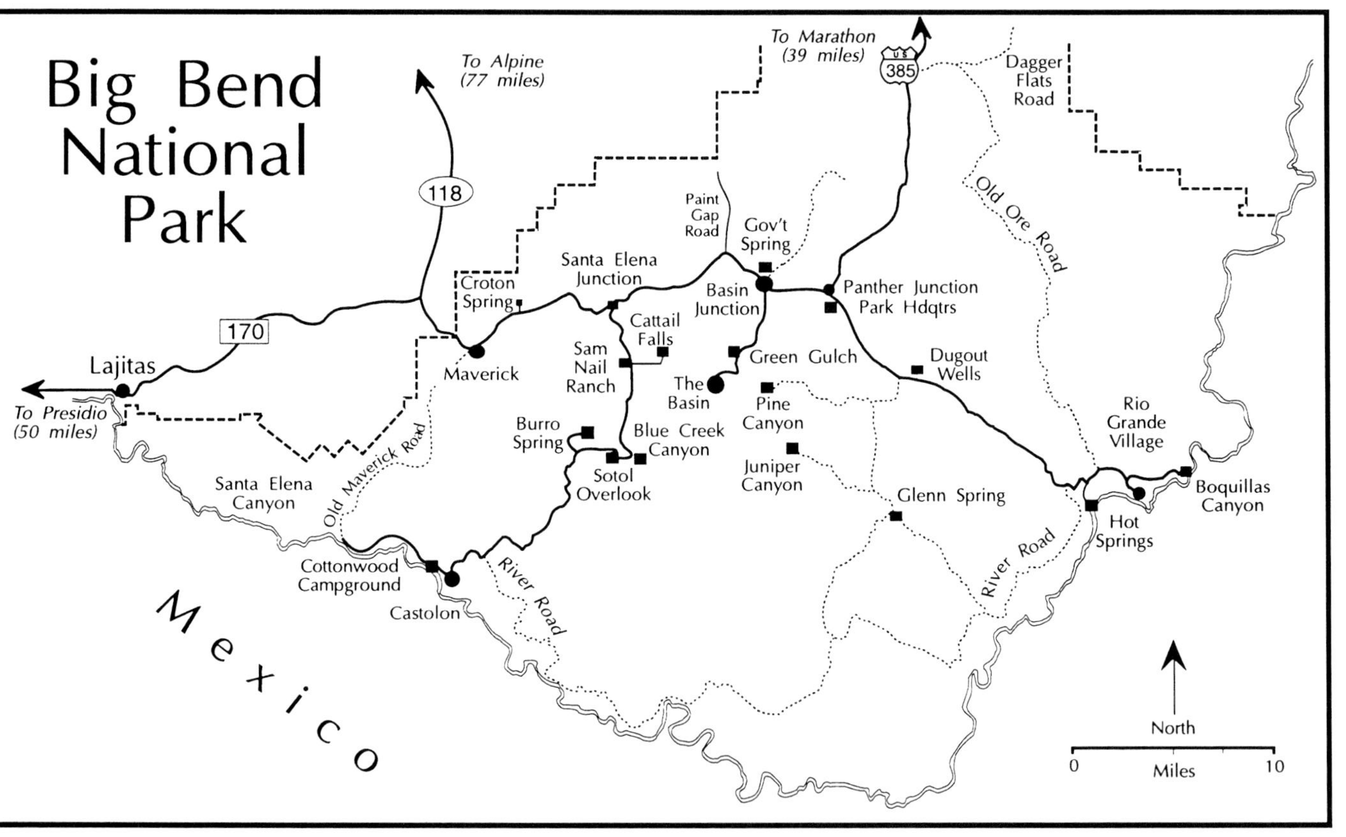
Big Bend
National
Park
To Alpine
(77 miles)
118
170
Lajitas
To Presidio
(50 miles)
To Marathon
(39 miles)
US 385
Dagger
Flats
Road
Old Ore Road
Paint
Gap
Road
Gov't
Spring
Croton
Spring
Santa Elena
Junction
Basin
Junction
Panther Junction
Park Hdqtrs
Maverick
Sam
Nail
Ranch
Cattail
Falls
Green Gulch
Dugout
Wells
The
Basin
Pine
Canyon
Rio
Grande
Village
Burro
Spring
Blue Creek
Canyon
Sotol
Overlook
Juniper
Canyon
Glenn Spring
Boquillas
Canyon
Hot
Springs
Santa Elena
Canyon
Old Maverick Road
River Road
Cottonwood
Campground
Castolon
River Road
Mexico
North
0
Miles
10

Yellow-bellied and Red-naped Sapsuckers, Blue-gray and Black-tailed Gnatcatchers, Brown Thrasher, American Robin, Ruby-crowned and Golden-crowned Kinglets, Orange-crowned and Yellow-rumped Warblers, American Goldfinch, and Dark-eyed Junco. In migration seasons you might find anything. Slate-throated Redstart has been reported here twice. Yellow-green Vireo has also been spotted twice. Thick-billed Kingbird has nested here. A Ruddy Ground-Dove spent the winter and spring of 1988 here. The Sennett's race of the Hooded Oriole found here is almost red about the face. In early November 1991, a Tufted Flycatcher (*Mitrephanes phaeocercus*) was seen at various locations in Rio Grande Village.

The road to the right of the store goes past the trailer campsites to the river (0.7). The cottonwoods and thickets in this area can be very productive. One year a Least Grebe stayed on the little pond here, but you will probably have to settle for a Black Phoebe. Soras can be common in migration. Gray Hawks have nested in the tall cottonwoods here for the past several years. Great Horned Owls are almost always present, and keep an eye overhead for Zone-tailed Hawks.

The road to the left from the store also leads to the river. On a little pond on the right just past the entrance to the campground, you may find a Pied-billed Grebe, an American Coot, or a Ring-necked Duck. Here is where the world's entire native population of *Gambusia affinis* lives; the water is swarming with this tiny mosquitofish. Verdin, Pyrrhuloxia, Canyon Towhee, and, in summer, Bell's Vireo can be found in the nearby thickets of mesquite.

Go back and carefully check the campground. Many campers put out feed, and there is often something good around. A Black-vented Oriole stayed around from September of 1968 to September 1970. Elf Owls are sometimes found in the utility poles, utilizing cavities made by Ladder-backed Woodpeckers. In general, though, you should find the same species here as mentioned above.

A short nature trail starts opposite campsite #18. Here, from the boardwalk among the tangle of willows and Carrizo Cane, you may find Yellow-billed Cuckoo, Painted Bunting, Bell's Vireo, Orchard Oriole, and many migrants in season. The trail ends on a high point above the river. From this vantage point, you can scan the cattail-filled ponds and surroundings. Watch for Belted Kingfisher, Common Yellowthroat, and Yellow-breasted Chat. This is an excellent spot for migrants. Shorebirds can sometimes be found along the shoreline of the river, and, in summer, the air may be filled with Northern Rough-winged, Barn, and Cliff Swallows. Even the Cave Swallow has been seen here, but use great care in identifying them. The race of Cliff Swallow found here may not have a white forehead.

Boquillas Canyon (Bow-KEY-yas) This canyon is better for photography than for birds, but Canyon Wrens and White-throated Swifts can be found along the cliffs. On summer nights, Common Poorwills are usually common along the entrance road. Sage Thrashers will utilize the mesquite flats upcanyon in the fall and early winter.

Old Ore Road This 25-mile primitive road runs from a spot just west of the tunnel to the Dagger Flats Road. Geologists will find it of interest, but birders should take it only if they still need a Cactus Wren, rattlesnake, or tarantula.

Hot Springs One must traverse a rather rough two-mile road and then hike a one-mile trail to reach this deserted spot, but it is one of the more picturesque spots along the river. Say's Phoebes have nested about the ruins of the old motel, and Hooded Orioles nest in the cottonwoods. Verdins and Bell's Vireos frequent the mesquite thickets, and Black-tailed Gnatcatchers can be found in the dry washes.

River Road This very primitive road crosses the southern end of the park from Rio Grande Village to Castolon. It takes less time to go by way of Panther Junction on the paved road, so do not take this road if your time is limited, and do not go at any time of year other than winter. It is long, hot, dry, rough, and almost birdless, but geologists and botanists find it fascinating. The display of Big Bend Bluebonnets in February can be breathtaking.

Dugout Wells It takes about 20 minutes to check this little oasis, and it is usually a waste of time; however, it can be good during migration. Resident species which can be found are Scaled Quail, Greater Roadrunner, Ladder-backed Woodpecker, Northern Mockingbird, and Black-throated Sparrow. Bell's Vireo nests; listen for its two-part song which seems to ask a question and then answers itself. The surrounding creosote flats are good for Verdin and Black-tailed Gnatcatcher.

Pine Canyon The turnoff is about 2.5 miles south of the main road along the graveled Glenn Spring Road. The primitive road goes up the canyon another 5 miles, but the last few are steep, rocky, and sometimes impassable. The road ends at the old Wade Ranch, from which a short trail leads to a waterfall. During the rainy season, the falls can be very impressive.

The canyon is well-wooded and full of birds. Here, among the Arizona Cypress, Ponderosa and Mexican Pinyon Pines, Douglas-fir, Texas Madrone, Big-toothed Maple, and Emory and Grave Oaks, look in summer for Broad-tailed and Black-chinned Hummingbirds, Ash-throated Flycatcher, Gray-breasted Jay, Tufted (Black-crested) Titmouse, Bushtit, Bewick's Wren, Blue-gray Gnatcatcher, Hutton's Vireo, Hepatic Tanager,

Black-headed Grosbeak, Rufous-sided Towhee, and Rufous-crowned Sparrow. The Colima Warbler and several other uncommon species have been found here, but are not to be expected.

Juniper Canyon This is a good birding area, but is difficult to reach. The turnoff is 4.4 miles down the Glenn Spring Road beyond the Pine Canyon Road. From here a very rough and primitive road leads another 7.5 miles into the canyon. A four-mile hiking-trail continues up the canyon to the cabin at Boot Spring. It can be a rough hike, but you should see numerous birds.

Glenn Spring This spot is not worth a special trip, but stop if you are in the area. It is 3 miles beyond the turnoff to Juniper Canyon.

Green Gulch (3.3 miles west of Highway 385) The first 7 miles of the 11-mile road leading into the Basin go through Green Gulch. The birding starts rather slowly but gets better as you go higher. In the desert scrub at the bottom, you may find Greater Roadrunner, Scaled Quail, Curve-billed Thrasher, Verdin, Black-tailed Gnatcatcher, and Black-throated Sparrow. As the brush gets thicker, look for Ladder-backed Woodpecker, Phainopepla, Bell's Vireo, Pyrrhuloxia, and Varied Bunting. When you see the first Drooping Junipers, start watching for flowering agaves. Their tall flowering-stalks furnish a banquet for Scott's Oriole, White-winged Dove, and Black-chinned Hummingbird. The rare Lucifer Hummingbird is sometimes found in the agaves, particularly in mid-summer. (Later in the summer the agaves are not blooming, and then the Lucifers are at higher altitudes.)

Lost Mine Trail The road up Green Gulch tops out at Panther Pass (El. 5,800 ft.), where you will find the start of the Lost Mine Trail. The view into Juniper Canyon at the end of this two-mile trail is one of the finest in the park, but most hikers settle for the magnificent view at the end of the first mile. Buy a pamphlet at the trailhead to follow the self-guiding tour. It will give you a better understanding of the area. The early-morning birders will find this a good area.

The Basin This large bowl-shaped valley sits in the very center of the Chisos Mountains at about 5,500 feet of elevation. The beauty of the surrounding peaks and the cool, highland climate makes this a favorite spot for both birds and people in summer. The Chisos Lodge and a large campground are located here. Gray-breasted Jays and Canyon Towhees are often abundant, and you may hear Elf Owls and Common Poorwills during the campfire talks on summer nights, but the best birding is along the trails that emanate from the Basin. There are 32 hiking-trails in the park totaling more than 150 miles. These are listed in the *Hiker's Guide* published by the Big Bend Natural History Association and available at park

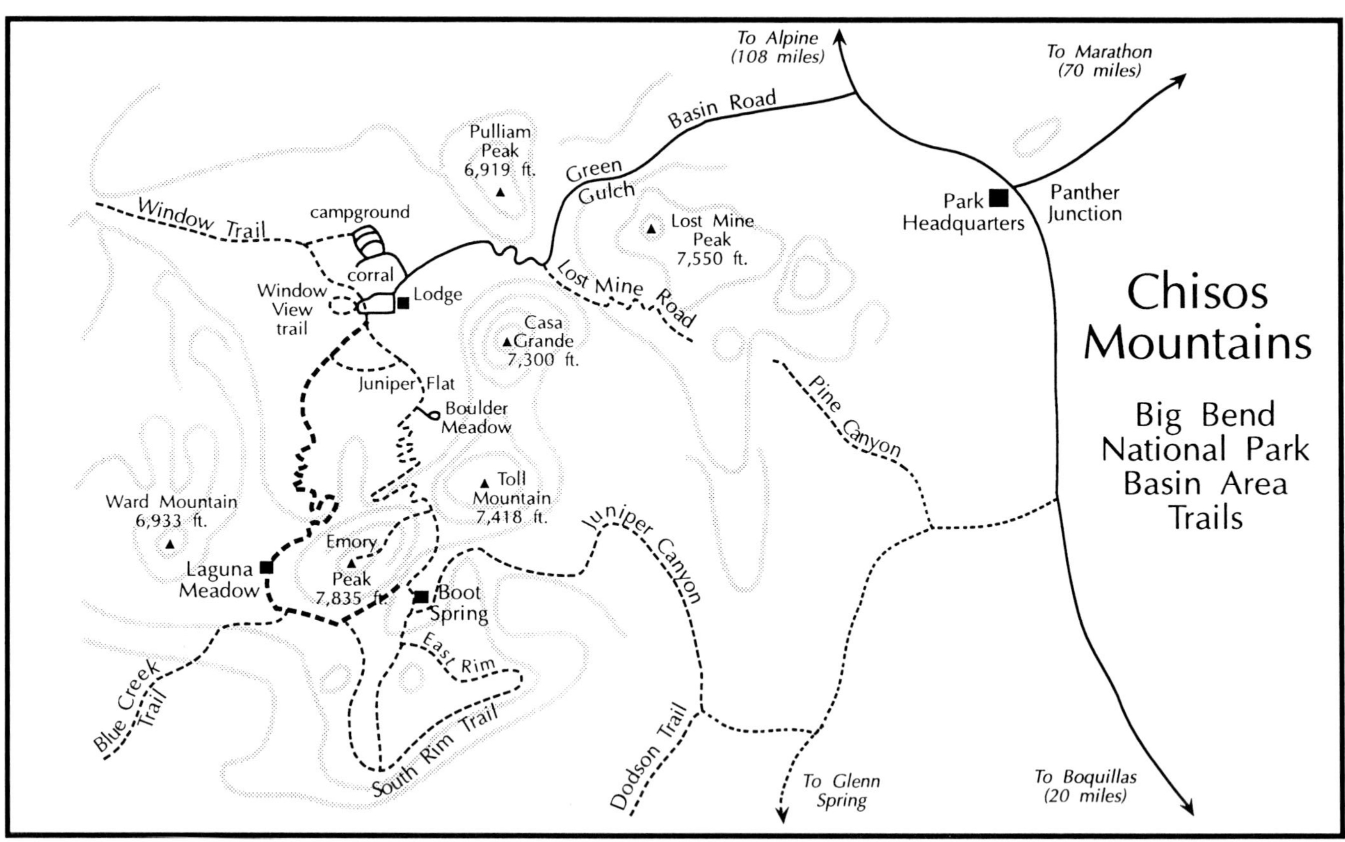
Chisos Mountains
Big Bend National Park Basin Area Trails
To Alpine (108 miles)
To Marathon (70 miles)
Basin Road
Park Headquarters
Panther Junction
Pulliam Peak 6,919 ft.
Green Gulch
Lost Mine Peak 7,550 ft.
Lost Mine Road
Window Trail
campground
corral
Window View trail
Lodge
Casa Grande 7,300 ft.
Pine Canyon
Juniper Flat
Boulder Meadow
Toll Mountain 7,418 ft.
Ward Mountain 6,933 ft.
Juniper Canyon
Emory Peak 7,835 ft.
Laguna Meadow
Boot Spring
East Rim
Blue Creek Trail
South Rim Trail
Dodson Trail
To Glenn Spring
To Boquillas (20 miles)

headquarters or from the ranger station at the Basin. Campground (fee) limit is 14 days.

The Window Trail This 5.2-mile round-trip trail starts at the Basin Trailhead across the parking lot from the lodge, but it is a mile shorter if you catch it along the southwest edge of the campground. The trail crosses a brushy grassland interspersed with oaks, pinyon, and juniper. In the early morning you should find Ladder-backed Woodpecker, Say's Phoebe, Bewick's and Cactus Wrens, Scott's Oriole, Pyrrhuloxia, Blue Grosbeak, Canyon Towhee, and Black-chinned and Rufous-crowned Sparrows. With luck you may find a Gray Vireo or a Varied Bunting. The bunting is usually found below the sewer ponds. Even an Elegant Trogon has been spotted along this trail.

Campground Canyon There is no well-defined trail into Campground Canyon on the southern slope of Pulliam Ridge, the ridge that forms the northwest edge of the Basin, but it is of great interest to birders because Gray and Black-capped Vireos and rare Rufous-capped Warblers have been found on its slopes. Access is difficult here, and you might decide to spend the time more wisely birding elsewhere.

Boot Spring In summer this is the most exciting area for birding in the park. The Colima Warbler is the main attraction, but there are other tantalizing possibilities. When you are this close to the border, who knows what may wander up from Mexico? Yellow-eyed Juncos have been reported here; there have been thrushes and warblers from Mexico, and once there was a intriguing and unconfirmed report of an Imperial Woodpecker from south of the border.

The hike to the springs is exciting and very hard on the muscles. All of the routes into the canyon require long hikes. (The shortest way is up Juniper Canyon, a mere 4-mile hike; it is also a rigorous, difficult, and confusing trail. If you survive, you deserve a medal. Avoid this alternative.) The Boot Canyon Trail via Boulder Meadow and Pinnacle Pass (El. 7,100 ft.) is only 4.5 miles straight up the side of the canyon. Of course, it does seem longer as you slide back down.

The 11-mile loop-route used by most birders goes up the South Rim Trail from the Basin Trailhead via Laguna Meadow, across the Boot Canyon Cutoff, and back down the Boot Canyon Trail through Boulder Meadow. Following this route is 5.5 miles to the springs, but the hiking is much easier and the birding is far better. However, you will never forget those last 4 miles down from Pinnacle Pass. (A good point to remember, however, is that, as indicated below, Colima Warblers can be present all summer at Laguna Meadow. If this is your only, target you may not have to go the whole loop-route, though the Boot Spring area itself is excellent for many other birds as well.)

There is no drinking-water at Boot Spring. Be sure to take along plenty. This is usually a long, hot trip, but it is sometimes cold even in midsummer.

If hiking is not your cup of tea, you can rent a horse. This is not always the most satisfactory means of birding because you are accompanied by a wrangler, who is usually more interested in getting to the end of the trail than in stopping for birds. It may be better to arrange a special trip. The stables will make almost any arrangement for which you are willing to pay. An alternative solution is to ride up and hike down—that is if you can still walk after getting off the horse.

Agave in the Chisos Basin attracts a variety of birds — Ty and Julie Hotchkiss

Mid-April through mid-June is the best time to find the breeding birds of the lower elevations, but some of the highland species do not start to nest until the summer rains begin in early July. By late June many of the lowland birds have moved into the mountains, and by late August there are postbreeders from the Rockies.

As soon as you leave the Basin Trailhead, start watching for Ash-throated Flycatcher, Bewick's Wren, and Rufous-crowned Sparrow. Crissal Thrasher and Black-chinned Sparrow have nested on the brushy hillsides at Laguna Meadow (3.5). When the red-flowered Mountain Sage and the yellow-flowered Century Plant are in bloom, this meadow is a great spot for Scott's Oriole and Black-chinned Hummingbird. With luck you may find post-nesting Lucifer and Rufous Hummingbirds as well.

Above Laguna Meadow you will enter the woodlands of deciduous oaks and maples that are preferred by the Colima Warbler. In early summer the new leaves of the oaks stand out in sharp contrast to the surrounding vegetation, making it easy to pick out clumps where the warbler might be found. The birds can sometimes be found at lower elevations when they first arrive in mid-April or just before they leave in mid-September, but the nesting sites are all above 5,900 feet in elevation. (The nests are built on the ground.)

Although this warbler responds well to squeaks, pishes, and owl calls, it can be hard to see clearly because it is neither gaudy nor very active. It is usually located by its trilling song, which is suggestive of that of a Pine Warbler or a Chipping Sparrow. Luckily, the males are persistent singers from late April to about mid-June. The females can often be found by their sharp *psit* call-notes.

At the start of the South Rim Trail, 0.5 mile above Laguna Meadow, there is a trail junction. The trail to the right continues along the rim and joins the East Rim Trail, which eventually comes back to the Boot Canyon Trail after 3 miles. You should turn left and follow the Boot Canyon Trail; this portion of the trail is called the "Colima Warbler Trail." It is 1.5 miles to the cabin at the springs, which are located in about the middle of the canyon. Boot Canyon is well wooded with Arizona Cypress, Ponderosa Pine, Douglas-fir, Texas Madrone, Big-tooth Maple, and Emory and Grave Oaks.

The Colima Warbler can be found either above or below the cabin. Also watch for Band-tailed Pigeon, and Broad-tailed, Blue-throated, and Magnificent (rare) Hummingbirds. During fall migration, hundreds of Rufous and Broad-tailed Hummingbirds are seen every day. In August 1991 a Berylline Hummingbird was found here. Watch for Acorn Woodpecker, Cordilleran Flycatcher, Violet-green Swallow, Gray-breasted

Jay, Tufted Titmouse, Bushtit, White-breasted and Pygmy (sporadic in fall) Nuthatches, Hutton's and Solitary Vireos, Painted Redstarts (some summers), and Hepatic Tanager. Warbler migration is fabulous with Nashville, Virginia's, Yellow, Yellow-rumped, Black-throated Gray, Townsend's, Hermit, Grace's, Wilson's, and Black-and-white Warblers. Aztec Thrush has been found here on at least three occasions. Red-faced Warbler has been reported about six times (usually August), and a Slate-throated Redstart was seen here in the spring of 1990. If you camp here overnight, you should hear Whip-poor-will, Eastern (rare) and Western Screech-Owls, Flammulated Owl, and perhaps a Long-eared Owl.

About a half-mile below the cabin on your way back to the Basin, you will find the Boot, a volcanic spire shaped like an upside-down cowboy boot. In the same area, you will find the Emory Peak Trail, which goes one mile to the top of the highest peak (El. 7,835 ft.) in the park. There are not many birds on the mountain, but the view is terrific.

A half-mile below the Emory Peak Trail is Pinnacle Pass (El. 7,100 ft.), from which you can get a fine view of the Basin far below. From this high vantage point, you can see Red-tailed Hawks, White-throated Swifts, an occasional Golden Eagle, and Turkey Vultures. Carefully check all of the vultures to make sure that none of them has a black-and-white-banded tail. This is the best area to find the Zone-tailed Hawk, and in flight it looks very much like a Turkey Vulture.

A 1.5-mile series of steep switchbacks will bring you to the floor of the Basin at Boulder Meadow only 1.5 miles from the lodge. You may be too tired to care about the birds in this little meadow, but if you take time to come back another day, you will find it a good spot. Lucifer Hummingbirds are sometimes common in summer about the agaves.

Government Spring This spring is on the left side of the road to the Grapevine Hills (0.3 mile west of Basin Junction) about a half-mile north of the main road from Panther Junction to Maverick. A few birds come here to drink. Look for Scaled Quail, Pyrrhuloxia, Varied Bunting (in wet years), Canyon Towhee, Black-throated Sparrow, and migrants. Many wintering sparrows feed at the horse corral. Early in the morning or just at dusk, you can often see Mule Deer, Collared Peccary, Coyote, and Desert Cottontail coming to the spring, and you might even see a Gray Fox, a Bobcat, or even a Mountain Lion.

The rest of the road to the Grapevine Hills is hot and dusty and, usually, not worth the effort. But it can be good habitat for Lucifer Hummingbirds since they do prefer the arroyos here in the grasslands. The same may be said of the Paint Gap Road, too. Croton Spring can be good for mammals, but the spring is not so productive since it was "improved" a few years ago.

Chisos Basin and Pulliam Ridge from the top of Emory Peak *Ro Wauer*

Sam Nail Ranch The parking area for the ranch is 3.0 miles south of the Santa Elena Junction. Most of the buildings are gone, but the windmill still creaks out a trickle of water that lures numerous birds and mammals. In season, it is an excellent migrant trap. The birds are concentrated in a very small area. By spending an hour or two in this peaceful spot (a bench in the shade is provided for your comfort), you may see Lucifer and Black-chinned Hummingbirds, Yellow-billed Cuckoo, Long-billed Thrasher (last 3 years), Bell's Vireo, and Painted Buntings. Orange-crowned, Virginia's, Yellow, Nashville, Blackburnian, Prairie, and Wilson's Warblers have been found in migration. Look for Yellow-breasted Chat, Northern Cardinal, Pyrrhuloxia, Blue Grosbeak, Summer Tanager, Scott's Oriole, House Finch, and Black-throated Sparrow. Crissal Thrasher and Varied Buntings are fairly common here. They come to the water, but are more often seen in the area between the parking area and the old buildings.

Cattail Falls This is a beautiful spot if you can find it. Cattail Creek starts on the north side of Ward Mountain and flows westward. During periods of heavy rain, it actually crosses the highway just north of the Sam Nail Ranch. To reach the falls, go east on Oak Canyon Road, which starts almost opposite the Sam Nail Ranch parking area. This dirt road soon bears left and crosses the dry bed of Cattail Creek. Park and walk up the creekbed.

Blue Creek Canyon On the left near the highest point on the Santa Elena Road, you will come to the Blue Creek Overlook, from which a trail drops into the canyon and goes 5.5 miles up to Laguna Meadow. About a mile above the old Wilson Ranch and near a spectacular formation of red rock spires, a narrow canyon branches off to the north. A rare live-oak (*Quercus graciliformis*), not found anywhere else, occurs far up the canyon. The canyon is particularly good for Lucifer Hummingbirds, Gray Vireos, and Varied Buntings in April and May. Even Black-capped Vireos have been seen here.

Sotol Vista There are not many birds here, but the view is terrific.

Burro Spring This is one of the better springs in the desert areas of the park, and it attracts many animals. The one-mile trail to it starts from the road that leads to the Burro Mesa Pour-off. There is another trail that goes to the pour-off, but it is not worth the effort.

The spring attracts the usual mammals, such as Mule Deer, Collared Peccary, and Coyote, but you may also see Burro. Most of the Burros have just wandered up from Mexico, but they have adapted quickly and well to the hostile environment. The tourists may consider these hardy animals to be cute, but they can be very detrimental to the fragile habitat and to the native mammals.

Castolon (25.0 miles from Santa Elena Junction) The weedy fields near Castolon are at their best in early winter, when you can find great flocks of sparrows. The common sparrows are Vesper, Clay-colored, Brewer's, and White-crowned. With a little more effort, you may find Savannah, Grasshopper, Baird's, Cassin's, Chipping, Field, White-throated, Lincoln's, Swamp, and Song.

Cottonwood Campground is located here (fee, primitive). Turkey Vultures may try to share your evening meal with you, for they like to scavenge food from the tables. Greater Roadrunners are very tame, and White-winged Doves wake you early in the morning. Migrant warblers such as Yellow-rumped (Audubon's) are common in spring. Other nesting species include Inca, Mourning, and White-winged Doves, Western Screech-Owl (common in this area), Great Horned Owl, Common Poorwill, Ash-throated Flycatcher, Thick-billed (nested last three years) and Western Kingbirds, Black-tailed Gnatcatcher, Lucy's Warbler (nested last five years in mesquite thicket on north edge of campground), Summer Tanager, and Orchard Oriole.

The mesquite thickets and willows along the river may yield Ladder-backed Woodpecker, Common Yellowthroat, Vermilion Flycatcher, and

Painted Redstart
Gail Diane Luckner

Canyon Towhee. Other birds to be found in summer are Yellow-billed Cuckoo, Black-chinned Hummingbird, Bell's Vireo, Yellow-breasted Chat, Orchard Oriole, Summer Tanager, Blue Grosbeak, and Painted Bunting. Lucy's Warbler can be found in the mesquite thickets from Castolon to Santa Elena Canyon.

Santa Elena Canyon (8.0) You might want to visit this very scenic spot, but it is not particularly good for birds. However, you will be impressed by the Peregrine Falcons and the White-throated Swifts that zoom up and down the canyon, and who can forget the Canyon Wrens, whose beautiful songs echo down from the cliffs? The 1.7-mile round-trip trail into the canyon has markers identifying the plants and features. Be on the alert for rarities; on at least two occasions Rufous-capped Warblers have made an appearance in this canyon.

Old Maverick Road This 14-mile gravel road leading from Santa Elena Canyon to Maverick (west entrance to park) does not have much in the way of birdlife, but it makes an interesting alternative to retracing your way back up the main road. At the turn of the century, this was prime grassland with cottonwood-lined streams. By the end of World War I, overgrazing and drought had reduced it to its present state.

Highway 118 to Alpine Of all the routes into the park, this one offers the best opportunities for birding. In winter the grasslands along the way abound with sparrows and Lark Buntings. About midway there is a wooded rest area that should be checked for migrants. Golden-fronted

Woodpecker is resident. North of that, you will find Calamity Creek, which sometimes attracts a few birds.

The Lajitas-Presidio Route and Alternate The route to Marfa via Highways 170 and 67 is longer and rougher, but offers a scenic trip along the river. The headquarters for the Big Bend Ranch State Natural Area (16.0) are on the south side of the road. Stop here at the Warnock Center for information on this new state recreation area.

In Lajitas (1.2) turn south (toward the river) at the center of town where there are signs advertising the trading post, golf course, and RV campground. Down this dirt road there are four ponds, two on each side of the road (0.1). The two closest to the road are the least productive. The other two have vegetation all around them and are difficult to see; however, they are worth the time to check. A Ruddy Ground-Dove spent a month here in 1990. Resident species which you may find include "Mexican Duck" Mallard, Inca and White-winged Doves, Lucifer Hummingbird (rare), House Finch, and Black-chinned Sparrow. In winter also look for Green-backed Heron, Swamp Sparrow, and Lesser Goldfinch. Migrants include various western warbler species, Grasshopper Sparrow, and Lazuli Bunting. Several unusual sightings include Sora, American Swallow-tailed Kite, and Common Grackle.

Between Lajitas and Redford, the land is characterized by Prickly Pear, agave, and Ocotillo, typical plants of the Chihuahuan Desert. At least one pair of Zone-tailed Hawks nests in this canyon. Take a few minutes and check all the "Turkey Vultures" you see overhead for one with a banded tail. Common Ravens are also seen overhead. At any of the higher overlooks in the canyon, in summer, you should see White-throated Swifts flying in the updrafts along with Violet-green, Cliff, and, in migration, Cave (rare) Swallows. In the desert itself watch for residents such as Inca Dove, Common Ground-Dove, Verdin, and Crissal Thrasher. In winter look for Sage Thrashers and Sage Sparrows.

At Redford (34.0) the land starts becoming more agricultural. In summer you can find Yellow-breasted Chat, Northern Cardinal, and Painted and Varied Buntings. After crossing Alamito Creek (9.0), between the road and the Rio Grande River, a small marshy area can be loaded with migrant waterfowl and shorebirds. Most of the shorebirds are Least Sandpipers, but Westerns are also common, and there will be fewer Baird's.

For a little history, stop at Fort Leaton (2.8). This is also the western headquarters for permits to Big Bend Ranch State Natural Area. The permits cover all park activities, such as rafting, fishing, hiking, and camping. Bus tours are available.

At Presidio (3.5) you have another choice. You can turn north to Marfa on US 67 or continue northwest on River Road 170 to Ruidosa (36.0). The road to Ruidosa is narrow and undulating. Drive carefully because loose cattle and other livestock are common. Along the way watch for Turkey Vultures, Greater Roadrunner, White-winged and Mourning Doves, Verdin, Cactus Wren, and Crissal Thrasher. Black Vultures are rather common here, part of a small population of forty to sixty birds in the Ruidosa-Candelario area. (One must travel 150-200 miles east to see more Black Vultures.) As you near Ruidosa, a pair of Harris's Hawks is resident, and you may begin to see Gambel's Quail.

The best birding is beyond Ruidosa along the road to Candelaria (12.0). Along this stretch watch the skies carefully, for Common Black-Hawk, Zone-tailed Hawk, and Peregrine and Prairie Falcons have all nested in this area. Golden Eagles are fairly common, especially in migration. Near Candelaria an oxbow of the river can be alive with spring migrant waterfowl and shorebirds. In the sandy draws and in the trees look for migrating warblers and possibly a Lazuli Bunting. In summer such species as Ladder-backed Woodpecker, Bell's Vireo, Common Yellowthroat, Yellow-breasted Chat, Summer Tanager, Varied Bunting, and Hooded and Scott's Orioles may be present. In May and June you may be lucky enough to hear the high-pitched trill of, or actually see, a Lucy's Warbler. This area around Candelaria is one of the few reliable places in Texas where this bird nests. In winter numerous species of sparrows are found.

This road ends at Candelaria, so return to Ruidosa, and if you are really adventurous, take Ranch Road 2810 to the left over the Chinati Mountains (*not recommended for low-clearance vehicles*) to Marfa (52.0). This road is dirt and narrow, but very scenic. (There are no bridges on 2810. If it is raining or has recently rained, watch out for low-water crossings which may be washed out.) After going over the pass (20.0), the road is paved for the last 32 miles.

(Alternately, you can go all the way back to Presidio before turning north onto US 67 to Marfa.) Phainopeplas and Scrub Jays are rather common around cottonwoods and junipers. In winter you might find Williamson's Sapsucker and Steller's Jay. All land off the road is private; do not trespass.

Presidio (36.0) is said to be the oldest settlement in the United States. The Indians inhabited this region long before Spaniards arrived in the sixteenth century. North of Presidio, on US 67, you will find the ghost town of Shafter (19.0), where some $18,000,000 worth of silver was mined. Check the cottonwoods along Cibolo Creek here for birds.

Just before you reach Marfa (40.0), one mile south, on the east side of US 67 you will find an area flooded with water from the sewage-treatment plant. Here you should see in winter White-faced Ibis, Snow Goose, "Mexican Duck" Mallard, other dabbling ducks, Yellow-headed Blackbird, and migrant shorebirds (yellowlegs, peeps, etc.).

If you are going to the Davis Mountains, you may take Highway 17 north from Marfa, or visit Alpine first.

Highway 90 — Marfa to Alpine

The prairies along Highway 90 between Marfa and Alpine are good for Eastern and Western (winter only) Meadowlarks, Horned Lark, an occasional Prairie Falcon, Golden Eagle, and, in winter, flocks of sparrows and McCown's and Chestnut-collared Longspurs. Occasionally, Swainson's Hawks nest on power poles along the way.

With a little luck, you will see Pronghorns, which may run along the fence in a mad race with your car before disappearing across the plains with their white tails flashing. These curious animals can sometimes be lured closer by waving a white handkerchief from the window of your car.

During World War II, the now-overgrown airport at Marfa was a busy military base. Most of the airmen stationed there were bored stiff. An adventuresome few spent their spare time looking for the ghost light. Ghost or no ghost, there is definitely a light on most nights (still true as of this writing in 1991). From Highway 90 near the airport, it appears to be in the foothills of Chinati Peak some 20 miles away in a southwesterly direction. It looks like a lantern or bonfire, which brightens, flicker, fades, and brightens again. It even seems to move around. Some people think that it is the lights of a distant car, but there are no roads in that area. A hundred years ago, when the light was first observed, there were no cars.

Several explanations for the light have been offered, but none verified. Many a doubting-Thomas has called it swamp gas. Swamp gas in the middle of the desert? Other unromantic and scientific types explain it away as a phosphate deposit that glows on dark nights after a rain, but it can be seen on moonlit nights in dry weather. Local legends say that it is the ghost of Alsate, an ancient Indian chief, looking for his lost wives.

Many people have tried to find the light. The airmen dropped sacks of flour on it at night and then tried to find it in the daytime. But it does not stay in one spot. Cowboys and tourists have covered the area on foot and by horseback and have found nothing unusual. More-organized groups have spent months trying to triangulate the light from different directions, but to no avail.

Next to the former entrance to the base, the State Highway Department has opened a sizable picnic area as the official Marfa Light viewing position.

ALPINE

You may think of Alpine (population 5,700, elevation 4,484 ft.) as a small town, but it is the largest town in the largest county (5,935 square miles) in Texas. It is the home of Sul Ross State University, named after a former governor and Civil War general. To most travelers Alpine is only a rest stop, and it has been one for centuries because several old Indian trails passed this way. Cabeza de Vaca, the first European to cross Texas, camped about a mile north of the present town in 1532.

Cabeza de Vaca and three others were the sole survivors of the 600-man Narvaez Expedition, which set out to colonize Florida in 1528. Beset by hostile Indians and a shortage of food, the dwindling colony sailed westward in small boats, hoping to find more hospitable conditions. The boats were caught in the currents of the mighty Mississippi River and pushed out into the Gulf. Eventually, some were cast ashore on Galveston Island. For seven years the survivors were treated alternately as slaves and gods by the various Indian tribes that they encountered on their way across Texas. After camping near Alpine, they crossed the Rio Grande near Presidio and reached other Spanish forces in Sinaloa in 1536.

Northwest of Alpine lie the gentle-looking Davis Mountains. If you are going west from Alpine, it is only a few miles farther to Van Horn by way of Highway 118 through Fort Davis than along the rather barren Highway 90. After the hot, dry stretches of the Chihuahuan Desert, you will find the green slopes of the mountains a welcome relief.

Going north from Alpine on Highway 118 on the way to Fort Davis, you will find a large pond (16.0) next to the road. View it from the stone wall. *Do not cross the fence.* In winter you should find various ducks, including Cinnamon Teal, "Mexican Duck" Mallard, Ring-necked Duck, Bufflehead, Northern Shoveler, Gadwall, and others. Look for Eastern Phoebes and Eastern Bluebirds. There are two records for Common Goldeneye. In summer you might look for Anna's Hummingbird (one nesting record in 1976), Black Phoebe, Vermilion and Ash-throated Flycatchers, Phainopepla, Black-headed and Blue Grosbeaks, Summer Tanager, and Hooded Oriole (one record). In migration look for Osprey, *Empidonax* flycatchers, five species of swallows, House Wren, Western Tanager, Indigo Bunting, and warblers such as Yellow-rumped, Wilson's, Yellow, MacGillivray's, and Common Yellowthroat.

A picnic-area rest stop is just a mile and a half up the road. A traveler can overnight here.

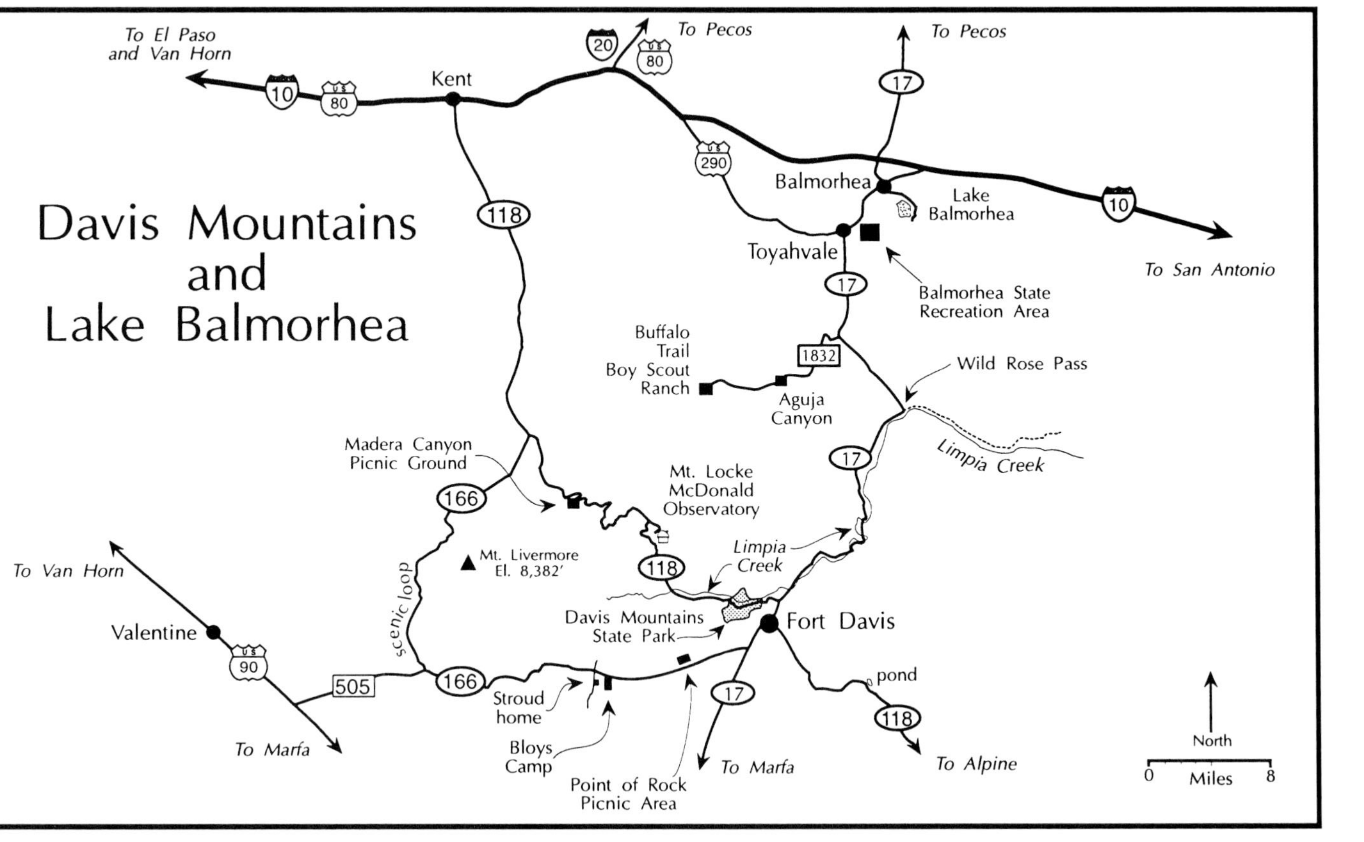
Davis Mountains and Lake Balmorhea
To El Paso and Van Horn
10
80
Kent
20
80
To Pecos
17
To Pecos
290
Balmorhea
Lake Balmorhea
10
To San Antonio
118
Toyahvale
17
Balmorhea State Recreation Area
Buffalo Trail Boy Scout Ranch
1832
Aguja Canyon
Wild Rose Pass
Limpia Creek
Madera Canyon Picnic Ground
166
17
Mt. Locke McDonald Observatory
Mt. Livermore El. 8,382′
Limpia Creek
118
To Van Horn
scenic loop
Davis Mountains State Park
Fort Davis
Valentine
90
505
166
Stroud home
17
pond
118
North
To Marfa
Bloys Camp
Point of Rock Picnic Area
To Marfa
To Alpine
0 Miles 8

DAVIS MOUNTAINS AND LAKE BALMORHEA

The Davis Mountains have a park-like look of grassy expanses and scattered trees. They seem to welcome the visitor—not to challenge him as do the other mountains of the Trans-Pecos. This genial appearance is due in part to a rather ample rainfall of 20 inches a year, and to the fact that these mountains are composed of a series of lava flows which are recent, geologically speaking. The hills are rounded and well-vegetated, not rugged and bare like those of the Chisos. The few cliffs are not very high, and they only add to the charm. Only along the northern edge of the mountains, where streams have cut their way out of the highlands, are there rugged canyons.

Mount Livermore (El. 8,382 ft.) is the highest peak in these mountains and the second highest in Texas. In fact, there is not a higher mountain east of this point until one reaches the Alps in Europe. The upper parts of the peak are privately owned and closed to public access. This is regrettable because the forests of Gambel's Oak, Ponderosa and Limber Pines, and aspen on top are a relic of another era when the climate was wetter and the flora of the Rocky Mountains extended farther south.

The rich birding areas around the lower parts of the mountain are accessible from the 74-mile scenic loop that encircles the peak. The starting point for this trip is 24 miles north of Alpine at Fort Davis, which has stores, motels, cafes, and service stations.

This little town has only 900 people, but it is the largest in Jeff Davis County. The other town, Valentine, has only 330. The entire county has a population of about one person for each of its 2,363 square miles. Cattle, sheep, deer, and Pronghorns far outnumber people.

This area is off the beaten path today, but during the last half of the 19th century it was not. After the discovery of gold in California, thousands of people migrated west via the San Antonio/El Paso Trail, which passed this way to take advantage of the abundance of grass and water. The wagon trains and cattle of the migrants were prime targets for the raiding Mescalero Apaches and Comanches. To provide protection, the United States Army, in 1854, established Fort Davis, named after Jefferson Davis, then Secretary of War. The fort was used off and on until 1891. In 1963 it was made a National Historical Site. The site is open 8am-5pm all year, except Christmas and New Year's Day. It encompasses 460 acres, has several miles of hiking-trails, and a shaded picnic area.

Check the area by the gate or along the Tall Grass Nature Trail for Eastern and Western Meadowlarks (Western in winter only), Horned Lark, and Cassin's Sparrow. Look for Rock and Canyon Wrens, Canyon Towhee, and Rufous-crowned Sparrow by the rocky cliffs. In summer Cassin's Kingbirds and Orchard Orioles nest in the trees along the highway.

There are three distinct birding areas in the Davis Mountains: (1) The Scenic Loop around the mountains, (2) Limpia Creek, and (3) Aguja Canyon. Although many birds are common to all three areas, each has a few species that are not seen elsewhere in the mountains. Some 235 species of birds have been recorded in Jeff Davis County, and the Davis Mountains Christmas Counts average over 100 species. All of these birds are seen from the roadsides, because West Texas birders make it a rule never to trespass on private property. Visitors should behave accordingly.

The Scenic Loop

To follow this 74-mile loop go north from Fort Davis on Highway 17. Travel in a counter-clockwise direction, turning left at both Highway 118 (1.0) and Highway 166 (29.0) until returning to Fort Davis. The first few miles of Highway 118 follow Limpia Creek, which will be discussed later.

After leaving Limpia Creek behind, Highway 118 traverses grassy hillsides with scattered clumps of Gray and Emory Oaks, Pinyon Pine, and Alligator and One-seeded Junipers. Especially note the Alligator Juniper with its conspicuous squarish bark-scales, which resemble the hide of an alligator. During June, another feature of this part of the loop is the 12-foot stalks of the yellow-blossomed Century Plants. When these are in bloom, watch for Scott's Orioles and Black-chinned Hummingbirds around the flowers. Another favorite of the hummingbirds is the Scarlet Bouvardia, which blooms most of the summer. It is an attractive shrub with neat foliage and clusters of bright red, honeysuckle-like flowers.

Davis Mountains State Park (1,869 acres) is about 3 miles up Highway 118, located in the foothills between the grassland and the mountains (entrance fee $3.00 weekdays, $4.00 weekends). It has an excellent campground (fee) and the Indian Lodge (Box 786, Fort Davis, TX 79734; phone 915/426-3254). The lodge has good food, comfortable rooms, and a heated pool. It is a great spot to spend a few days; advance reservations are highly recommended. An elevation of 4,900 to 5,500 feet provides

Davis Mountains — Ro Wauer

mild winters and cool summers, with average rainfall of 19 inches. There is a 4.5-mile hiking trail connecting the park with Fort Davis.

Campers are usually awakened by the noisy Cassin's Kingbirds and Scrub Jays. Other birds to look for here and along the highway are Ladder-backed and Acorn Woodpeckers, White-winged Dove, Say's Phoebe, Tufted (Black-crested) Titmouse, Bushtit, Rock and Bewick's Wrens, Western Bluebird, Phainopepla, Chipping Sparrow, and House Finch. In summer look for White-throated Swift, Common Poorwill, Western and Summer Tanagers, Pyrrhuloxia, Black-headed Grosbeak, Canyon Towhee, Cassin's and Lark Sparrows, and Orchard Oriole. In winter, in addition to the above residents, you should be able to find Red-naped Sapsucker, Rufous-sided and Green-tailed Towhees, and two to four races of Dark-eyed Junco. There is only one record of Williamson's Sapsucker, but they probably are annual in the mountains.

The park has become one of the better locations for seeing Montezuma Quail. Early in the morning, the birds take dust-baths in the bare spots along the perimeter of the camping areas. Sometimes they are easiest to find in and along the dry wash which runs through the middle of the

See Montezuma at this campground area at Host site

Elf Owls
Charles H. Gambill

campground. In evening they may stroll right through the campground, adding people to their life-lists. Also look for them along the road to Indian Lodge and in the canyon behind the lodge. They are either fearless or foolish, because crowds frighten them not at all. Along the highway they usually freeze when a car approaches; however, sharp-eyed birders may find them by driving slowly and watching closely. The best location is along Highway 118 on either side of the Mount Locke Road during the two hours before dark in the evening. The quail seem to be most common during the year following a wet year.

Those interested in astronomy should take the trip up the steepest and highest road in the state of Texas to the McDonald Observatory atop Mount Locke (El. 6,802 ft.). The facility is operated by the University of Texas. Tours are given each afternoon year-round (also in the mornings in summer), and the view from the top is excellent. In the residential area at the base of the mountains, you may find Montezuma Quail.

Beyond the Mount Locke Road, the highway soon passes the mile-high marker and stays above that elevation for several miles. This higher country is more forested, and the birdlife changes. The best birding spot is the **Madera Canyon Picnic Grounds**. Plan to spend an hour or so in the vicinity. *Do not cross any fences*—all land around the picnic area is privately owned.

Band-tailed Pigeons should be watched for throughout the high country, and flocks of Bushtits can be found. Acorn Woodpeckers nest in the dead pines across the creek. Violet-green Swallows nest in the old woodpecker holes. Black-headed Grosbeaks and Hepatic Tanagers nest in the Ponderosa Pines. On June nights Common Poorwills and Elf Owls can be heard. Mountain Chickadees and Steller's Jays sometimes wander down from their home on the slopes of Mount Livermore after the nesting season or in winter, when you can also find Townsend's Solitaire, Mountain Bluebird, and Dark-eyed Junco. In migration Black-throated Gray, Townsend's, and Grace's Warblers may be found. If Pinyon Jays are in the neighborhood, they will make themselves known by their raucous cries. The birder need not worry about missing them. Also, in winter, watch for Lewis's Woodpecker, Williamson's Sapsucker, and Golden Eagle overhead.

After a few more miles of high country, the scenic loop turns left onto Highway 166 and drops into lower, more-open country. Bison and Pronghorn are sometimes seen along this road. You also may see White-tailed and Mule Deer, Rock Squirrel, Black-tailed Jack Rabbit, Eastern Cottontail, and Mexican and Spotted Ground Squirrels. At night there may be Spotted, Striped, Hooded, and Hog-nosed Skunks, Raccoon,

Gray Fox, Coyote, Bobcat, and Porcupine. In winter this open stretch is the most favorable spot for seeing Golden Eagle, Ferruginous Hawk, and McCown's and Chestnut-collared Longspurs. Zone-tailed Hawks (rare) are resident in the Davis Mountains and might be seen in the air at almost any location. Other birds of this area are Prairie Falcon, Western Meadowlark, Say's Phoebe, and Cassin's Sparrow.

A sure place to see Montezuma Quail is at the Stroud home (no permission necessary). The owners always have water out for the quail. The home is on your left one mile down the road to the right (opposite the Crow's Nest RV Park sign). Early morning and late afternoon are best.

After several miles of open country, scattered oaks again appear. An excellent place to see birds of this habitat is the **Bloys Camp Meeting Ground** (ask permission). Montezuma Quail may stroll about the grounds. Acorn Woodpeckers are common, and Phainopeplas frequent the area in fall and winter.

At Point of Rock roadside picnic area (5.0) you can easily hear the down-the-scale song of Canyon Wrens, and may possibly be able to locate one with your binoculars. The grasslands along the way back to Fort Davis could be harboring a few Mountain Plovers (nesting records) and good numbers of McCown's and Chestnut-collared Longspurs in winter. Watch for Pronghorn.

LIMPIA CREEK

It is worth the picnicking fee of $1.00 to have the privilege of birding among the cottonwoods and willows about the private campground on Limpia Creek at the junction of Highways 17 and 118. In winter at least 40 species can be found in 2 hours, including Vermilion Flycatcher, Black Phoebe, Lesser Goldfinch, Eastern, Western, and Mountain Bluebirds, and White-throated, Lincoln's, Swamp, and Song Sparrows. In summer Western Wood-Pewee and Summer Tanager are among the nesting birds. For several years a pair of Common Black-Hawks has nested in the cottonwoods farther up the creek.

After birding the campground, go northeast on Highway 17, which follows Limpia Creek all the way to Wild Rose Pass. After 0.8 mile stop at the *Litter Barrel* sign. Common Black-Hawks have nested in recent years in the tall cottonwood across Limpia Creek. Stop at each bridge and beside all oak groves and thickets. In summer Cliff Swallows nest under the bridges, and in winter Green-tailed and Rufous-sided Towhees are common in the brush. Canyon Towhees and Rufous-crowned Sparrows are present all year, but Inca Doves and Common Ground-Doves are seen only occasionally in the fields. Some 15 species of sparrows winter in the grassy areas, and small flocks of Lark Buntings sometimes find their way this far into the mountains.

Where the canyon is narrow and the road approaches the palisade-like cliffs, Canyon Wrens may be heard singing at almost any time of year. Great Horned Owls sit in crevices, and hawks soar above the cliffs. The Red-tailed Hawk is the most common, but in winter watch for Ferruginous as well. (Note: the morph of Red-tailed found here is very pale, and care should be taken not to confuse it with the Ferruginous Hawk.)

Common Black-hawk
Gail Diane Luckner

Aguja Canyon

After crossing Wild Rose Pass (22.6), continue north on Highway 17 to the sign indicating Road 1832 to the Buffalo Trail Boy Scout Ranch (12.1). Turn left (west) here through typical foothill brush country. This paved road has lots of room, so you can pull over to birdwatch.

This is the habitat of such typical desert species as Greater Roadrunner, Western Kingbird, Ash-throated Flycatcher, Verdin, Cactus Wren, Curve-billed and Sage Thrashers, Pyrrhuloxia, and Black-throated and Brewer's Sparrows. After 8.5 miles the road enters a wide-mouthed canyon, and the scrub gives way to larger trees.

At the first place the road fords the creek, look in summer in the stream-side thickets for Varied and Painted Buntings, White-winged Dove, Summer Tanager, and Bell's Vireo. At the second ford look in winter for Black-chinned Sparrow. At the entrance to the Boy Scout Ranch (12.0), watch along the cliffs for the White-throated Swifts, which are present the year round and may be seen even in winter on warm days. Near the ranch headquarters Scott's Orioles may be seen. If you enjoy hiking, ask permission to walk up Aguja Canyon (Ah-WOO-ha, "needle" in Spanish) on the trail along the creek. Canyon Wrens are heard on all sides, Black Phoebes are common, and Acorn Woodpeckers inhabit the oak groves. Spring and fall are the best times for this hike because the canyon is hot in summer.

Return to Highway 17, go north to the town of Toyahvale and Highway 290 (7.0), and turn right. Just beyond is **Balmorhea State Recreation Area** (entrance fee $3.00 weekdays, $4.00 weekends; camping and showers available), a fine place for birding. (Accommodations are available at San Solomon Springs Courts: Box 15, Toyahvale 78786; phone 915/375-2370). The park is noted for the 26-million-gallon per day artesian San Solomon Spring, around which is built a natural-like swimming-pool. These spring waters are home to two very rare, endangered desert fishes, the Comanche Spring Pupfish and the Pecos Mosquitofish. Cave Swallows have nested under the eaves of the entrance station and other buildings along with Barn and Cliff Swallows.

Resident birds include Scaled Quail, White-winged and Inca Doves, Greater Roadrunner, Ladder-backed Woodpecker, Black and Say's Phoebes, Cactus Wren, Curve-billed Thrasher, Loggerhead Shrike, Pyrrhuloxia, Canyon Towhee, Black-throated Sparrow, Eastern Meadowlark, Great-tailed and Common (uncommon) Grackles, and House Finch. Other nesters include Black-chinned Hummingbird, Cassin's and Western Kingbirds, Bewick's Wren, and Blue Grosbeak. In winter, look for Northern Flicker, Marsh Wren, Ruby-crowned Kinglet, Hermit

Thrush, Cedar Waxwing, Yellow-rumped Warbler, Green-tailed and Rufous-sided Towhees, Chipping, Clay-colored, Brewer's, Vesper, Savannah, Song, Lincoln's, and White-crowned Sparrows, Lark Bunting, Dark-eyed Junco, and Western Meadowlark. Migrations should bring Wilson's Warbler, Summer Tanager (spring), and Orchard and Northern (uncommon) Orioles.

LAKE BALMORHEA

In the town of Balmorhea (4.0), turn right at the sign for Lake Balmorhea onto Houston Street and drive to the lake (2.6). Check in at the store; there is a charge of $2.00 per day for birdwatching, fishing, and primitive camping at this private lake. The water in the lake, which is a storage area for irrigation projects, comes from San Solomon Springs at the State Recreation Area. Lake Balmorhea is the premier place in all of the Trans-Pecos for waterbirds in migration and winter.

Some 40 species of waterbirds winter here, including the "Mexican Duck" Mallard. This duck is most often seen in the irrigation canals leading into or out of the lake. This is about the only place in Texas where the Western and Clark's (10 percent) Grebes winter regularly. Many shorebirds can be seen during spring and fall migrations, including American Avocet, Long-billed Curlew, Pectoral and Stilt Sandpipers, Common Snipe (also winters), and Wilson's and Red-necked Phalaropes. The lake is well-known for its nesting Snowy Plovers. Black-necked Stilts also nest in good numbers. Neotropic Cormorants are becoming regular in the fall. Rarities include Red-throated and Pacific Loons, Brown Pelican, Tricolored Heron, Reddish Egret, Ross's Goose, all three scoters, and Sabine's Gull.

A scope is a must. The lake is large (573 acres), and the ever-present West Texas wind creates waves that are large enough to make birds in the center difficult to see. The dirt roads around the lake can be rough driving and are often impassable after rains. Many raptors can be found wintering around the lake or migrating through, including Osprey, Northern Harrier, Ferruginous and Rough-legged (rare) Hawks, Golden Eagle (rare), American Kestrel, and Prairie Falcon. Many of the birds mentioned in the list for the State Recreation Area can also be found here, plus Lesser and Common (rare) Nighthawks and Common Poorwill. Ash-throated and Scissor-tailed Flycatchers may be found as summer nesters. Western Wood-Pewee and Willow, Least, and Dusky Flycatchers are regular but rare migrants. Common Ravens are resident. American Pipit is common in winter. Ring-necked Pheasant and Verdin are resident in the surrounding fields. (The pheasant, a white-winged race, was introduced many years ago. It is now ranging north and west of Balmorhea.)

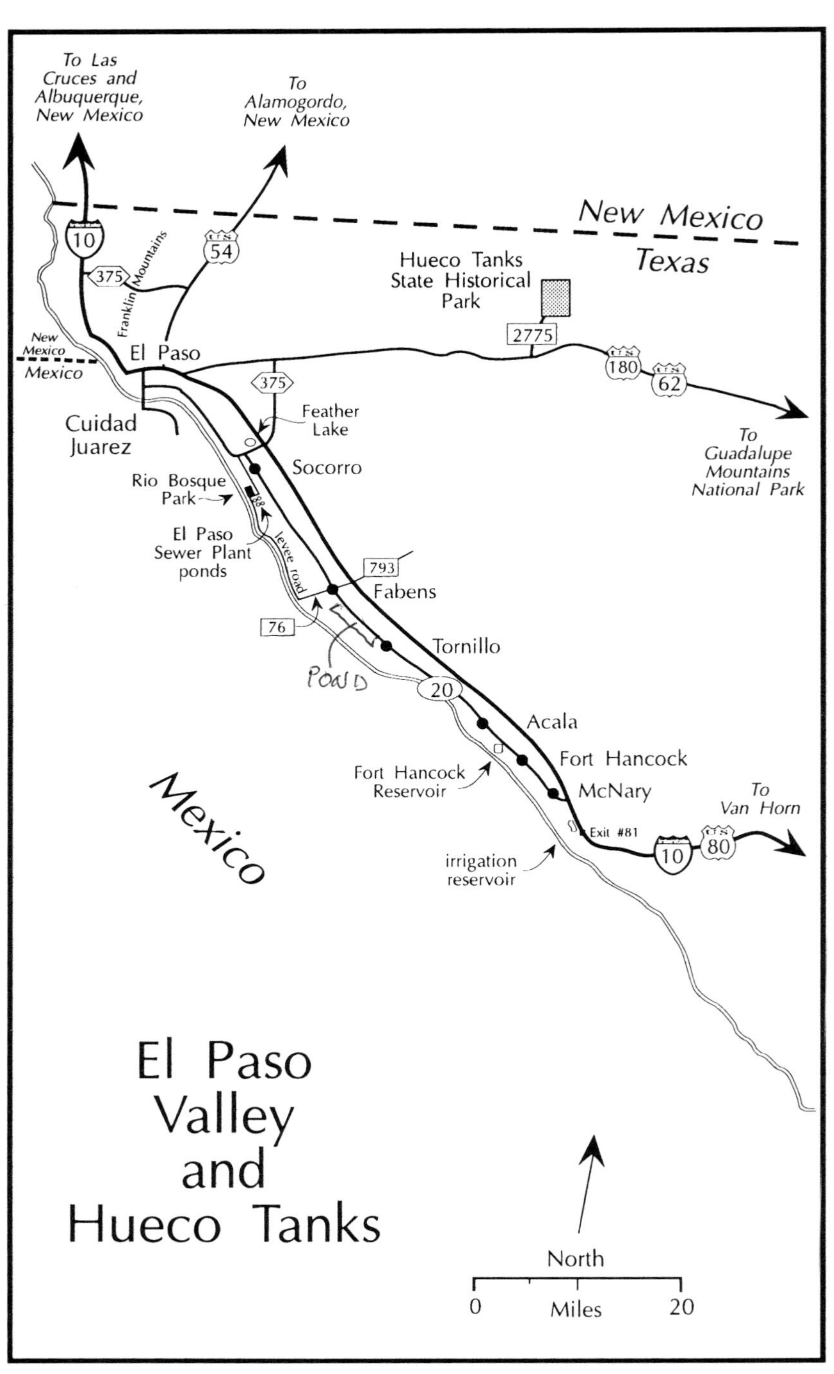
To Las Cruces and Albuquerque, New Mexico
To Alamogordo, New Mexico
New Mexico
Texas
10
54
375
Franklin Mountains
Hueco Tanks State Historical Park
2775
New Mexico
Mexico
El Paso
180
62
375
Feather Lake
To Guadalupe Mountains National Park
Cuidad Juarez
Socorro
Rio Bosque Park
El Paso Sewer Plant ponds
levee road
793
Fabens
76
Tornillo
POND
20
Acala
Fort Hancock
Fort Hancock Reservoir
McNary
To Van Horn
Exit #81
10
80
irrigation reservoir
Mexico
El Paso Valley and Hueco Tanks
North
0
Miles
20

El Paso Valley and Hueco Tanks

To continue west after your visit to Lake Balmorhea and the Davis Mountains, take Interstate 10 to Van Horn (68.0 miles). At the junction with Highway 54, you have a choice of continuing west to El Paso or driving north to the Guadalupe Mountains. If you opt for El Paso, continue west on Interstate 10 to Sierra Blanca (33.0 miles). About 28 miles west of Sierra Blanca, you can leave busy Interstate 10 at the McNary turnoff to follow the old Highway 20 through the farmlands of the El Paso Valley. Most of the little towns along the way are practically deserted now, but the road is still good and the traffic is light. There are a few good birding spots in this oasis, and you will find the green cotton-fields a pleasant relief from the desert.

The first missionaries came through the valley in 1581, but the first mission was not established until 1659. On Socorro Road (FM 258) near Clint, you will find the San Elizario Mission and several historic buildings. One is the original El Paso County Courthouse, and another is reported to be the oldest building in Texas. This is also the site of the first introduction by Europeans of domestic animals into the United States. They were brought here in 1598 when Don Juan de Oñate established the first military garrison.

The Spaniards, on entering this area in the 16th century, found large and prosperous settlements occupied by the Tigua Indians, whose ancestors built the famous cliff houses of Mesa Verde. They had developed a complex irrigation system, some of which is still in use today. Their principal crops were maize and squash.

To reach this area, watch for Exit #81 to FM 2217. [You may be able to reach a large irrigation reservoir from this exit. It lies just off to the west. You can cross over the interstate to a gate on the right which is usually open (0.3). At the corral you may be able to drive onto a dike leading to the north end of the reservoir. (See map of McNary and Fort Hancock.) Alternately, if you are unable to reach the reservoir by this route (where access conditions may change without notice), try the following route.]

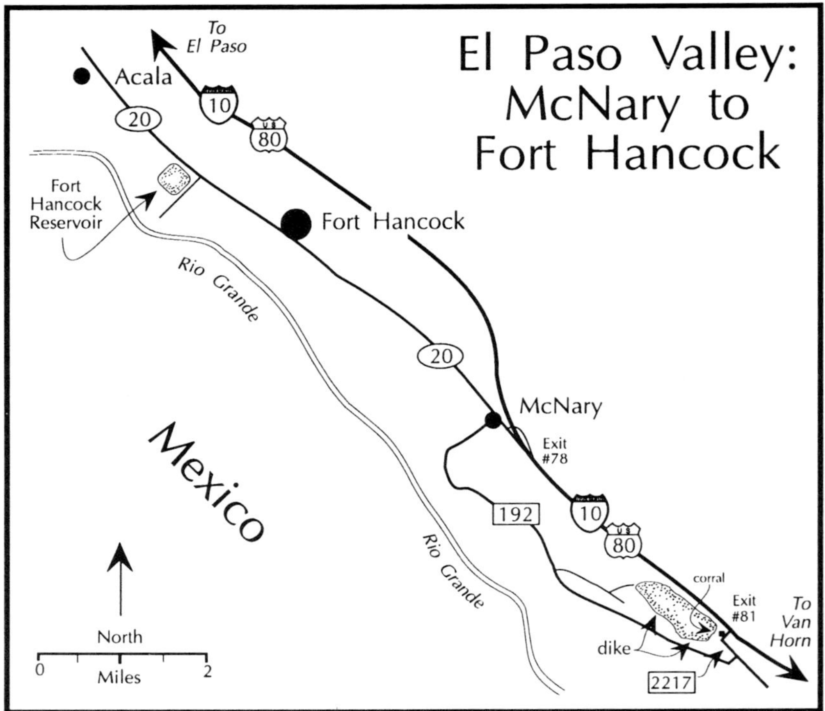

Continue past Exit #81 for 3.0 miles before leaving the freeway at the McNary Exit. Where the off-ramp passes under the highway, pull over and check the overpass for nesting Cave Swallows, a very recent colonizer of the area. This swallow now nests under a number of bridges throughout the county. This particular location is not necessarily the best spot in the county, but it is on the route to other birding locations. In 1991, 8 pairs of Cave Swallows were found here.

Continue under the overpass until the road joins Highway 20 (0.2 mile). Turn right, go 0.2 mile, and turn left onto FM 192. Follow this road through arid brushland and plowed fields until you reach a small bridge (3.2 miles). Just before the bridge turn left onto a small dirt road that parallels an irrigation ditch. Go 1.0 mile and turn left at the fork, continuing on this road for 0.6 mile, and park at the cattle-guard. Beyond is a large irrigation reservoir, sometimes called Lake 2217, Holding Reservoir #3, or McNary Reservoir. The water-level in this reservoir varies drastically in the course of the year, and you may find it rather full or bone dry. As long as water is present, this is a great place for migrant waterfowl and waders. In addition to the regular species of ducks and geese, this spot has attracted Greater White-fronted and Ross's Geese, Greater Scaup, and Oldsquaw. The number of waders is often spectacular, with hundreds of migrant White-faced Ibis and Snowy, Cattle, and Great Egrets joining the resident Black-crowned Night-Herons, Green-backed Herons, and Great Blue Herons. When water-levels are low, with resultant exposed shoreline, the shorebirding can be exciting. Such local rarities as Red Knot, Ruddy Turnstone, Semipalmated Sandpiper, and Short-billed Dowitcher have all been recorded, along with multitudes of the more common species.

The salt-cedar (Tamarisk) and mesquite that line the road leading to the reservoir are home to Gambel's Quail, Greater Roadrunner, White-winged Dove, Cactus Wren, Crissal Thrasher, Bell's Vireo (summer), Yellow-breasted Chat (summer), Summer Tanager, Pyrrhuloxia, Blue Grosbeak (summer), Painted Bunting (summer), Lark Sparrow (summer), and Northern (Bullock's) Oriole. The ditches should be checked for Common Moorhen, Black Phoebe, Vermilion Flycatcher (winter), and Swamp Sparrow (winter).

Return to Highway 20 and turn left. You will soon come to the small town of Fort Hancock (5.0 miles). Continue west on Highway 20 for another 2.1 miles, at which point you will see a large dirt impoundment on the left. This area is known locally as the Fort Hancock Reservoir. A small dirt road at the far (west) end leads up onto the dike surrounding the lake. Vehicle traffic is not allowed around the reservoir, but the current lessee allows birders on foot to view the area from the dike. If water conditions are right, this large pond may contain thousands of migrant/wintering ducks and transient shorebirds. This spot has hosted small numbers of wintering/migrant Ross's Geese in recent years. It is also a good spot for winter gulls (Mew, California, and Thayer's have been seen here), grebes (Western and Clark's), and mergansers (all three have been here). Bring your scope.

Continue on Highway 20 toward El Paso. Watch telephone poles and treetops anywhere along Highway 20 for Harris's Hawk. A small population of these beautiful raptors persists (especially around the little town of Acala) despite loss of habitat and pressure from gunners and falconers.

At 8.1 miles you will come to a small rest-area on the left. The cottonwoods here are good for nesting Yellow-breasted Chat, Northern and Orchard Orioles, Summer Tanager, and Blue Grosbeak. In winter there are usually Phainopeplas here. The roadside rest, however, is most productive during migration, when the cottonwood trees serve as a magnet to migrants passing through.

Plainview Lake, a small, private fishing-lake on the left (2.8), may have a few wintering waterfowl and shorebirds.

One of the most interesting drives is along the levee of the Rio Grande, which you have paralleled for many miles. To reach the levee, turn left in Fabens (10.5) onto Farm Road 76. When this turns left (1.5), continue straight ahead and follow the road as it bends first right and then left. On reaching the levee (2.5), turn right. You may see signs reading *Not Authorized for Public Use*, but you are allowed to drive on the levee. (If you are pulling a trailer or driving a large motorhome, however, avoid this route because of a narrow bridge after 17 miles.)

At this point the river is often only a trickle, but its banks can be good for Greater Roadrunner, Gambel's Quail, and, in winter, hawks. In the early morning or late evening, Burrowing Owls may be common in summer.

The "Mexican Duck" Mallard may be found feeding in the irrigated fields in the early morning. During the day, it often stays along the canals. The main canal, which borders the levee on the right 5.4 miles ahead, is one of the better spots for finding one. Watch the vegetation along the banks carefully. This duck can often hug the shore when a car approaches; other times it is highly visible and active.

You will eventually see some large ponds (12.0) on the right. These are a part of the El Paso Sewer Plant at Socorro. At the west end of the ponds, bear right following the canal to Socorro Road. (Rio Bosque Park, undeveloped and good for Yellow-breasted Chat, Blue Grosbeak, and Painted Bunting, is on your left.) The road along the canal is dirt. Cross the canal on a narrow bridge. If you go farther on the levee, there is a border checkpoint, which can be a hassle. For a better look at the ponds, try turning right onto Socorro Road and driving 0.2 mile to the second road to the right (the entrance to the sewage-treatment plant), then left just before the chain-link fence. If the gate is locked, the ponds will have to be viewed from the levee. Ducks may be common here in winter, and shorebirds during migration.

After checking the ponds, continue west on Socorro Road toward El Paso. At the Socorro Mission (1.3), which is the oldest active church building in the United States, having been founded in 1682, keep left on Farm Road 258. At Loop Road 375 (Avenue of the Americas)(1.5), turn right. However, if you wish to visit the metal-domed Ysleta Mission, which was founded in 1681, continue straight on Farm Road 258 for another mile.

Feather Lake

After turning right onto Loop Road 375, watch for the signal light (1.2), and turn left onto North Loop Drive (Farm Road 76). Pull off just beyond the first little bridge (0.4). To the left is **Feather Lake**. It is protected by the El Paso/Trans-Pecos Audubon Society, which is responsible for the fence and the *No Trespassing* signs. Birders are welcome, but they must first call the society (phone: 915/852-3119) for information. It may be possible to see some of the area by walking along the fence in both directions.

The lake offers a haven for numerous ducks, shorebirds, Common Moorhen, and Yellow-headed Blackbird. It is a good spot for Cinnamon Teal, Ruddy Duck, and "Mexican Duck" Mallard. White-faced Ibis is common in migration. Common Merganser is sometimes present in winter and Least Bittern has been a summer resident in recent years.

To reach El Paso, take Loop Road 375 north to Interstate 10.

El Paso

El Paso County is located at the western extremity of Texas, in the valley of the Rio Grande at the base of the Franklin Mountains, and is surrounded by the Chihuahuan Desert. The county has an average annual rainfall of about 8 inches. El Paso's birdfinding habitats are varied, though somewhat limited. Finding birds here means finding places where there is water. Yet El Paso County has a very impressive list of over 360 species of birds.

Some of the resident and nesting birds include "Mexican Duck" Mallard, Swainson's Hawk, Gambel's and Scaled Quail, Common Moorhen, Inca and White-winged Doves, Greater Roadrunner, Burrowing Owl, Lesser Nighthawk (summer), Common Poorwill (summer), White-throated Swift, Say's Phoebe, Ash-throated Flycatcher (summer), Chihuahuan Raven, Verdin, Cactus, Rock, and Canyon Wrens, Crissal Thrasher, Phainopepla, Scott's (summer) and Hooded (uncommon, but local) Orioles, and Black-throated Sparrow. A bird checklist for El Paso County may be obtained from El Paso/Trans-Pecos Audubon Society, P.O. Box 9655, El Paso 79986. Send 50 cents and a stamped, self-addressed envelope.

Memorial Park

This city park is located in downtown El Paso and is a favorite with local birders. To reach it from Interstate 10, drive north on Piedras Street seven blocks and turn right onto Grant Avenue, which leads to the park. Resident

birds are Inca and White-winged Doves, Great-tailed Grackle, and House Finch. Spring migration can be great for western warblers, including Orange-crowned, Virginia's, Yellow, Yellow-rumped (Audubon's), Black-throated Gray (rare), Townsend's, MacGillivray's, and Wilson's. Also look for Western Wood-Pewee, Western Tanager, Black-headed Grosbeak, and Hooded and Northern (Bullock's) Orioles. In the fall migrations, there are probably more warblers, though they are spread out over a longer period. *Empidonax* flycatchers are present in spring or fall—Willow, Hammond's, Least (rare), Dusky, Gray (rarer in spring), and Cordilleran—if you can identify them when they are silent. Also in fall look for a possible Flammulated Owl along with Red-naped and Williamson's Sapsuckers, Red-breasted, White-breasted, and Pygmy Nuthatches, Mountain Chickadee, Golden-crowned Kinglet, and Red Crossbill (in the pines). Some of these montane species will be common in some winters and completely absent in others. In addition, watch for Dark-eyed (Oregon and Gray-headed) Juncos, Green-tailed Towhee, and Lesser Goldfinch. Be sure to get here early in the morning before the crowds arrive.

After birding Memorial Park you may want to drive over the Scenic Drive to **Arroyo Park**. To reach the area from Memorial Park, return to Piedras Street and go north five blocks to Copper Avenue. Take Copper Avenue west to Alabama Street and turn north six blocks, then left onto Richmond Avenue, which becomes Scenic Drive. After 1.4 miles stop at the scenic overlook for a great view of the city. Here you should hear and see Rock or Canyon Wrens. Continuing down, watch for and turn right onto Robinson Avenue (0.6), which follows the north edge of Arroyo Park. Pull over on the left, park anywhere, and walk into the park. Here you should find Gambel's Quail, Inca and White-winged Doves, Verdin, Cactus Wren, Crissal Thrasher, Pyrrhuloxia, and Black-throated Sparrows among other desert-type species.

McKelligon Canyon Park is reached by driving north on Alabama Street about 2 miles. Turn left onto McKelligon Canyon Road (just before Alabama Street swings to the right). The park is up the canyon 2.4 miles. Although this park is crowded with people unless you go early, birding can be good anywhere along the way.

The **Franklin Mountains** which tower above the city to the north look very dry and barren, but they harbor some desert species such as Scaled Quail, Verdin, Cactus, Rock, and Canyon Wrens, Verdin, Rufous-crowned and Black-throated Sparrows, and House Finch. There is good birding in several of the canyons off Trans-Mountain Road (Loop 375), which crosses the mountains. To reach Loop 375 drive north on Interstate 10 about 15 miles and turn east. Franklin Mountains State Park (undeveloped as of this

Black-throated Sparrow
Charles H. Gambill

writing, but still with an entrance fee of $3.00 per day) (3.3) at the arch on the left has picnicking only. Follow the road in for 1.0 mile, and park in the picnic area on your right. Walk the wide, rocky path that heads toward the large canyon half a mile to the east. This is West Cottonwood Spring Canyon, one of the best locations for birds in the Franklins. Walk up the trail into the canyon, continuing straight onto a smaller trail where the main trail turns to the left. This will take you to West Cottonwood Spring, a great area in fall migration for Calliope, Broad-tailed, and Rufous Hummingbirds, especially in August and September. Warblers such as Orange-crowned, Virginia's, Black-throated Gray, Townsend's, and MacGillivray's, and even rare warblers such as Hermit Warbler and Painted Redstart, have been found here. Scrub Jays can be found some years in fall and winter, along with Black-chinned Sparrows, which may also be found in summer.

Return to the entrance to the park and continue driving east. After 4.1 miles you will find a small pull-off on the left. A trail leads from here to Whispering Spring, the longest-flowing spring in the Franklins. Here in the hackberries, ash, and Western Soapberry, you will find a few nesting birds such as Ladder-backed Woodpecker, Ash-throated Flycatcher, Bewick's Wren, Indigo Bunting (sporadic), Canyon Towhee, and Rufous-crowned Sparrow. Watch overhead for White-throated Swifts, and check for Rock and Canyon Wrens. Migrations bring some warblers, including Virginia's, Townsend's, and MacGillivray's.

After another 2.1 miles you will find a much larger turn-off on your left. Here you will find another trail leading across the flats and arroyos to Indian Spring Canyon. Resident birds found here include Red-tailed Hawk, White-throated Swift, Canyon Wren, Crissal Thrasher, Verdin, and Rufous-crowned and Black-throated Sparrows. Additionally, in summer you should find Ash-throated Flycatcher, Blue Grosbeak, and Scott's Oriole. In winter you should also find Pyrrhuloxia, and Chipping, Brewer's, Black-chinned, and White-crowned Sparrows. Sage Thrasher may be found in migration.

The Wilderness Park Museum 0.3 mile on the left is worth a visit. It features dioramas and displays of primitive man and Indians of the region. The museum also has a nice Nature Trail along which you could find some of the above-mentioned species.

At Gateway Boulevard (0.6) you can turn right (south) to return to downtown El Paso. Or if you want to visit the **Fred Hervey Water Reclamation Plant ponds** continue east on Loop 375 to its end at Railroad Drive (3.0). Turn left (north) to the entrance road on your right (3.6). (From downtown, take US 54 north to Loop 375 and turn east to Railroad Drive, then follow directions above.) When the gate is open, drive across the railroad tracks (make sure that you come to a complete stop at the stop-sign for the very wide dirt track used by Fort Bliss training vehicles) and follow the paved road to the buildings. Do not go inside (permission is not necessary), but turn right before the gate onto the unpaved road and drive to the area of large trees and cattails surrounding the large ponds. You can drive up on the levees or walk there. This is a great area for waterfowl, shorebirds, and landbirds all year-round. Many species use the area for nesting, for wintering, and in migration. Resident birds include Pied-billed and Eared Grebes, Green-backed Heron, "Mexican Duck" Mallard, Ruddy Duck, American Kestrel, Scaled and Gambel's Quails, Common Moorhen, American Coot, Killdeer, White-winged, Mourning, and Inca Doves, Greater Roadrunner, Ladder-backed Woodpecker, Say's Phoebe, Verdin, Cactus Wren, American Robin, Northern Mockingbird, Curve-billed and Crissal Thrashers, Loggerhead Shrike, Pyrrhuloxia, and Black-throated Sparrow. Additional summer nesters are Mississippi Kite, Swainson's Hawk, Black-necked Stilt, American Avocet, Lesser Nighthawk, Western Kingbird, Blue Grosbeak, and Painted Bunting. Winter brings in many waterfowl of numerous species, including Bufflehead and Common Merganser, and many raptors. Of the shorebirds coming through, the Least Sandpiper is most common, followed by Greater Yellowlegs, Long-billed Dowitcher, Common Snipe, and in lesser numbers Spotted Sandpiper and Lesser Yellowlegs. Ring-billed Gulls are fairly common in winter, but Franklin's, Bonaparte's, California, and Herring Gulls have also been found. Also in winter watch for Northern Flicker (the "red-shafted" form is more common than the "yellow-shafted" form), Black Phoebe, Horned Lark, Bewick's and Marsh Wrens, American Pipit, and Green-tailed and Rufous-sided Towhees. The many species of sparrows include Brewer's, Savannah, Song, Lincoln's, White-crowned, and rarely Cassin's, Sage, Swamp, and Harris's.

HUECO TANKS

Hueco Tanks State Park (WAY-co) ($3.00 plus camping) is an excellent place to study the Chihuahuan Desert. To reach the 860-acre park, go east from downtown El Paso on Interstate 10 and take the Highway 62/180 exit (3.8) toward Carlsbad. Turn left at Farm Road 2775 (21.8) and proceed to the park (8.0). Within the first mile or so in winter watch for Sage Sparrows among the patches of Creosote Bush and Tar Bush, along with a few other wintering sparrows. Cassin's Sparrows nest here in summer. After about two miles, a small dirt road on the left leads to a stock pond and a small clump of mesquite. Crissal Thrasher and Verdin are found here year-round. In summer Black-tailed Gnatcatcher may sometimes be found. Migrant Gray Flycatchers are consistent in fall, and in winter look for Green-tailed Towhee.

The park was created to preserve the Indian pictographs, but it is great for birds. You should find some around the campground and picnic area. There are six ponds in wet winters. The largest is over the dike behind the "Old Ranch House" across the road from headquarters. Two others are to the right among the rocks of Mescalero Canyon, which is the best birding area.

At any season you should find Red-tailed Hawk, Scaled and Gambel's Quails, Greater Roadrunner, Great Horned Owl, White-throated Swift, Ladder-backed Woodpecker, Say's Phoebe, Verdin, Cactus, Rock, and

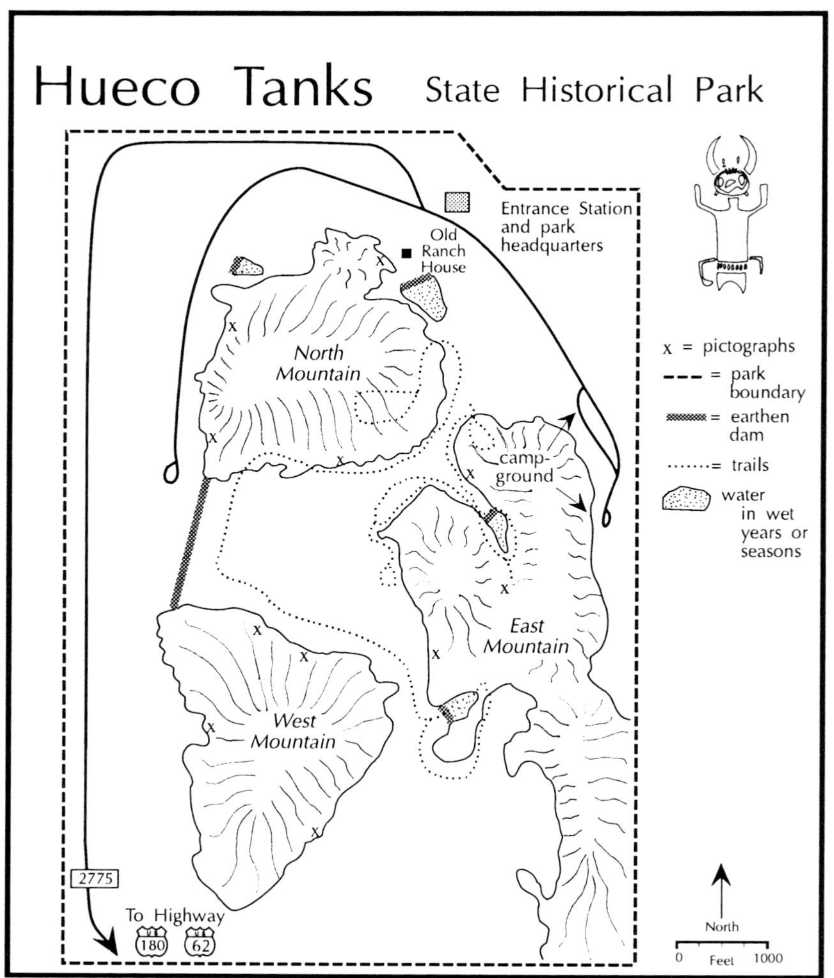

Hueco Tanks State Historical Park John Sproul

Canyon Wrens, Northern Mockingbird, Crissal and Curve-billed Thrashers, Loggerhead Shrike, Pyrrhuloxia, Canyon Towhee, and Rufous-crowned and Black-throated Sparrows. In summer watch for Swainson's Hawk, Burrowing Owl, Lesser Nighthawk, Common Poorwill, Black-chinned Hummingbird, Western Kingbird, Ash-throated Flycatcher, Cliff and Barn Swallows, Scott's Oriole, Blue Grosbeak, Cassin's Sparrow, Eastern Meadowlark, and Brown-headed Cowbird. Winter is often the best time to visit the park. Not only is it cooler, but also there is usually water in the ponds. Look here for waterfowl and Black Phoebe (all rare). At this season look for Northern Harrier, American Kestrel, Long-eared Owl (rare), Western and Mountain Bluebirds (sporadic), Townsend's Solitaire, American Robin, Sage Thrasher, Green-tailed and Rufous-sided Towhees, Chipping, Brewer's, Black-chinned, Vesper, Sage, Savannah, Song, Lincoln's, and White-crowned Sparrows, Dark-eyed (Gray-headed) Junco, Red-winged Blackbird, Western Meadowlark, and American Goldfinch. Migration brings flycatchers, swallows, Solitary and Warbling Vireos, Western Tanager, Black-headed Grosbeak, Lazuli Bunting, and warblers of 19 species.

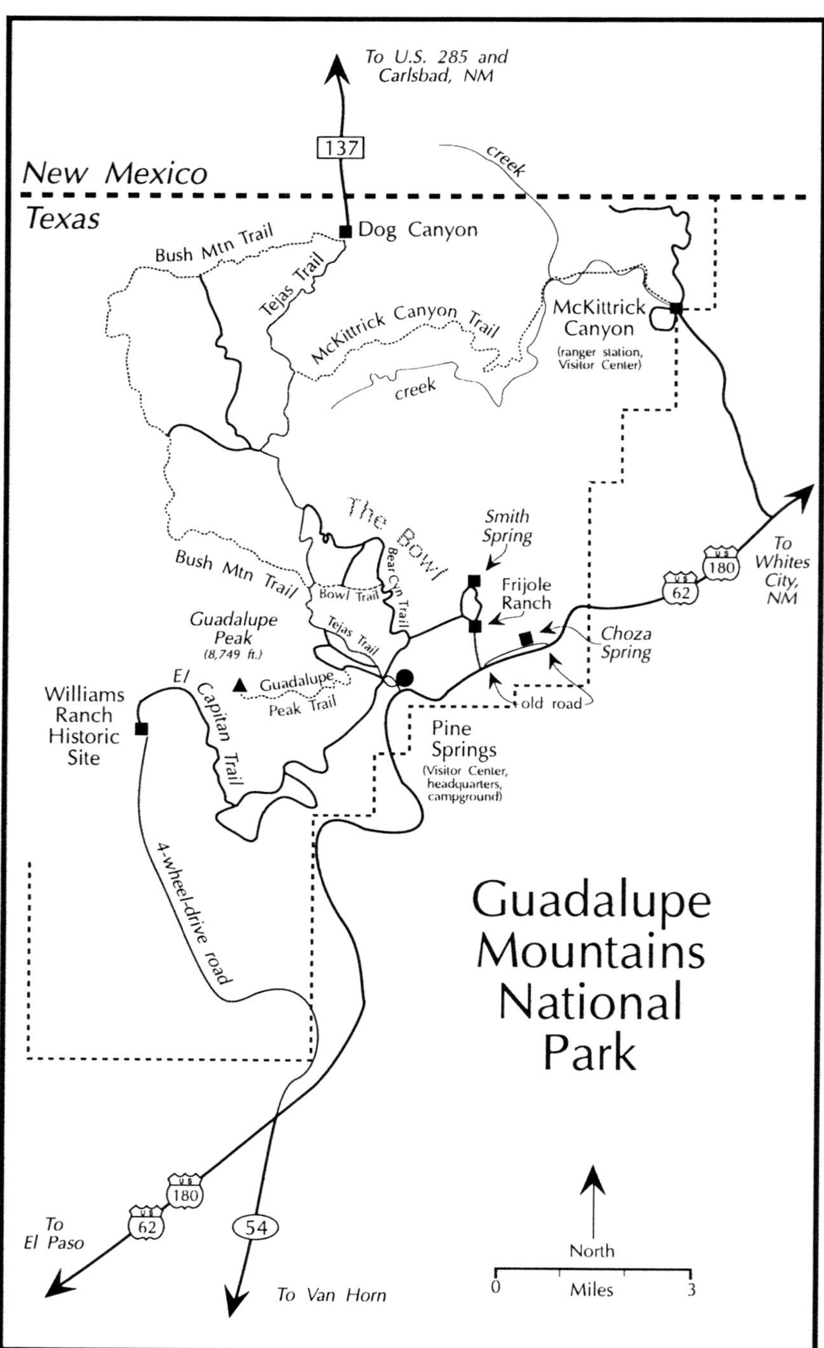
To U.S. 285 and Carlsbad, NM
137
New Mexico
Texas
creek
Dog Canyon
Bush Mtn Trail
Tejas Trail
McKittrick Canyon Trail
McKittrick Canyon
(ranger station, Visitor Center)
creek
The Bowl
Smith Spring
Frijole Ranch
Bush Mtn Trail
Bear Cyn Trail
Bowl Trail
Tejas Trail
Guadalupe Peak
(8,749 ft.)
Choza Spring
To Whites City, NM
US 180
US 62
El Capitan Trail
Guadalupe Peak Trail
old road
Williams Ranch Historic Site
Pine Springs
(Visitor Center, headquarters, campground)
4-wheel-drive road
Guadalupe Mountains National Park
US 180
US 62
To El Paso
54
To Van Horn
North
0
Miles
3

GUADALUPE MOUNTAINS NATIONAL PARK

Birders who are trying to build up their Texas list will find a visit to the Guadalupe Mountains a must. This is the only place in the state where some Rocky Mountain species can be found. To reach this interesting area, drive east from Hueco Tanks Highway 62/180 for 88 miles (the park is 110 miles east of El Paso). This 76,293-acre park was created in 1972, but is intended to have only limited development. There is a primitive campground and a number of trails. Stop at the new Visitor Center for more information. Pick up a bird checklist as well as maps, books, and other literature.

Approaching from the south, the most impressive view of the Guadalupe Mountains is the towering cliffs of El Capitan (El. 8,078 ft.), the most-photographed natural landmark in Texas. This majestic peak marks the southern end of the Capitan Reef, an ancient limestone formation that was laid down beneath the oceans of long ago. From El Capitan the reef rises to the top of Guadalupe Peak (El. 8,751 ft.), the highest point in Texas, and then slopes downward into New Mexico. The edges of the reef have been eroded into deep canyons. The center has been partially dissolved to form huge caves such as those of the Carlsbad Caverns, which are in the northern part of the reef.

The Visitor Center and Headquarters (opened in 1990) is located at **Pine Springs**, the first road to the left, 0.9 mile north from the south park-boundary sign. The campground is located nearby at the trailhead for El Capitan and Guadalupe Peak. To really see Guadalupe Mountains National Park, one must be prepared to hike. There are 63 miles of hiking trails. There are over 250 species of birds to be found, and most are seen only by hiking, although some are found at the campground and several other places to which one can drive. Resident birds around Pine Springs are Red-tailed Hawk, Golden Eagle (overhead), American Kestrel, Scaled Quail, White-winged and Mourning Doves, Greater Roadrunner, Western

Screech-Owl, Great Horned Owl, Common Poorwill, Acorn and Ladder-backed Woodpeckers, Phainopepla (summer), Pyrrhuloxia, Green-tailed (rare in summer), Rufous-sided, and Canyon Towhees, and Rufous-crowned, Chipping, Black-chinned, Lark, and Black-throated Sparrows. In winter look also for Mountain Chickadee, Western Bluebird, Sage Thrasher, Dark-eyed Junco, and Lesser and American Goldfinches.

Continuing north on Highway 62/180, turn left at the road(1.2) leading to **Frijole Ranch** (0.7). This old ranch house has a spring in the yard with Pecan and Chinkapin Oak trees. Another trailhead is also located here. In winter, rare woodpeckers, such as Red-headed Woodpecker, Lewis's Woodpecker, and Williamson's Sapsuckers, have been found here. All three bluebirds can be rather common some winters. Look for Townsend's Solitaire, Scrub Jay, Plain Titmouse (in surrounding junipers), and, in good years, American Robin and Cassin's Finch.

When you return to the highway, turn left directly onto the old road which parallels the highway for about a mile, and park where you see a group of large Texas Madrone (Manzanita) trees some little distance on your left, or you can continue and park by the bridge over **Choza Spring**. This growth along the spring is great for Plain Titmouse, which is resident in the junipers above the spring, as well as for Great Horned Owl. In winter it can be good for Wood Duck (several records), Cedar Waxwing, and Fox (uncommon), Song, Lincoln's, Swamp (rare), White-throated (irregular), and White-crowned Sparrows. Dark-eyed Juncos and Cassin's Finches (in good years) are also here. *Do not walk along the spring-edge itself, but make your way along the outside of the growth there—this area is very fragile.* Continue on as this old road returns to the present Highway 62/180.

McKITTRICK CANYON

Possibly the prettiest spot in the park is **McKittrick Canyon**, which is reached by continuing on Highway 62/180 some 5 miles to the turn-off on the left, and then to the end of this road (4.4). There is a small ranger station and Visitor Center here. The trail starts in the low desert, but as you climb higher, the canyon closes in and the walls get higher and higher, reaching over 2,000 feet in places. The canyon eventually forks. The north fork is rugged and much drier. The south fork has a permanent supply of water, which is first encountered as scattered puddles, then as a quiet brook, and finally as a rushing, rock-hopping stream.

In the desert brushlands at the mouth of the canyon, you should find Scaled Quail, Greater Roadrunner, Verdin, Cactus and Rock Wrens, Curve-billed and Crissal Thrashers, Canyon Towhee, Pyrrhuloxia, House Finch, and Rufous-crowned and Black-throated Sparrows. In winter look for Ladder-backed Woodpecker, Sage Thrasher, Rufous-sided Towhee, and numerous sparrows, including Chipping, Brewer's, Song, Lincoln's, and White-crowned. You may also see Desert Cottontail, Black-tailed Jack Rabbit, Texas Antelope Squirrel, Rock Squirrel, Porcupine, Badger, Striped and Hog-nosed Skunks, Bobcat, and Mule Deer.

Farther up the canyon, the talus slopes become covered with dense brush, and the streamside forest of Alligator Juniper, Gray Oak, Black Walnut, Velvet Ash, and Texas Madrone gets thicker. Scattered throughout are huge Faxon Yuccas, an endemic species that may reach 20 feet in height. An unforgettable sight is to see the Scott's Orioles feeding in the yucca's six-foot stalks of snowy-white flowers.

In the spring the canyon rings with the songs of Solitary, Warbling, and Gray Vireos and Black-headed Grosbeak. It is an excellent location for Black-chinned Sparrow. Every stunted Yellow Pine may seem to have a Grace's Warbler singing from its tip, and you might see a Hepatic Tanager, Wild Turkey, or Zone-tailed Hawk. However, the one sound which dominates the canyon is the song of the Canyon Wren. It comes tripping down from every ledge and cliff.

Other birds to look for in the canyon are White-throated Swift, Blue-throated and Black-chinned Hummingbirds, Acorn and Ladder-backed Woodpeckers, Say's Phoebe, Ash-throated Flycatcher,

Scaled Quail
Charles H. Gambill

Cassin's Kingbird, Cliff Swallow, Scrub Jay, Bushtit, Bewick's Wren, Orange-crowned and Virginia's Warblers, Western Tanager, Blue Grosbeak, Green-tailed and Canyon Towhees, and Rufous-crowned, Chipping, and Lark Sparrows, Hooded Oriole (rare), and Lesser Goldfinch. In winter look for Cooper's and Sharp-shinned Hawks, Golden Eagle, Steller's Jay, Mountain Chickadee, Golden-crowned Kinglet, and Hermit Thrush. There are two recent records for American Dipper, and in one recent winter a Yellow-eyed Junco stayed the season.

The upper reaches of the canyon have never been open to cattle, thanks to the far-sighted conservation attitude of its owners, J.C. Hunter Jr. and Wallace Pratt. These men realized that the fragile balance of nature would have been destroyed by grazing. Because of their enlightened vision, the park has a canyon that is little changed from its pristine condition. Let us hope that the park administrators do not let a recreation-happy public ruin it.

The high country along the top of McKittrick Ridge is well-forested with Douglas-fir, Limber and Ponderosa Pines, and even Quaking Aspen. In this forested area you should find Band-tailed Pigeon, Hairy Woodpecker, Steller's Jay, Mountain Chickadee, White-breasted and Pygmy Nuthatches, Brown Creeper, Western Bluebird, Hermit Thrush, Dark-eyed Junco, Red Crossbill (irregular), and Pine Siskin. In summer there may be Blue-throated, Magnificent (rare), Black-chinned, and Broad-tailed Hummingbirds, Olive-sided and Cordilleran Flycatchers, Western Wood-Pewee, Violet-green Swallow, Blue-gray Gnatcatcher, Orange-crowned, Virginia's, and Yellow-rumped Warblers, Hepatic and Western Tanagers, and Black-headed Grosbeak. Also watch for Gray-footed Chipmunk, Porcupine, Mule Deer, and Elk.

THE BOWL

There are several ways to get to the high country. Most people hike up one of the various trails. The 4-mile trail to the top of Guadalupe Peak is quite popular and offers an excellent view. The best birding spot is an area known as The Bowl. It can be reached by a roundabout trail via Pine Canyon, or by the 2.5-mile trail up Bear Canyon.

Most birders use the Bear Canyon Trail, but it has one little drawback. Although relatively short, it goes almost straight up the side of the escarpment. Be sure to get an early start and take lots of water. As you rest at the top of each switchback, enjoy the magnificent view and scan the sky for Golden Eagles and Zone-tailed Hawks. Near the top of the trail, if you are very lucky you may flush a Spotted Owl, but you will have to stay overnight to see or hear the Western Screech-Owl, Flammulated Owl,

Whip-poor-will, and Common Nighthawk. Most of the birds found in the Bowl are similar to those found along McKittrick Ridge.

An easier way to reach forested areas in the Guadalupe Mountains is to drive to Dog Canyon. This means traveling into New Mexico. On your way, be sure to stop at Rattlesnake Springs, which is to the left off Highway 62/180 about 10.5 miles north of the Texas border. This lush oasis is the best birding spot in the Carlsbad Caverns National Park. An unbelievable number of birds can be found here.

A visit to Carlsbad Caverns themselves could prove interesting. Look for the Cave Swallows flying over the parking lot. To reach the Caverns

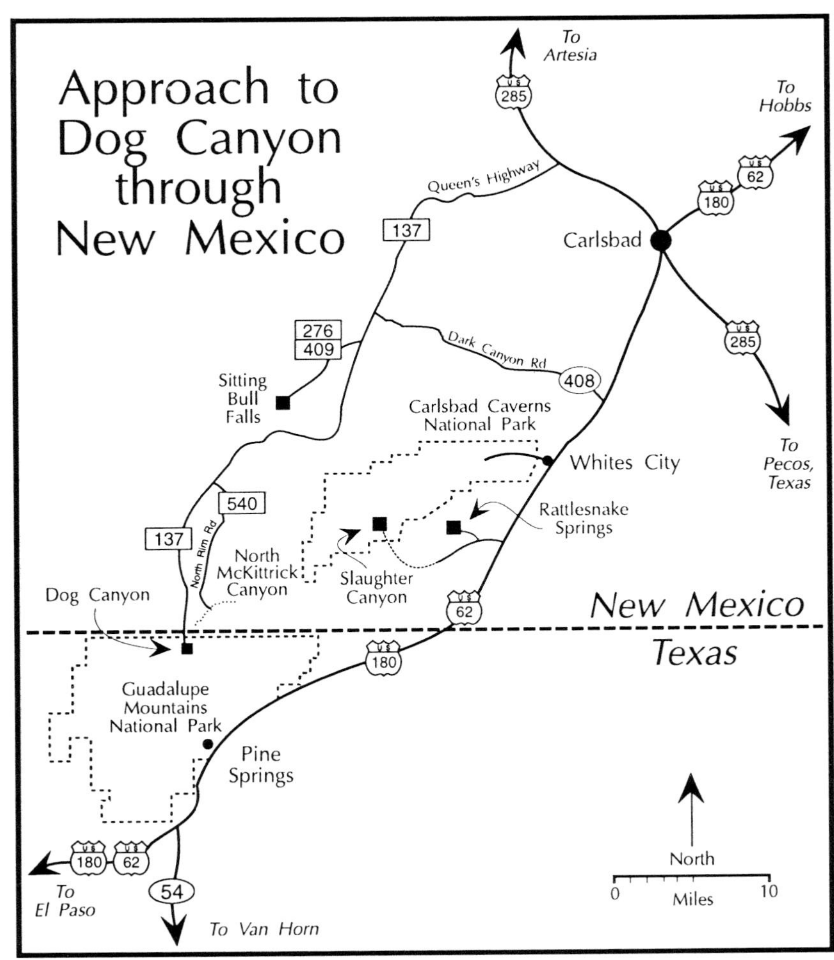

continue north from Rattlesnake Springs on Highway 62/180 to Whites City. Follow the entrance road into the park.

The northern portion of the Guadalupe Mountain range lies mostly in New Mexico and is part of the Lincoln National Forest. The Dog Canyon area is a good birding spot and well worth the visit. To reach it, drive 9.5 miles north of Whites City on Highway 62/180 and turn left onto Highway 408 (Dark Canyon Road). After 22.6 miles, turn left onto State Highway 137 and follow it into Dog Canyon. The road is paved all the way except for the last half-mile into Dog Canyon. By the way, the Canyon is back in Texas, so you should keep your state lists shuffled properly. The campground there has water and modern rest-rooms, and there is a trailhead for several trails with relatively easy grades.

In this forested area of junipers, pines, maples, and oaks are a good number of high-country birds. You should find Band-tailed Pigeon, Hairy Woodpecker, Cordilleran Flycatcher, Steller's Jay, Mountain Chickadee, Pygmy Nuthatch, and Dark-eyed (Gray-headed) Junco. In summer there should also be Olive-sided Flycatcher, Violet-green Swallow, Western Bluebird, Hermit Thrush, Warbling Vireo, Yellow-rumped (Audubon's) Warbler, Western and Hepatic Tanagers, Black-headed Grosbeak, and Red Crossbill. You may also find some of the less common species such as Flammulated Owl, Wild Turkey, and Broad-tailed Hummingbird. Some rare possibilities are Blue-throated and Magnificent Hummingbirds, Gray Flycatcher, Brown Creeper, and Grace's and Virginia's (dry canyon slopes) Warblers. In winter look for Acorn Woodpecker, Pinyon Jay (sporadic), and Plain Titmouse.

After exploring the Dog Canyon area, you may wish to bird the North Rim Road (FR 540) for wonderful views down into North McKittrick Canyon. Birds of this area will include many of the same species seen in The Bowl and other higher park elevations. The North Rim trail eventually crosses back into Texas and ends at the escarpment overlooking the mouth of McKittrick Canyon. *Do not descend into the canyon.* This is an extremely fragile area and each hiker's passage carries the potential of increasing the damage that it has already sustained.

A detour to Sitting Bull Falls on FR 409 on the way out of the area is a wonderful way to spend an afternoon. The falls are quite impressive and the climb into the cool caves behind them is worth the effort. Birding is excellent in the riparian area above the falls where the stream feeds the falls themselves. There are several deep pools for swimming. A rough trail to the top of the falls leaves from the parking area and follows switchbacks to the top. It is fairly easy, is short, and promises many of the same birds found in McKittrick Canyon.

END OF TRIP

If you have followed this book from beginning to end, you will have undoubtedly logged many long miles and wonderful birds on your journey. But, do not forget the people whose paths you have crossed. Jim Lane wrote of them in an earlier edition of this book:

By now you must have noticed that most Texans have a serious affliction, known as Southern Hospitality. Those suffering from this malady are easily recognized because they will speak to complete strangers on the street, offer their seat on a bus, or even wave another car through an intersection first. In severe cases they have been known to stop when they see a car parked along the highway and to back up to see if any help is needed. In some areas this plague is so pandemic that even waitresses and clerks will smile and greet you.

This affliction is highly contagious, but if you are willing to take a chance, you might ask the local people about other places to bird or about birds that you have missed. You may have to struggle to keep them from personally taking you off to see the bird or inviting you into their homes for coffee. If you are not careful, they will trick you into staying in Texas and never going home again.

Specialties of the Region

Least Grebe—Irregular permanent resident of freshwater ponds from about Eagle Pass to the Gulf and northward beyond our region to about Rockport. Sometimes scarce, but can usually be found at Laguna Atascosa National Wildlife Refuge, along Highway 281, Old Cannon Pond, and Santa Ana National Wildlife Refuge.

Neotropic Cormorant—Uncommon but increasing permanent resident from about Del Rio to the Gulf and northward to Louisiana. Normally found in areas of fresh water except during the nesting season, when it inhabits the islands of coastal bays. Fairly easy to find along the river or about fish-producing ponds such as at Falcon Dam, Santa Ana National Wildlife Refuge, and Laguna Atascosa National Wildlife Refuge.

Jabiru—One shot by a hunter in 1973. One reported by the press as the *Big Bird* in 1976. The latter bird may be the same one that was reported by William Keil, wildlife biologist, as having stayed on the King Ranch for over a week. Two birds were photographed near Encino, north of McAllen in late October 1979. One appeared near Bentsen-Rio Grande Valley State Park for four days in August 1985.

Fulvous Whistling-Duck—Mainly a rare migrant through the Lower Valley, but occasionally found at other times. Look for it on ponds at Laguna Atascosa National Wildlife Refuge and along Highway 281.

Black-bellied Whistling-Duck—Fairly common summer resident of tree-lined ponds from Rio Grande City to the Gulf and northward to Corpus Christi. Occasionally found elsewhere and in winter. Can usually be found from early April through September at Laguna Atascosa National Wildlife Refuge, Santa Ana National Wildlife Refuge, and the McAllen Sewage Ponds. Range expanding.

Muscovy Duck—These ducks have been present on the lower Rio Grande since 1984. Apparently, this species has been increasing recently in northeastern Mexico, responding to a Ducks Unlimited of Mexico nest-box program. Usually seen between Frontón and Falcon Dam, though there are reports from as far upriver as San Ygnacio. The sighting is often a fly-by seen from the riverbank.

"Mexican Duck"—Now considered conspecific with Mallard. Uncommon permanent resident of rivers, ponds, and irrigation canals from Lake Balmorhea and Big Bend National Park westward to Arizona. Can be found on irrigation canals and the Rio Grande at El Paso, on irrigated fields south of Marfa, on small ponds in the Davis Mountains, and on canals into and out of Lake Balmorhea. Found increasingly in Falcon Dam area in winter, sometimes even in mixed flocks with Mottled Ducks—a good opportunity for duck studies!

Masked Duck—Irregular visitor and possibly very rare resident of ponds with emerging vegetation from Santa Ana National Wildlife Refuge to the Gulf and northward beyond our region to Anahuac National Wildlife Refuge near Galveston. The distribution and seasonal movements of this bird are not known. It has occurred several times at both Laguna Atascosa and Santa Ana National Wildlife Refuges, but that is where the birders congregate, too.

Hook-billed Kite—First nested at Santa Ana National Wildlife Refuge in 1965 and again in 1976, when up to five individuals were seen. Now resident in small numbers to Falcon Dam, but most common at Bentsen-Rio Grande Valley State Park and Santa Ana.

Black-shouldered Kite—Uncommon permanent resident of coastal prairies and farmlands from about Falcon Dam to the Gulf and northward to about Houston. Occasionally elsewhere. Often seen at Laguna Atascosa National Wildlife Refuge, along Highway 281 west of Brownsville, and near Santa Ana National Wildlife Refuge.

Crane Hawk—One bird stayed at Santa Ana National Wildlife Refuge from December 1987 until April 1988. This first record for North America was seen by many birders during its five-month stay.

Common Black-Hawk—A rare migrant and winter visitor at the Santa Ana National Wildlife Refuge and elsewhere in the Valley. In 1976 a pair attempted to nest at the Santa Margarita Ranch near Roma. Has nested successfully for several years along Limpia Creek in the Davis Mountains; still there in 1991.

Harris's Hawk—Common but decreasing permanent resident in the brushlands of South Texas. Still easy to find beyond our region on the King Ranch, at Laguna Atascosa National Wildlife Refuge, at Santa Ana National Wildlife Refuge, and westward from La Joya.

Gray Hawk—Uncommon summer resident and a rare migrant and winter visitor. Most often seen at the Santa Ana National Wildlife Refuge, but there are recent breeding records from Big Bend National Park.

Roadside Hawk—One record from near Brownsville in 1901. This is a common hawk in Mexico, but, if it were found in the United States, it would probably be passed off as a Broad-winged. A second one was at Santa Margarita Ranch in January 1979. A third stayed at Bentsen-Rio Grande Valley State Park from October 1982 to January 1983.

White-tailed Hawk—Far more common just north of the region (especially along Highway 77 through the King Ranch and the Coastal Bend area) than in the Lower Valley. Look for it along the roads through the Rudman Tract north of Hargill. Can also be found at Laguna Atascosa National Wildlife Refuge, however, where it has nested.

Zone-tailed Hawk—Uncommon summer resident in the mountains of Trans-Pecos and Edwards Plateau; an occasional migrant and winter visitor in the Lower Valley. Has nested in Upper Sabinal Canyon and near Camp Wood on the Edwards Plateau, at Pinnacle Pass in Big Bend National Park, in the Davis Mountains, and in McKittrick Canyon in the Guadalupe Mountains. The surest location for seeing one is the Boot Spring Trail at Pinnacle Pass.

Golden Eagle—Uncommon permanent resident in the mountains of Trans-Pecos. More common in winter, when it reaches the Edwards Plateau and elsewhere. Your best bet for seeing this bird in summer is probably at Big Bend National Park, but it is sometimes seen along the Trans-Mountain Road at El Paso. In winter it is easy to find in the Davis Mountains, along Highway 90 west of Alpine, and along Interstate 10 near McNary.

Crested Caracara—Fairly common permanent resident of the brushlands of South Texas. Usually active in the early morning, when it can be seen feeding on roadkills. Most often seen north of our region on the King Ranch, but has nested at Laguna Atascosa National Wildlife Refuge and can be found from Falcon Dam westward to Eagle Pass.

Aplomado Falcon—Formerly a summer resident in the Trans-Pecos and a migrant in the Lower Valley. There are very few recent records, and most of those are probably not valid. A reintroduction program was started in 1985 at Laguna Atascosa National Wildlife Refuge by hacking. Releases have been seen as far away as Bentsen-Rio Grande Valley State Park. The program is continuing.

Peregrine Falcon—Rare summer resident in Big Bend National Park and in the Guadalupe Mountains. Most often seen as a migrant along the coast. Has been found recently wintering at Santa Ana National Wildlife Refuge and along the coast at Boca Chica.

Prairie Falcon—Rare permanent resident of the mountains of West Texas. Seen over the plains in winter. Your best bet is Big Bend National Park or along Highway 17 between Fort Davis and Marfa.

Plain Chachalaca—Fairly common permanent resident of thickets along the river from Falcon Dam to the Gulf. Formerly abundant at Santa Ana National Wildlife Refuge, but many of these birds are being trapped for stocking elsewhere along the river. Unmissable at Bentsen-Rio Grande Valley State Park.

Wild Turkey—Fairly common permanent resident beyond our region in the brushlands of the King Ranch and also on the Edwards Plateau. Often seen from the highways.

Montezuma Quail—Uncommon and unpredictable permanent resident of the Davis Mountains. At present, being seen regularly right in the campground at Davis Mountains State Park. Also seen on the scenic loop through the mountains, on the lower slopes of Mount Locke, and at Bloys Camp. Has been known to saunter across the main street of Fort Davis.

Scaled Quail—Common permanent resident of arid brushlands throughout. Can usually be found about the trailer section of Falcon State Park. More common farther west.

Gambel's Quail—Uncommon to common permanent resident of mesquite thickets and salt-bush flats from Big Bend National Park westward. Best seen early in the morning along Highway 20 from McNary to El Paso or along the levees of the Rio Grande above and below El Paso.

Northern Jacana—Straggler to the Lower Valley. Several recent records, including at least one near Bentsen-Rio Grande Valley State Park.

Red-billed Pigeon—A rare summer resident of river woodlands from Falcon Dam to the Gulf. Occasional at other seasons and locations (e.g., San Ygnacio). At the Santa Ana National Wildlife Refuge or Bentsen-Rio Grande Valley State Park, it flashes across the road at tree-top level like a dark falcon. When you are standing along the river below Falcon Dam watching for a Ringed Kingfisher, you may see a pigeon flying up the river and get a fairly good look.

Band-tailed Pigeon—Fairly common summer resident of the higher mountains of the Trans-Pecos. Sporadic in winter and in other locations. Easiest to see along the Boot Spring Trail in Big Bend National Park, at The Bowl in the Guadalupe Mountains, or along the scenic loop in the Davis

Mountains. In spring when the mulberries are ripe, it may be seen at Fort Davis.

White-winged Dove—Common summer resident of brushlands along the entire river; occasional in winter. Its *who cooks for you* call is heard everywhere after about the 10th of April. You are bound to see one—or a hundred.

Common Ground-Dove—Fairly common permanent resident of the farmlands and brushlands along the entire river. You are bound to see one.

Ruddy Ground-Dove—Accidental in the Lower Valley, but there are some recent records from Anzalduas County Park, Laguna Atascosa and Santa Ana National Wildlife Refuges, and elsewhere. It is accidental at Big Bend National Park.

Inca Dove—Common resident of cities and farms throughout. Its *no hope* call is frequently heard. Easy to see.

White-tipped Dove—Uncommon and secretive resident of thickets from Falcon Dam to the Gulf. Easiest to see at Santa Ana National Wildlife Refuge, Bentsen-Rio Grande Valley State Park, or the National Audubon Society's Sabal Palm Grove Sanctuary, where it walks along the roads and trails like a pigeon.

Parrots and parakeets—are often seen in the Lower Valley. Most, if not all, are escapees. However, several species occur just south of the border in Mexico. It is possible that some of the small flocks seen at Santa Ana National Wildlife Refuge and elsewhere are wild, but you may have a hard time convincing everyone. Green Parakeets are often seen in Brownsville and McAllen, but have yet to find their way onto the *ABA Checklist*. The Red-crowned Parrot has been found regularly at Brownsville, Santa Ana, and McAllen since 1976 and recently has nested.

Groove-billed Ani—Fairly common summer resident from mid-April through September in the wooded parts of the Lower Valley. Rare in winter and in other locations. Fairly easy to find in summer at Santa Ana and Laguna Atascosa National Wildlife Refuges and Falcon Dam.

Ferruginous Pygmy-Owl—Rare permanent resident of the woodlands in the Lower Valley and the King Ranch. Has recently been found on the Santa Margarita Ranch, but it is most often seen below Falcon Dam and just beyond the range of this book along Highway 77 on the King Ranch.

Elf Owl—Fairly common in woodlands of Lower Valley and at Rio Grande Village in Big Bend National Park.

Mottled Owl—One was found dead just outside the entrance to Bentsen-Rio Grande Valley State Park in February 1983. This woodland owl resides as close as southern Tamaulipas and Nuevo Leon in Mexico.

Lesser Nighthawk—Common summer resident of the open areas from El Paso to Falcon Dam. Easy to find. Less common in the Lower Valley, but numerous at Laguna Atascosa National Wildlife Refuge.

Pauraque—Common permanent resident in wooded areas of the Lower Valley. Fairly easy to see at Bentsen-Rio Grande Valley State Park if you drive the roads at night. Can often be flushed out during the day by prowling through the brush.

Common Poorwill—Common summer resident of the brushlands of West Texas and the Edwards Plateau. Can often be seen at night by driving the back roads and watching for its orange eyeshine. Common in Big Bend National Park, Davis Mountains, and off the Trans-Mountain Road at El Paso.

Chuck-will's-widow—Fairly common summer resident in the wooded areas of the Edwards Plateau; migrant elsewhere. Can be heard at night at most of the state parks on the plateau.

White-throated Swift—Common summer resident of cliffs and mountain peaks in West Texas. Easy to find in Boquillas and Santa Elena Canyons at Big Bend National Park, and at McKittrick Canyon in the Guadalupe Mountains.

Green Violet-ear—Reported at least nine times since 1961 from the Lower Valley north to the Austin area.

Broad-billed Hummingbird—Very rare summer resident along the Rio Grande in Big Bend National Park, where it has been found at Rio Grande Village.

Berylline Hummingbird—One record from Boot Canyon at Big Bend National Park in August 1991.

White-eared Hummingbird—Accidental summer visitor in the Chisos Mountains. There are several recent records.

Buff-bellied Hummingbird—Uncommon summer resident of woodlands and cities in the Lower Valley. Rare in winter. Easiest to find at the National Audubon Society's Sabal Palm Grove Sanctuary, near the old headquarters site at Santa Ana National Wildlife Refuge, or at someone's feeder.

Violet-crowned Hummingbird—One recorded in El Paso in December 1987.

Blue-throated Hummingbird—Rare summer resident of the Chisos, Davis, and Guadalupe Mountains.

Magnificent Hummingbird—Very rare summer resident of the Davis, Chisos, and Guadalupe Mountains.

Lucifer Hummingbird—Fairly common to uncommon summer resident in the Chisos Mountains of Big Bend National Park. Easiest to find in June, July, and August when the agaves and sages are in bloom. Often found in Green Gulch, Blue Creek Canyon, Laguna Meadow, and along the lower part of the Window Trail.

Ruby-throated Hummingbird—Common migrant and uncommon winter visitor to the Lower Valley and elsewhere. Often found about the red-flowered Turk's Cap in the Sabal Palm Grove Sanctuary and at the headquarters of Santa Ana National Wildlife Refuge.

Black-chinned Hummingbird—Common summer resident in the cities and brushlands of West Texas and the Edwards Plateau. Reaches the coast in migration. Easy to find at feeders near Hunt, in Big Bend National Park, and at El Paso.

Anna's Hummingbird—Rare winter visitor along Rio Grande in Big Bend and El Paso regions. Sporadic elsewhere.

Broad-tailed Hummingbird—Uncommon summer resident in the Davis, Chisos, and Guadalupe Mountains. Elsewhere in migration, particularly at El Paso. Can be found along the Boot Spring Trail in Big Bend National Park or at The Bowl in the Guadalupe Mountains.

Elegant Trogon—A rare visitor, with three records at Big Bend and a smattering of records for the Lower Valley. The most recent sighting was in late January 1990.

Ringed Kingfisher—Uncommon but often-seen permanent resident along the river below Falcon Dam. The way to see this bird is to stand along the river and wait for it to fly by. Usually found just below the dam, at Chapeño, or at the Santa Margarita Ranch. Uncommon at Santa Ana National Wildlife Refuge. Stragglers have shown up as far away as the Aransas National Wildlife Refuge and on the Edwards Plateau.

Green Kingfisher—Uncommon to rare permanent resident of the Edwards Plateau and the area below Falcon Dam. It seems to be more common below the dam in winter and more common on the plateau in summer. Has been seen just below the dam, at Chapeño, Salineño, Santa Margarita Ranch, and Frontón. Also found at the lakes in Santa Ana National Wildlife Refuge, and rarely at Bentsen-Rio Grande Valley State Park. Most often seen in the early morning when the water is low and it fishes from the rocks in the river. At other times it may be flushed from the overhanging limbs along the shore. On the plateau it is most often seen in shallow stretches of the Guadalupe River along Farm Road 1340 and Highway 39 near Hunt, on the Rio Frio at Garner State Park and Neal's Lodge, and on the Nueces River near Camp Wood.

Acorn Woodpecker—Fairly common permanent resident of oak woodlands in the Chisos, Davis, and Guadalupe Mountains. Very local and rare resident on the Edwards Plateau. Can be found anywhere in the Chisos Mountains in Big Bend National Park and at the Madera Canyon Picnic Area in the Davis Mountains.

Golden-fronted Woodpecker—Common permanent resident of woodlands and brushlands of the Lower Rio Grande Valley, South Texas, and the Edwards Plateau. If you miss this one here, you are not trying. Uncommon but increasing in Big Bend National Park.

Ladder-backed Woodpecker—Common permanent resident of the woodlands and brushlands along the entire river. Easy to find.

Northern Beardless-Tyrannulet—Rare and local permanent resident of thickets along the river in the Lower Valley. Has been found at Santa Ana National Wildlife Refuge, Anzalduas County Park, and Bentsen-Rio Grande Valley State Park. Most often identified by its *ee ee ee ee* call.

Tufted Flycatcher—One record at Rio Grande Village, Big Bend National Park, in early November 1991.

Olive-sided Flycatcher—Migrant throughout. Some nest in the Guadalupe Mountains, where it can be found around The Bowl.

Greater Pewee—Rare straggler to the Chisos and Davis Mountains.

Western Wood-Pewee—Fairly common summer resident of woodlands in the mountains of West Texas and in the southern part of the Edwards Plateau. Migrant throughout. Can be found at Boot Spring at Big Bend National Park or in the Davis Mountains.

Eastern Wood-Pewee—Migrant and rare winter visitor in the Lower Valley. Some nest along the eastern edge of the Edwards Plateau.

Cordilleran Flycatcher—Uncommon summer resident of the higher forests of the Chisos, Davis, and Guadalupe Mountains. Can be found near Boot Spring in Big Bend National Park or at The Bowl in the Guadalupe Mountains.

Black Phoebe—Uncommon permanent resident near water from the western edge of the Edwards Plateau through West Texas. Can be found along the Rio Frio at Neal's Lodge and along the Rio Grande in Big Bend National Park. Winters at El Paso and Falcon Dam.

Eastern Phoebe—Common migrant through South Texas. Nests on the Edwards Plateau. Winters in the Lower Valley.

Say's Phoebe—Uncommon summer resident from the western edge of the Edwards Plateau through West Texas. More widespread in winter, when it reaches Brownsville. Often nests about old buildings such as those at the Hot Springs in Big Bend National Park or about rocky cliffs such as those at the Hueco Tanks State Park.

Vermilion Flycatcher—Fairly common summer resident of brushlands throughout. Some winter in the Lower Valley. Not hard to find, except at El Paso.

Dusky-capped Flycatcher—Very rare spring migrant and summer visitor to West Texas. May nest.

Ash-throated Flycatcher—Fairly common summer resident of the brushlands of West Texas and the Edwards Plateau. Easy to find in Big Bend National Park and the Davis Mountains.

Great Crested Flycatcher—Abundant migrant through South Texas. Common summer resident of woodlands on the Edwards Plateau. Easy to find.

Brown-crested Flycatcher—Fairly common summer resident of woodlands from Eagle Pass to the Gulf. Occasional farther west. Fairly easy to find at Santa Ana National Wildlife Refuge, Bentsen-Rio Grande Valley State Park, and below Falcon Dam.

Great Kiskadee—Common permanent resident of woodlands near water from Laredo to the Gulf. Easy to find at Santa Ana National Wildlife Refuge and Bentsen-Rio Grande Valley State Park.

Social Flycatcher—Reported from Anzalduas County Park between mid-March and early April 1990. Looks like a miniature Great Kiskadee.

Sulphur-bellied Flycatcher—Very rare vagrant. A few birds reported irregularly from mid-1970s to 1980 in the Lower Valley, especially Santa Margarita Ranch. Also three reports in Big Bend National Park.

Couch's Kingbird—Common summer resident in woodlands along the Rio Grande from Big Bend National Park (rare) to the Gulf. Easy to find at Santa Ana National Wildlife Refuge, Bentsen-Rio Grande Valley State Park, and the Santa Margarita Ranch.

Tropical Kingbird—One bird was reported in March 1988 at Laguna Atascosa National Wildlife Refuge. A pair was found in the winter of 1990 in Brownsville and stayed to nest in 1991. Call is the best way to differentiate this bird from Couch's Kingbird—a twittering *pip-pip-pip* rather than the Couch's shrill *breeer*.

Western Kingbird—Fairly common summer resident in open areas of the Edwards Plateau and West Texas. Less common elsewhere.

Cassin's Kingbird—Common summer resident of the woodlands of the Trans-Pecos. Easy to find in the Davis Mountains, but less common in Big Bend National Park. Common migrant in West Texas.

Thick-billed Kingbird—Several records for Big Bend National Park, mostly in spring. Has nested at Cottonwood Campground and Rio Grande Village.

Eastern Kingbird—Mainly migrant in this area, but a few nest along the eastern edge of the Edwards Plateau.

Scissor-tailed Flycatcher—Abundant migrant through southern Texas and summer resident on the Edwards Plateau. Far less common along the river from Big Bend National Park to the Gulf.

Fork-tailed Flycatcher—One fairly old record from the Lower Valley (February 4, 1961) and several more records in the 1980s. More likely near the coast.

Rose-throated Becard—Rare summer resident of the woodlands in the Lower Valley. Has nested at Santa Ana National Wildlife Refuge, Anzalduas County Park, and Bentsen-Rio Grande Valley State Park. Occasional in winter.

Masked Tityra—One of these birds was observed from mid-February to early March 1990 at Bentsen-Rio Grande Valley State Park. There was also another report several years earlier.

Gray-breasted Martin—Formerly recorded in the Lower Valley. There are two specimens from the 1880s. Since it closely resembles a female Purple Martin, sight records are almost impossible.

Violet-green Swallow—Uncommon summer resident of wooded areas and canyons of the Chisos, Davis, and Guadalupe Mountains. A common migrant throughout West Texas. Can be found near Boot Spring in the Chisos and at The Bowl in the Guadalupe Mountains.

Cave Swallow—Common summer resident about caves and sinkholes on the Edwards Plateau and at Carlsbad Caverns. Also reported from Big Bend National Park. Since the mid-1980s, the species has made increasing use of bridges and culverts and has extended its range east to Kingsville and west almost to El Paso. It is even being seen in winter.

Steller's Jay—Locally common in the higher parts of the Davis and Guadalupe Mountains. Lower and more widespread in winter. Can be found at The Bowl in the Guadalupe Mountains.

Green Jay—Common permanent resident of river thickets in the Lower Valley. Although shy for a jay, in breeding season it can be found at Santa Ana National Wildlife Refuge, Bentsen-Rio Grande Valley State Park, and upriver to Salineño.

Brown Jay—First reported in the United States in 1969 from just below the Falcon Dam. Now a permanent resident of the river thickets from Falcon Dam to Roma. At present, easiest to find on the Santa Margarita Ranch and at Salineño. This large, noisy jay is easy to hear when present, but not always easy to see.

Scrub Jay—Common permanent resident of brushlands on the Edwards Plateau and in the mountains of West Texas. Easy to find at Garner State Park and in the Davis Mountains.

Gray-breasted Jay—Common permanent resident of the oak woodlands of the Chisos Mountains. Easy to find at the Basin in Big Bend National Park.

Mexican Crow—Reported in the United States for the first time in 1968 near Brownsville. Sometimes abundant in fall and winter, but hard to find in spring. Prefers cow lots and garbage dumps. The most reliable spot for finding it has been the Brownsville dump, where it recently has been found nesting. **American Crow**—does not occur along the Rio Grande except in winter at El Paso, but the Chihuahuan Raven is common at the dump. The Mexican Crow is about the size of a female Great-tailed Grackle and sounds like a small frog.

Chihuahuan Raven—Common permanent resident of the plains along the entire river. Becomes abundant in the Lower Valley in winter and less common in West Texas, but still easy to find. It is replaced on the Edwards Plateau and in the higher mountains of West Texas by the Common Raven.

Mountain Chickadee—Fairly common in the coniferous forests at the higher elevations in the Davis and Guadalupe Mountains. Can be found near The Bowl in the Guadalupe Mountains.

Tufted Titmouse—The Black-crested race is common in the woodlands from the Lower Valley to Big Bend National Park, in the Davis Mountains, and on the Edwards Plateau. Not hard to find.

Verdin—Fairly common permanent resident of mesquite thickets and brushlands along the entire river. Easy to find except in the Lower Valley.

Bushtit—Fairly common in the brushlands of West Texas and on the Edwards Plateau. Goes around in flocks and twitters constantly. If you learn the call, this bird is fairly easy to find.

Pygmy Nuthatch—Fairly common permanent resident of mature pine forests at higher elevations in the Davis and Guadalupe Mountains. Occasionally found elsewhere in West Texas in winter. Can be found near The Bowl in the Guadalupe Mountains.

Cactus Wren—Common permanent resident of cactus patches and thorny brushlands throughout. Noisy and conspicuous. Perhaps easiest to see in campgrounds at Falcon State Park.

Rock Wren—Common permanent resident of dry, rocky areas from West Texas to the Edwards Plateau. Easy to find in Big Bend National Park.

Canyon Wren—Fairly common permanent resident of rocky canyons and cliffs from West Texas through the Edwards Plateau. Preferred sites are usually near water, probably because insects are more common there. Can be hard to find unless you learn its song, which is loud, clear, and unmistakable. Easy to find along the Guadalupe River, in the river canyons of Big Bend National Park, and at Hueco Tanks.

Black-tailed Gnatcatcher—Fairly common permanent resident of thorny brushlands from El Paso to about Rio Grande City. Easy to find in Big Bend National Park.

Mountain Bluebird—Uncommon to rare and irregular winter visitor to the plains and farmlands throughout. More common westward.

Townsend's Solitaire—Fairly common but irregular winter visitor to areas of berry-producing bushes such as juniper, Squaw Bush, or Mistletoe throughout. Fairly easy to find in the Chisos Mountains.

Clay-colored Robin—Rare straggler to woodlands and river thickets from Big Bend National Park to the Gulf. Most recent records have been from the Santa Ana National Wildlife Refuge and Bentsen-Rio Grande Valley State Park, usually from December to April. In the early spring, it sings in the early morning. There are a few nesting records.

White-throated Robin—A bird of this species accompanied three Clay-colored Robins in February 1990 in a residential area in Cameron County. A previous sight record was for March 1984—also in Cameron County.

Rufous-backed Robin—There is a handful of records along the Rio Grande, from Santa Ana National Wildlife Refuge to Big Bend.

Aztec Thrush—At least four records for Big Bend, most at Boot Canyon.

Sage Thrasher—Uncommon winter visitor to arid plains throughout. Unpredictable and often hard to find.

Long-billed Thrasher—Fairly common but shy permanent resident of river thickets from Del Rio to the Gulf. Most easily seen at Santa Ana

National Wildlife Refuge and Bentsen-Rio Grande Valley State Park. Beware of Brown Thrashers which winter uncommonly in much of South Texas (except the Lower Valley).

Curve-billed Thrasher—Common permanent resident of arid brushlands throughout. Easy to find.

Crissal Thrasher—Fairly common but extremely shy permanent resident of dense brush in arid regions from El Paso to the Pecos River. Usually chanced upon along some desert wash. Easiest to find in Big Bend National Park or near El Paso.

Gray Silky-Flycatcher—Observed at Laguna Atascosa National Wildlife Refuge in October-November 1985. This neotropical species is largely fruit-eating, and may be prone to wandering.

Phainopepla—Uncommon to fairly common permanent resident of mistletoe-infected brushlands of the Trans-Pecos. Less common in winter, in Big Bend National Park, and farther east along the Rio Grande. Can usually be found in the Davis Mountains.

White-eyed Vireo—Common summer resident of woodland in South Texas and on the Edwards Plateau west to Big Bend National Park (rare). Less common in winter. Noisy and easy to find in spring.

Bell's Vireo—Common summer resident of brushlands (especially mesquite) from Laredo to Big Bend National Park and on the Edwards Plateau. Uncommon to rare in the Lower Valley and at El Paso. Easy to locate by its calls, but hard to see.

Black-capped Vireo—Uncommon and shy summer resident of ungrazed scrub-oak thickets (those with a low understory). Most common on the Edwards Plateau near Austin and Kerrville, but occurs westward to Big Bend National Park. Some known locations are Comanche Trail near Austin, Friedrich Wilderness Park in San Antonio, Lost Maples State Park, Johnson Canyon north of Medina, and Blue Creek Canyon in Big Bend National Park (rare).

Gray Vireo—Uncommon to rare summer resident in the brushy canyons of the Chisos, Davis, and Guadalupe Mountains, and western Edwards Plateau. In Big Bend National Park most often found on the Window Trail. In the Guadalupe Mountains fairly common in McKittrick Canyon.

Hutton's Vireo—Uncommon permanent resident of oak woodlands in the Chisos, Davis, and Guadalupe Mountains. Fairly common at Boot Spring in the Chisos Mountains and in McKittrick Canyon in the Guadalupe Mountains.

Red-eyed Vireo—Fairly common summer resident of woodlands of the Edwards Plateau. Migrant throughout, but rare westward.

Yellow-green Vireo—Very rare summer resident of woodlands and residential areas in the Lower Valley and occasionally farther upriver. This bird is usually passed off as a Red-eyed Vireo except in midsummer, when the Red-eyed is not around. You should check all Red-eyed Vireos seen in the Lower Valley to make sure that the under-tail coverts are white and not yellow. For the last several years Yellow-green Vireos have been found nesting at Laguna Atascosa National Wildlife Refuge.

Migrant Warblers and Other Landbirds—Many landbirds move through this area in the spring and fall although they are seldom seen in great numbers except along the coast. The Audubon Sabal Palm Grove Sanctuary and Santa Ana National Wildlife Refuge are good spots to find those that migrate along the coast. Rio Grande Village and the Boot Spring Trail in Big Bend National Park are good for western migrants. For a list of migrants, consult the bar-graphs.

Virginia's Warbler—Rare summer resident in the brush areas at higher elevations in the Guadalupe Mountains. Uncommon migrant through West Texas.

Colima Warbler—Fairly common but very localized summer resident of the oak woodlands in the Chisos Mountains. Easy to find along the Boot Spring Trail from late April to June when the males are singing; however, you may have some difficulty in seeing one because it is a shy, rather drab bird. It responds to squeaking and to pygmy-owl calls.

Lucy's Warbler—Very rare summer resident of thickets along Rio Grande from Big Bend National Park (Castolon) westward. It is found almost exclusively in areas of mesquite.

Tropical Parula—Rare permanent resident of woodlands in the Lower Valley and on the King Ranch. Found mainly after the Northern Parula has moved north. It is seen normally moving about the upper branches of a large tree. Most recent records have been just beyond our region from the first roadside-rest area south of Sarita on Highway 77 or at the last rest area near Norias. Formerly nested in the refuge manager's front yard at the Santa Ana National Wildlife Refuge, and in the last few years has again nested elsewhere on the refuge. Also to be looked for at Sabal Palm Grove Sanctuary near Brownsville.

Golden-cheeked Warbler—Locally fairly common summer resident of wooded areas with stands of mature junipers on the Edwards Plateau from Austin and San Antonio west to about Garner State Park. Seems to prefer the upper parts of wooded canyons, but may occur on hilltops or in valleys as long as there are mature junipers for nest-building. At present the best spot for finding one is along the road to Emma Long Metropolitan Park (City Park) in Austin. Other sites are Friedrich Wilderness Park in San Antonio, Johnson Canyon north of Medina, Kerrville State Park, Pedernales Falls State Park, Lost Maples State Park, and Highway 674 south of Rocksprings.

Grace's Warbler—Uncommon to fairly common summer resident of pine trees in the Davis and Guadalupe Mountains. Easy to find in McKittrick Canyon in late April and early May, when the males are singing from the tops of every pine tree.

Gray-crowned Yellowthroat—Formerly nested in river thickets in the Lower Valley. Four records from 1959 to 1965. Five recent records from the Lower Valley from 1987 to 1990, at Santa Ana and at Sabal Palm Grove Sanctuary.

Red-faced Warbler—Seven records for Big Bend National Park, all in summer, in Boot Canyon, Boot Spring, or the Basin.

Painted Redstart—Very rare summer resident near Boot Spring in the Chisos Mountains.

Slate-throated Redstart—Accidental at Big Bend National Park, including an individual seen at Boot Canyon from April 30 to May 15, 1990.

Golden-crowned Warbler—About nine records: two old ones from the 1890s, most of the others since 1979. Locations include Brownsville, Santa Ana, Weslaco, and Sabal Palm Grove Sanctuary; dates are overwhelmingly in winter.

Rufous-capped Warbler—First reported in 1973 from near Falcon Dam. There are almost a dozen subsequent records from Big Bend National Park (from the Chisos Basin or Santa Elena Canyon). Also, one record from Webb County, another in Kendall County on the Edwards Plateau.

Hepatic Tanager—Uncommon summer resident of the pine forests of the Chisos, Davis, and Guadalupe Mountains. Can be found at Boot Spring, at The Bowl in the Guadalupe Mountains, or at the Madera Canyon Rest Area in the Davis Mountains.

Western Tanager—Uncommon summer resident of the coniferous forests of the Chisos, Davis, and Guadalupe Mountains. More common as a migrant throughout the Trans-Pecos. Can be found along the Boot Spring Trail and at The Bowl in the Guadalupe Mountains.

Crimson-collared Grosbeak—First recorded in 1974 at Bentsen-Rio Grande Valley State Park, and there have been a couple of sight records in that area since. This is a common cage-bird in Mexico. Most recently one was found at Audubon's Sabal Palm Grove Sanctuary.

Pyrrhuloxia—Common resident of the brushlands throughout. Easy to find.

Blue Bunting—About eleven records for the area, including the following: two (photo) Bentsen-Rio Grande Valley State Park, March 12-16, 1980, and two birds observed at Anzalduas County Park, February 12, 1982. One bird December 1987 to February 1988, and also in December 1989 at Bentsen-Rio Grande Valley State Park, and one bird January 5 to March 1990 at Santa Ana National Wildlife Refuge.

Varied Bunting—Rare to uncommon and localized summer resident of dense thickets in Big Bend National Park and occasional elsewhere. Can be found along the Window Trail near the sewer ponds and at the Old Ranch in Big Bend National Park, in the lower part of Aguja Canyon in the Davis Mountains, and along a dirt road that parallels the Pecos River between Iraan and Sheffield.

Painted Bunting—Fairly common summer resident of brushlands throughout. Fairly easy to find after mid-April.

Dickcissel—Common but irregular summer resident of pastures and roadside thickets in South Texas and on the Edwards Plateau. Usually easy to find after mid-April. Often sits on fence lines along the roads.

Olive Sparrow—Common but shy permanent resident of thickets from Del Rio to the Gulf. Its loud, clear trill is often heard from the dense undergrowth, but the bird is seldom seen. It can sometimes be coaxed out by squeaking.

Green-tailed Towhee—Rare to fairly common winter visitor in brushy parts of the Trans-Pecos and along the Rio Grande to Falcon Dam. Has nested in the Guadalupe Mountains. It is an uncommon winter bird at Santa Ana National Wildlife Refuge.

Canyon Towhee—Fairly common permanent resident in arid brushlands of the Trans-Pecos, Big Bend National Park, and the Edwards Plateau. Not hard to find.

White-collared Seedeater—Very rare in thickets and weed patches in the Lower Valley. Apparently resident locally, but no recent nesting confirmed. Do not count on seeing this one, although it has recently been found about the town of San Ygnacio, upriver from Falcon Dam, and at Zapata.

Yellow-faced Grassquit—The first, and thus far only, U.S. record was for three days in late January 1990 at Santa Ana. This bird is a common resident within 150 miles of the U.S. border and should be watched for again.

Botteri's Sparrow—Uncommon permanent resident of brushy pastures in the Lower Valley, mainly east of Brownsville. Can be found at Laguna Atascosa National Wildlife Refuge. The Cassin's Sparrow also occurs here, and the two look very much alike. The best way of separating them is by song; however, the Botteri's is browner, particularly on the tail.

Cassin's Sparrow—Common permanent resident of brushy pastures and grasslands throughout. Skylarks continually in May and June. In winter it may be flushed by walking across the pastures.

Rufous-crowned Sparrow—Fairly common permanent resident of arid, rocky brushlands in the Trans-Pecos and on the Edwards Plateau. Easy to find at Big Bend National Park, Davis Mountains, and Hueco Tanks State Park.

Clay-colored Sparrow—Common migrant and winter visitor to grasslands and open brushlands throughout. Usually easy to find near El Paso, Big Bend National Park, and Falcon Dam, but sporadic.

Brewer's Sparrow—Common migrant and winter visitor to arid grasslands and open brushlands from El Paso to Del Rio. Easy to find in the Davis Mountains.

Field Sparrow—Fairly common permanent resident in brushy areas of the Edwards Plateau. More common and widespread in winter, when it can be found along the entire river.

Black-chinned Sparrow— Uncommon permanent resident of high-elevation brushlands in the Trans-Pecos. In mid-April and May, when the males are singing, it is easy to find in McKittrick Canyon in the Guadalupe Mountains. In winter, may be found in the Basin at Big Bend National Park and in Aguja Canyon in the Davis Mountains.

Black-throated Sparrow—Common permanent resident of arid, rocky, and thinly-vegetated brushlands from El Paso to Falcon Dam and on the western Edwards Plateau. Can be found at the trailer section of Falcon State Park, Big Bend National Park, and many other areas.

Lark Bunting—Abundant migrant throughout. Common winter visitor in the grasslands of South Texas. Since it goes about in large flocks, it is usually easy to find in season.

Baird's Sparrow—Uncommon but regular migrant and rare winter visitor in the grasslands and weedy fields of the Trans-Pecos. Can usually be found along Highway 118 south of Alpine and Highway 90 west of Marfa.

Yellow-eyed Junco—Three records for Big Bend, including two at Boot Spring. Also recorded in the Guadalupe Mountains.

Great-tailed Grackle—Abundant on the farmlands and brushlands of South Texas. Hard to miss. In fact, you will soon be sick of it.

Bronzed Cowbird—Common permanent resident of farms and brushlands in South Texas. Less common in winter from about October to mid-April. Not hard to find about cow-lots.

Black-vented Oriole—One record from Rio Grande Village at Big Bend National Park in 1968, and presumably the same bird from April 28 to September 29, 1969, and April 17 to October 10, 1970. These were probably all the same bird. One other was reported near San Ygnacio August 14, 1980. North of our area an adult male stayed just south of Kingsville from June 17 to October 4, 1989.

Hooded Oriole—Rare to uncommon summer resident of wooded areas and gardens all along the river, although quite rare near Brownsville. Often nests in palm trees in the cities such as Laredo or in cottonwoods as in Rio Grande Village.

Altamira Oriole—Fairly common permanent resident in woodlands of the Lower Valley. Often seen at Santa Ana National Wildlife Refuge, Bentsen-Rio Grande Valley State Park, or about hummingbird feeders in the cities.

Audubon's Oriole—Rare resident of wooded areas of South Texas. Usually chanced upon, but it can sometimes be attracted to a hummingbird feeder. Try Falcon Dam, Salineño, or Santa Margarita Ranch.

Scott's Oriole—Fairly common summer resident of woodlands and stands of yucca in the Trans-Pecos. Can usually be found in the Basin at Big Bend National Park, at Davis Mountains State Park, in McKittrick Canyon, and on the western part of the Edwards Plateau.

Lesser Goldfinch—Fairly common permanent resident of woodlands and brushlands from El Paso to the eastern part of the Edwards Plateau. Often seen sitting on phone wires or feeding in weedy fields.

Birds of the Region

All birds regularly occurring along the Rio Grande in an average year are listed in the following charts. There are also sections for the Edwards Plateau and the Guadalupe Mountains. No attempt is made to reflect yearly fluctuations, extremely early or late dates, or unusual occurrences. Birds that are seldom seen or accidental are in the previous "Specialties" section or are listed separately after the bar-graphs.

On the top left side of the bar-graphs are printed regional indicators which correspond roughly with parts of southern Texas treated in this book. *They do not correspond directly with the eight chapters in the book.* Instead, they cover arbitrary sections along the length of the Rio Grande in Texas, from the Gulf Coast through the El Paso area. The two side-trip areas in this book—the Edwards Plateau and Guadalupe Mountains National Park—are dealt with by two separate sections in the left side of the bar-graphs. The sections along the Rio Grande are clearly indicated by "marker locations" in vertical lines; the two side-trip sites are indicated by the spaces between vertical lines. The five "marker locations" for the bar-graph areas are as follows:

The Gulf—This covers the shore and adjacent areas along the Gulf Coast and westward through the Lower Rio Grande Valley (Cameron, Willacy, Hidalgo, and Starr counties) to the next location.

Falcon Dam—This area starts at the dam, and moves through the route beyond Falcon Reservoir, Laredo, and upriver to Del Rio.

Del Rio—This section includes from Amistad Reservoir upriver to the Big Bend area.

Big Bend—This area starts at Big Bend and covers that area plus the Davis Mountains.

El Paso—This covers just west of the Davis Mountains through the El Paso Valley.

The bar-graphs are also designed to give you an idea of occurrence through the year, and the bar-graphs will provide a conservative idea of your chances for finding a particular bird rather than the bird's actual abundance. Thus a large bird such as the Red-tailed Hawk may be shown as *hard to miss*, while a shy, hard-to-identify, or small bird such as Botteri's Sparrow may occur in greater numbers, but be shown as *lucky to find*. You may find birds at other seasons or in greater abundance than is indicated.

HARD TO MISS

SHOULD SEE

MAY SEE

LUCKY TO FIND

HOW LUCKY CAN YOU GET

Many local birders and others who bird the area frequently were consulted in determining the status of each bird. Since these people are familiar with the birds, their songs, habits, and habitats, they are good at finding the more elusive species. On your first trip to the area, you may think that some birds are harder to find than is indicated.

If you are in the RIGHT HABITAT and the RIGHT AREA at the RIGHT SEASON, you should be able to find the *hard to miss* birds on nearly every field trip; the *should see* birds on 3 out of 4 trips; the *may see* birds on 1 out of 4 trips, and the *lucky to find* birds on 1 out of 10 trips or less often.

Although *forget it* is the answer that you will probably receive when inquiring about your chances of seeing a very rare (*how lucky can you get*) species, do not stop looking. Adding one of these bonus birds to your list is what puts the topping on a trip. Besides, birding optimists in the area are often seen carrying *A Field Guide to Mexican Birds* by Peterson and Chalif. If you are positive of your identification, take careful notes and report your rare findings to the regional editors of *American Birds*, Greg Lasley (305 Loganberry Court, Austin TX 78745) and Chuck Sexton (101 E. 54th Street, Austin TX 78751).

✓	The Gulf	Falcon Dam	Del Rio	Big Bend	El Paso	Edwards Plateau	Guadalupes	January	February	March	April	May	June	July	August	September	October	November	December
☐ Common Loon																			
☐ Least Grebe																			
☐ Pied-billed Grebe																			
☐ Horned Grebe																			
☐ Eared Grebe																			
☐ Western Grebe																			
☐ Clark's Grebe																			
☐ American White Pelican																			
☐ Brown Pelican																			
☐ Double-crested Cormorant																			
☐ Neotropic Cormorant																			
☐ Anhinga																			
☐ American Bittern																			
" "																			
☐ Least Bittern																			
" "																			
☐ Great Blue Heron																			
☐ Great Egret																			
" "																			
☐ Snowy Egret																			
☐ Little Blue Heron																			
☐ Tricolored Heron																			
☐ Reddish Egret																			
☐ Cattle Egret																			
☐ Green-backed Heron																			
☐ Black-crowned Night-Heron																			
" "																			
☐ Yellow-crowned Night-Heron																			
" "																			
☐ White Ibis																			

✓	The Gulf	Falcon Dam	Del Rio	Big Bend	El Paso	Edwards Plateau	Guadalupes	January	February	March	April	May	June	July	August	September	October	November	December
☐ White-faced Ibis																			
" "																			
☐ Roseate Spoonbill																			
☐ Wood Stork																			
☐ Fulvous Whistling-Duck																			
☐ Black-bellied Whistling-Duck																			
☐ Tundra Swan																			
☐ Greater White-fronted Goose																			
☐ Snow Goose																			
☐ Canada Goose																			
☐ Muscovy Duck																			
☐ Wood Duck																			
" "																			
☐ Green-winged Teal																			
☐ Mottled Duck																			
☐ Mallard																			
" "																			
☐ Northern Pintail																			
☐ Blue-winged Teal																			
☐ Cinnamon Teal																			
☐ Northern Shoveler																			
" "																			
☐ Gadwall																			
☐ American Wigeon																			
☐ Canvasback																			
☐ Redhead																			
☐ Ring-necked Duck																			
☐ Greater Scaup																			
☐ Lesser Scaup																			
☐ Common Goldeneye																			
☐ Bufflehead																			

✓	The Gulf	Falcon Dam	Del Rio	Big Bend	El Paso	Edwards Plateau	Guadalupes	January	February	March	April	May	June	July	August	September	October	November	December
☐ Hooded Merganser																			
☐ Common Merganser																			
☐ Red-breasted Merganser																			
☐ Ruddy Duck																			
☐ Masked Duck																			
☐ Black Vulture																			
☐ Turkey Vulture																			
" "																			
☐ Osprey																			
☐ Hook-billed Kite																			
☐ Black-shouldered Kite																			
☐ Mississippi Kite																			
☐ Bald Eagle																			
☐ Northern Harrier																			
☐ Sharp-shinned Hawk																			
" "																			
☐ Cooper's Hawk																			
☐ Northern Goshawk																			
☐ Common Black-Hawk																			
" "																			
☐ Harris's Hawk																			
☐ Gray Hawk																			
☐ Red-shouldered Hawk																			
" "																			
☐ Broad-winged Hawk																			
☐ Swainson's Hawk																			
" "																			
☐ White-tailed Hawk																			
☐ Zone-tailed Hawk																			
" "																			
☐ Red-tailed Hawk																			
☐ Ferruginous Hawk																			

✓	The Gulf	Falcon Dam	Del Rio	Big Bend	El Paso	Edwards Plateau	Guadalupes	January	February	March	April	May	June	July	August	September	October	November	December
☐ Rough-legged Hawk																			
☐ Golden Eagle																			
" "																			
☐ Crested Caracara																			
☐ American Kestrel																			
" "																			
☐ Merlin																			
☐ Peregrine Falcon																			
" "																			
☐ Prairie Falcon																			
☐ Plain Chachalaca																			
☐ Ring-necked Pheasant																			
☐ Wild Turkey																			
☐ Montezuma Quail																			
☐ Northern Bobwhite																			
☐ Scaled Quail																			
☐ Gambel's Quail																			
☐ Clapper Rail																			
☐ King Rail																			
☐ Virginia Rail																			
☐ Sora																			
☐ Purple Gallinule																			
☐ Common Moorhen																			
☐ American Coot																			
☐ Sandhill Crane																			
☐ Black-bellied Plover																			
" "																			
☐ Lesser Golden-Plover																			
☐ Snowy Plover																			
☐ Wilson's Plover																			

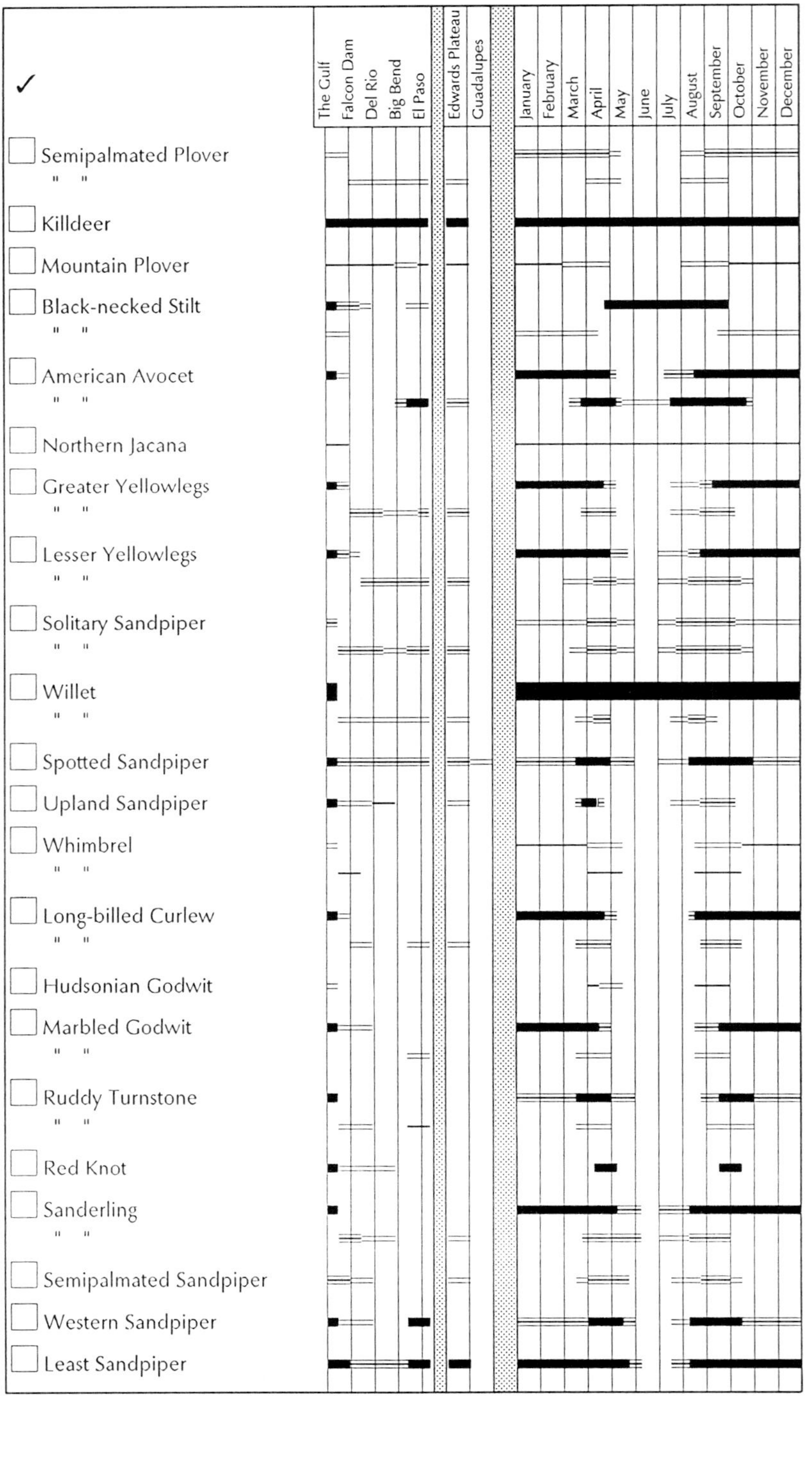

✓	The Gulf	Falcon Dam	Del Rio	Big Bend	El Paso	Edwards Plateau	Guadalupes	January	February	March	April	May	June	July	August	September	October	November	December
☐ Semipalmated Plover																			
" "																			
☐ Killdeer																			
☐ Mountain Plover																			
☐ Black-necked Stilt																			
" "																			
☐ American Avocet																			
" "																			
☐ Northern Jacana																			
☐ Greater Yellowlegs																			
" "																			
☐ Lesser Yellowlegs																			
" "																			
☐ Solitary Sandpiper																			
" "																			
☐ Willet																			
" "																			
☐ Spotted Sandpiper																			
☐ Upland Sandpiper																			
☐ Whimbrel																			
" "																			
☐ Long-billed Curlew																			
" "																			
☐ Hudsonian Godwit																			
☐ Marbled Godwit																			
" "																			
☐ Ruddy Turnstone																			
" "																			
☐ Red Knot																			
☐ Sanderling																			
" "																			
☐ Semipalmated Sandpiper																			
☐ Western Sandpiper																			
☐ Least Sandpiper																			

✓	The Gulf	Falcon Dam	Del Rio	Big Bend	El Paso	Edwards Plateau	Guadalupes	January	February	March	April	May	June	July	August	September	October	November	December
☐ White-rumped Sandpiper																			
☐ Baird's Sandpiper																			
☐ Pectoral Sandpiper																			
☐ Dunlin																			
" "																			
☐ Stilt Sandpiper																			
☐ Buff-breasted Sandpiper																			
☐ Short-billed Dowitcher																			
☐ Long-billed Dowitcher																			
" "																			
☐ Common Snipe																			
☐ Wilson's Phalarope																			
☐ Red-necked Phalarope																			
☐ Laughing Gull																			
☐ Franklin's Gull																			
☐ Bonaparte's Gull																			
☐ Ring-billed Gull																			
☐ Herring Gull																			
☐ Gull-billed Tern																			
☐ Caspian Tern																			
☐ Royal Tern																			
☐ Sandwich Tern																			
☐ Common Tern																			
☐ Forster's Tern																			
" "																			
☐ Least Tern																			
" "																			
☐ Black Tern																			
☐ Black Skimmer																			
☐ Red-billed Pigeon																			
☐ Band-tailed Pigeon																			

✓	The Gulf	Falcon Dam	Del Rio	Big Bend	El Paso	Edwards Plateau	Guadalupes	January	February	March	April	May	June	July	August	September	October	November	December
☐ White-winged Dove																			
☐ Mourning Dove																			
☐ Inca Dove																			
☐ Common Ground-Dove																			
☐ White-tipped Dove																			
☐ Red-crowned Parrot																			
☐ Black-billed Cuckoo																			
☐ Yellow-billed Cuckoo																			
☐ Greater Roadrunner																			
☐ Groove-billed Ani																			
☐ Barn Owl																			
☐ Flammulated Owl																			
☐ Eastern Screech-Owl																			
☐ Western Screech-Owl																			
☐ Great Horned Owl																			
☐ Ferruginous Pygmy-Owl																			
☐ Elf Owl																			
☐ Burrowing Owl																			
" "																			
☐ Spotted Owl																			
☐ Barred Owl																			
☐ Long-eared Owl																			
☐ Short-eared Owl																			
☐ Northern Saw-whet Owl																			
" "																			
☐ Lesser Nighthawk																			
☐ Common Nighthawk																			
☐ Pauraque																			
☐ Common Poorwill																			
" "																			

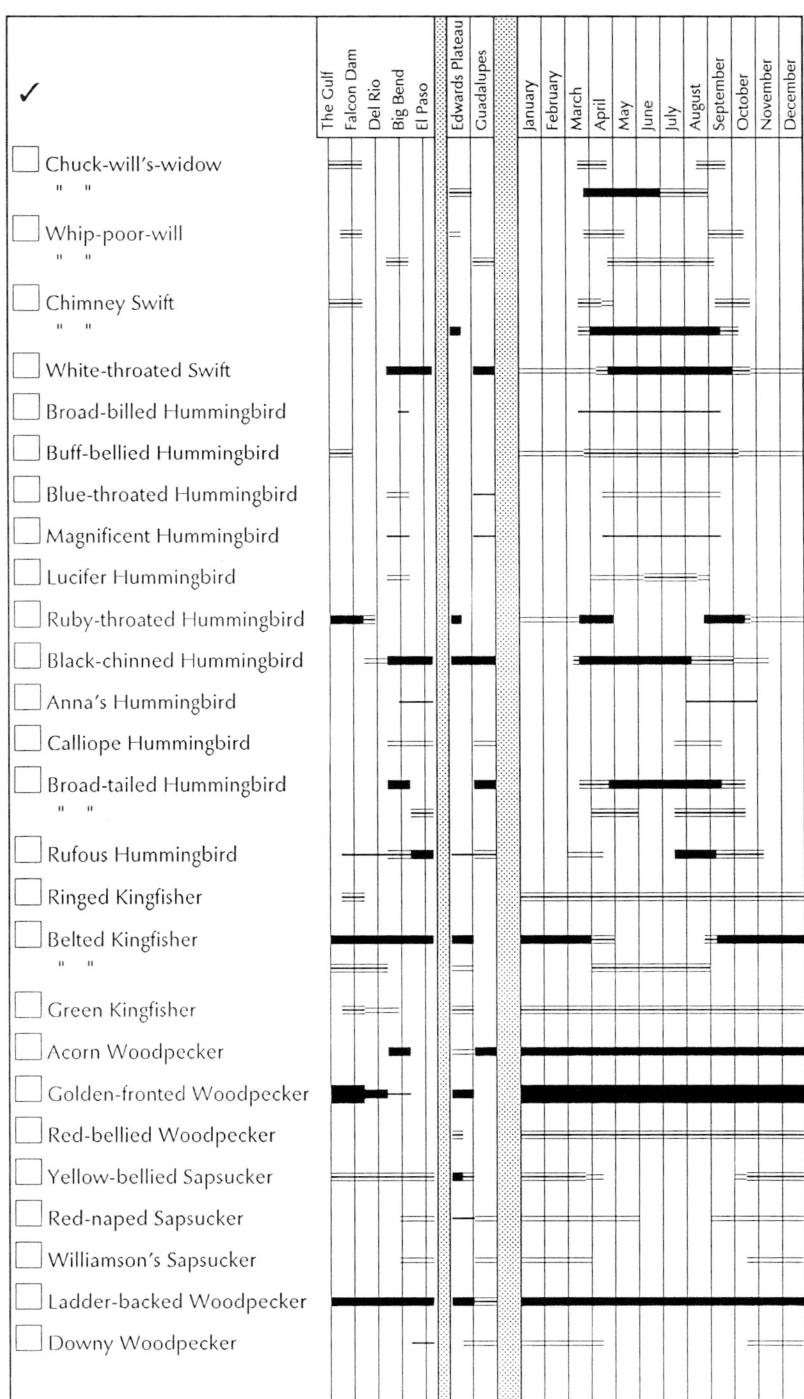
✓
The Gulf
Falcon Dam
Del Rio
Big Bend
El Paso
Edwards Plateau
Guadalupes
January
February
March
April
May
June
July
August
September
October
November
December
Chuck-will's-widow
" "
Whip-poor-will
" "
Chimney Swift
" "
White-throated Swift
Broad-billed Hummingbird
Buff-bellied Hummingbird
Blue-throated Hummingbird
Magnificent Hummingbird
Lucifer Hummingbird
Ruby-throated Hummingbird
Black-chinned Hummingbird
Anna's Hummingbird
Calliope Hummingbird
Broad-tailed Hummingbird
" "
Rufous Hummingbird
Ringed Kingfisher
Belted Kingfisher
" "
Green Kingfisher
Acorn Woodpecker
Golden-fronted Woodpecker
Red-bellied Woodpecker
Yellow-bellied Sapsucker
Red-naped Sapsucker
Williamson's Sapsucker
Ladder-backed Woodpecker
Downy Woodpecker

✓	The Gulf	Falcon Dam	Del Rio	Big Bend	El Paso	Edwards Plateau	Guadalupes	January	February	March	April	May	June	July	August	September	October	November	December
☐ Hairy Woodpecker																			
☐ Northern Flicker																			
" "																			
☐ Northern Beardless-Tyrannulet																			
☐ Olive-sided Flycatcher																			
" "																			
☐ Western Wood-Pewee																			
" "																			
☐ Eastern Wood-Pewee																			
" "																			
☐ Yellow-bellied Flycatcher																			
☐ Acadian Flycatcher																			
☐ Willow Flycatcher																			
☐ Least Flycatcher																			
☐ Hammond's Flycatcher																			
☐ Dusky Flycatcher																			
" "																			
☐ Gray Flycatcher																			
☐ Cordilleran Flycatcher																			
" "																			
☐ Black Phoebe																			
☐ Eastern Phoebe																			
" "																			
☐ Say's Phoebe																			
" "																			
☐ Vermilion Flycatcher																			
" "																			
☐ Dusky-capped Flycatcher																			
☐ Ash-throated Flycatcher																			
" "																			
☐ Great Crested Flycatcher																			
" "																			
☐ Brown-crested Flycatcher																			

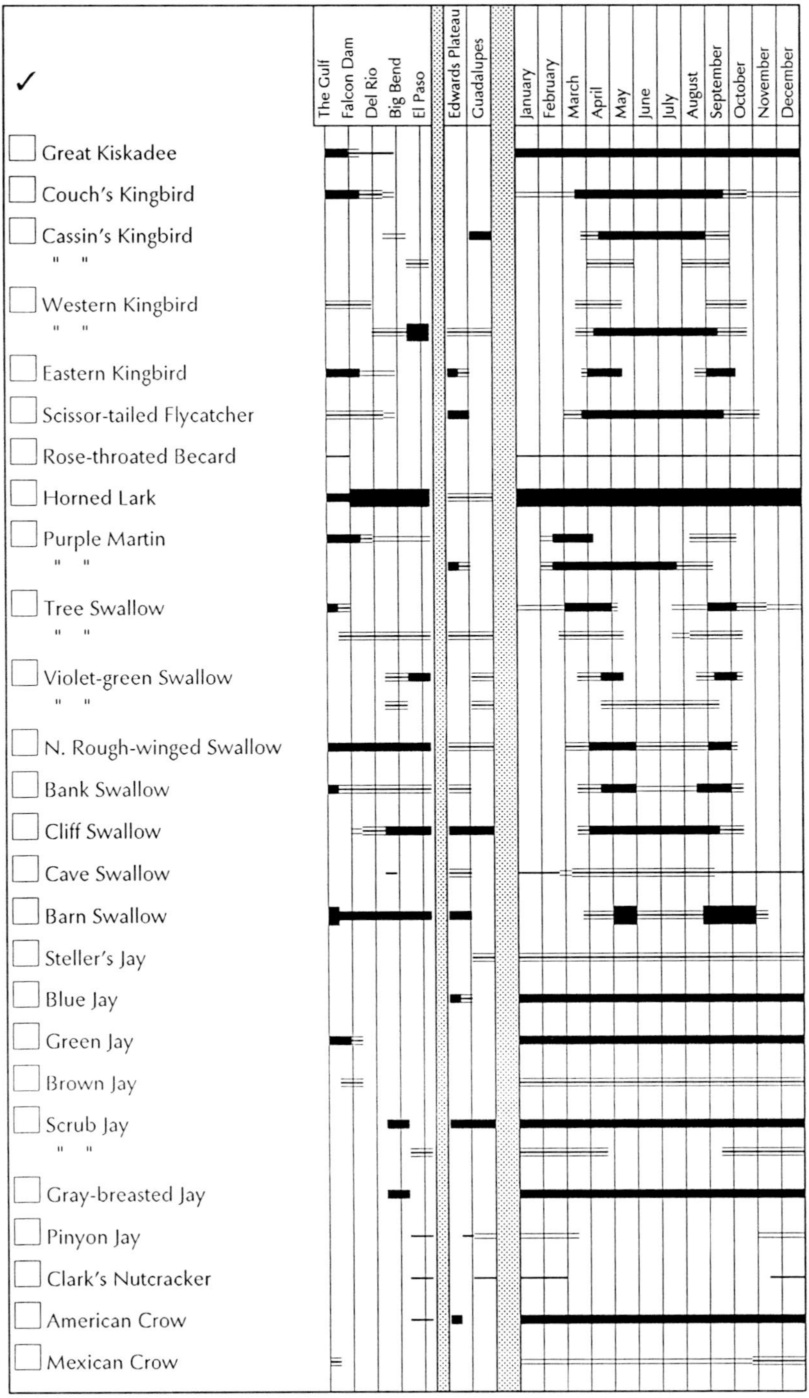

✓	The Gulf	Falcon Dam	Del Rio	Big Bend	El Paso	Edwards Plateau	Guadalupes	January	February	March	April	May	June	July	August	September	October	November	December
☐ Great Kiskadee																			
☐ Couch's Kingbird																			
☐ Cassin's Kingbird																			
" "																			
☐ Western Kingbird																			
" "																			
☐ Eastern Kingbird																			
☐ Scissor-tailed Flycatcher																			
☐ Rose-throated Becard																			
☐ Horned Lark																			
☐ Purple Martin																			
" "																			
☐ Tree Swallow																			
" "																			
☐ Violet-green Swallow																			
" "																			
☐ N. Rough-winged Swallow																			
☐ Bank Swallow																			
☐ Cliff Swallow																			
☐ Cave Swallow																			
☐ Barn Swallow																			
☐ Steller's Jay																			
☐ Blue Jay																			
☐ Green Jay																			
☐ Brown Jay																			
☐ Scrub Jay																			
" "																			
☐ Gray-breasted Jay																			
☐ Pinyon Jay																			
☐ Clark's Nutcracker																			
☐ American Crow																			
☐ Mexican Crow																			

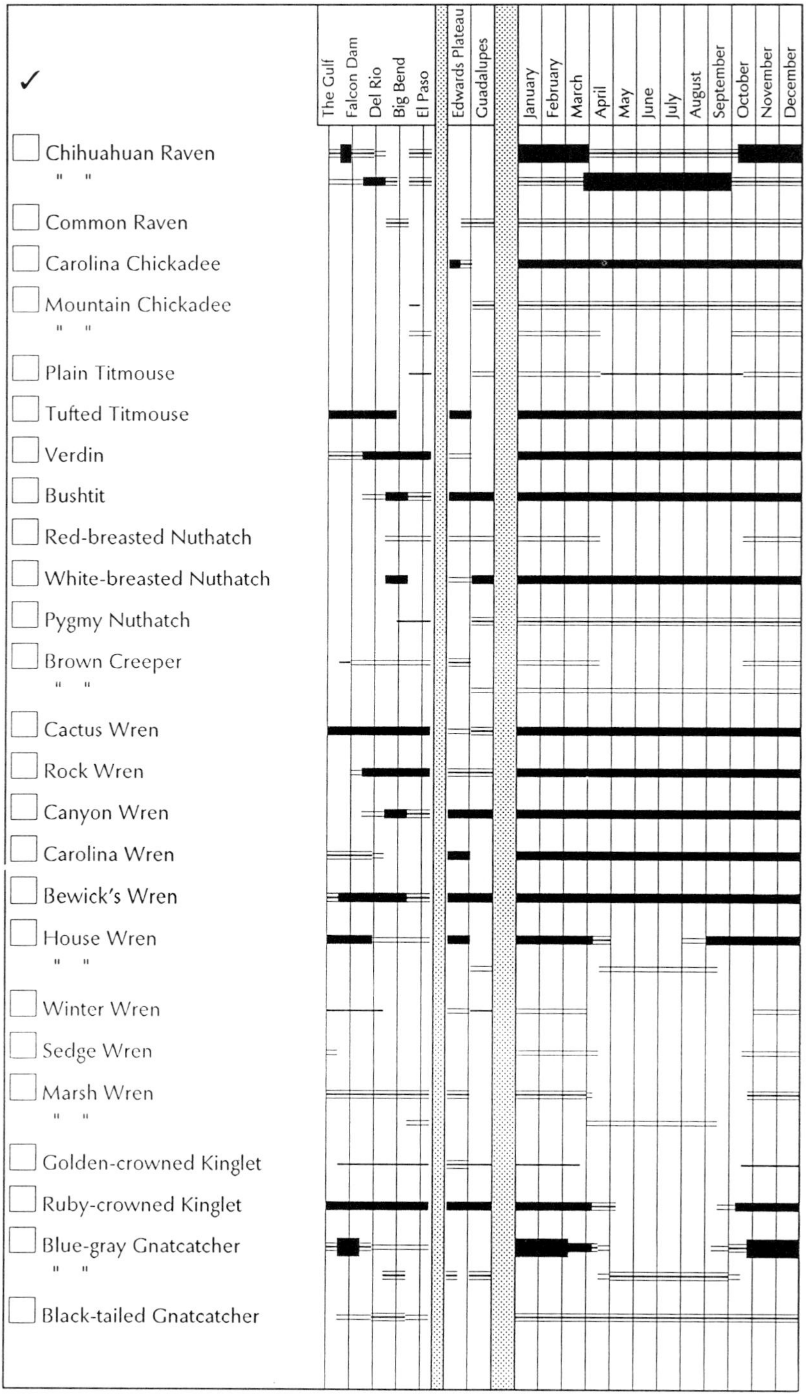

✓	The Gulf	Falcon Dam	Del Rio	Big Bend	El Paso	Edwards Plateau	Guadalupes	January	February	March	April	May	June	July	August	September	October	November	December
☐ Chihuahuan Raven																			
" "																			
☐ Common Raven																			
☐ Carolina Chickadee																			
☐ Mountain Chickadee																			
" "																			
☐ Plain Titmouse																			
☐ Tufted Titmouse																			
☐ Verdin																			
☐ Bushtit																			
☐ Red-breasted Nuthatch																			
☐ White-breasted Nuthatch																			
☐ Pygmy Nuthatch																			
☐ Brown Creeper																			
" "																			
☐ Cactus Wren																			
☐ Rock Wren																			
☐ Canyon Wren																			
☐ Carolina Wren																			
☐ Bewick's Wren																			
☐ House Wren																			
" "																			
☐ Winter Wren																			
☐ Sedge Wren																			
☐ Marsh Wren																			
" "																			
☐ Golden-crowned Kinglet																			
☐ Ruby-crowned Kinglet																			
☐ Blue-gray Gnatcatcher																			
" "																			
☐ Black-tailed Gnatcatcher																			

✓	The Gulf	Falcon Dam	Del Rio	Big Bend	El Paso	Edwards Plateau	Guadalupes	January	February	March	April	May	June	July	August	September	October	November	December
☐ Eastern Bluebird																			
" "																			
☐ Western Bluebird																			
" "																			
☐ Mountain Bluebird																			
☐ Townsend's Solitaire																			
☐ Veery																			
☐ Gray-cheeked Thrush																			
☐ Swainson's Thrush																			
☐ Hermit Thrush																			
" "																			
☐ Wood Thrush																			
☐ Clay-colored Robin																			
☐ American Robin																			
" "																			
☐ Gray Catbird																			
☐ Northern Mockingbird																			
☐ Sage Thrasher																			
☐ Brown Thrasher																			
" "																			
☐ Long-billed Thrasher																			
☐ Curve-billed Thrasher																			
☐ Crissal Thrasher																			
☐ American Pipit																			
☐ Sprague's Pipit																			
☐ Cedar Waxwing																			
☐ Phainopepla																			
☐ Loggerhead Shrike																			
" "																			
☐ European Starling																			
" "																			
☐ White-eyed Vireo																			

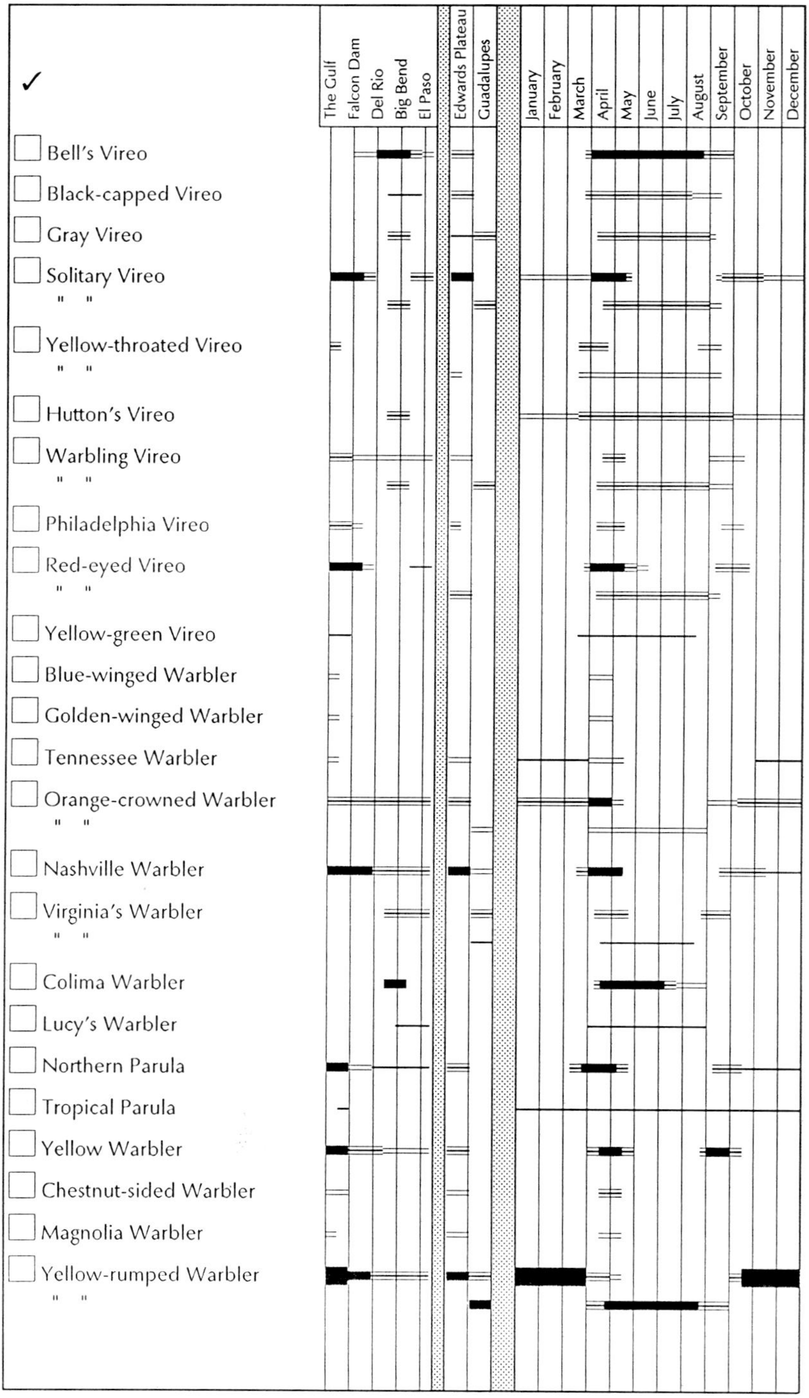

✓	The Gulf	Falcon Dam	Del Rio	Big Bend	El Paso	Edwards Plateau	Guadalupes	January	February	March	April	May	June	July	August	September	October	November	December
☐ Bell's Vireo																			
☐ Black-capped Vireo																			
☐ Gray Vireo																			
☐ Solitary Vireo																			
" "																			
☐ Yellow-throated Vireo																			
" "																			
☐ Hutton's Vireo																			
☐ Warbling Vireo																			
" "																			
☐ Philadelphia Vireo																			
☐ Red-eyed Vireo																			
" "																			
☐ Yellow-green Vireo																			
☐ Blue-winged Warbler																			
☐ Golden-winged Warbler																			
☐ Tennessee Warbler																			
☐ Orange-crowned Warbler																			
" "																			
☐ Nashville Warbler																			
☐ Virginia's Warbler																			
" "																			
☐ Colima Warbler																			
☐ Lucy's Warbler																			
☐ Northern Parula																			
☐ Tropical Parula																			
☐ Yellow Warbler																			
☐ Chestnut-sided Warbler																			
☐ Magnolia Warbler																			
☐ Yellow-rumped Warbler																			
" "																			

✓	The Gulf	Falcon Dam	Del Rio	Big Bend	El Paso	Edwards Plateau	Guadalupes	January	February	March	April	May	June	July	August	September	October	November	December
☐ Black-throated Gray Warbler																			
" "																			
☐ Townsend's Warbler																			
" "																			
☐ Hermit Warbler																			
☐ Black-throated Green Warbler																			
☐ Golden-cheeked Warbler																			
☐ Blackburnian Warbler																			
☐ Yellow-throated Warbler																			
" "																			
☐ Grace's Warbler																			
☐ Pine Warbler																			
☐ Bay-breasted Warbler																			
☐ Blackpoll Warbler																			
☐ Cerulean Warbler																			
☐ Black-and-white Warbler																			
" "																			
☐ American Redstart																			
☐ Prothonotary Warbler																			
☐ Worm-eating Warbler																			
☐ Ovenbird																			
☐ Northern Waterthrush																			
☐ Louisiana Waterthrush																			
☐ Kentucky Warbler																			
☐ Mourning Warbler																			
☐ MacGillivray's Warbler																			
☐ Common Yellowthroat																			
☐ Hooded Warbler																			
☐ Wilson's Warbler																			
☐ Canada Warbler																			
☐ Painted Redstart																			

✓	The Gulf	Falcon Dam	Del Rio	Big Bend	El Paso	Edwards Plateau	Guadalupes	January	February	March	April	May	June	July	August	September	October	November	December
☐ Yellow-breasted Chat																			
" "																			
☐ Hepatic Tanager																			
☐ Summer Tanager																			
☐ Scarlet Tanager																			
☐ Western Tanager																			
" "																			
☐ Northern Cardinal																			
☐ Pyrrhuloxia																			
☐ Rose-breasted Grosbeak																			
☐ Black-headed Grosbeak																			
" "																			
☐ Blue Grosbeak																			
☐ Lazuli Bunting																			
☐ Indigo Bunting																			
☐ Varied Bunting																			
☐ Painted Bunting																			
☐ Dickcissel																			
" "																			
☐ Olive Sparrow																			
☐ Green-tailed Towhee																			
" "																			
☐ Rufous-sided Towhee																			
" "																			
☐ Canyon Towhee																			
☐ White-collared Seedeater																			
☐ Botteri's Sparrow																			
☐ Cassin's Sparrow																			
☐ Rufous-crowned Sparrow																			
☐ Chipping Sparrow																			
" "																			
☐ Clay-colored Sparrow																			

✓	The Gulf	Falcon Dam	Del Rio	Big Bend	El Paso	Edwards Plateau	Guadalupes	January	February	March	April	May	June	July	August	September	October	November	December
☐ Brewer's Sparrow																			
☐ Field Sparrow																			
" "																			
☐ Black-chinned Sparrow																			
" "																			
☐ Vesper Sparrow																			
☐ Lark Sparrow																			
☐ Black-throated Sparrow																			
☐ Sage Sparrow																			
☐ Lark Bunting																			
" "																			
☐ Savannah Sparrow																			
☐ Baird's Sparrow																			
☐ Grasshopper Sparrow																			
" "																			
☐ Le Conte's Sparrow																			
☐ Fox Sparrow																			
☐ Song Sparrow																			
☐ Lincoln's Sparrow																			
☐ Swamp Sparrow																			
☐ White-throated Sparrow																			
☐ White-crowned Sparrow																			
☐ Harris's Sparrow																			
☐ Dark-eyed Junco																			
" "																			
" "																			
☐ McCown's Longspur																			
☐ Chestnut-collared Longspur																			
☐ Red-winged Blackbird																			
☐ Eastern Meadowlark																			
" "																			
☐ Western Meadowlark																			

✓	The Gulf	Falcon Dam	Del Rio	Big Bend	El Paso	Edwards Plateau	Guadalupes	January	February	March	April	May	June	July	August	September	October	November	December
☐ Yellow-headed Blackbird																			
☐ Brewer's Blackbird																			
☐ Great-tailed Grackle																			
☐ Common Grackle																			
☐ Bronzed Cowbird																			
☐ Brown-headed Cowbird																			
☐ Orchard Oriole																			
☐ Hooded Oriole																			
☐ Altamira Oriole																			
☐ Audubon's Oriole																			
☐ Northern Oriole																			
" "																			
☐ Scott's Oriole																			
☐ Purple Finch																			
☐ Cassin's Finch																			
☐ House Finch																			
☐ Red Crossbill																			
☐ Pine Siskin																			
" "																			
☐ Lesser Goldfinch																			
☐ American Goldfinch																			
☐ House Sparrow																			

OTHER SPECIES SELDOM SEEN BUT POSSIBLE

The bar-graphs illustrate species which regularly occur in the average year; the section on **Specialties of the Region** included local breeders, migrants, and virtually all the "Mexican Vagrants" seen in the area. The listing below includes other species—basically eastern and western birds—which have been seen in the region only rarely.

Pacific Loon
Magnificent Frigatebird
Ross's Goose
Eurasian Wigeon
Oldsquaw
Black Scoter
Surf Scoter
White-winged Scoter
Hooded Merganser
American Swallow-tailed Kite
Snail Kite
American Oystercatcher
Ruff
Red Phalarope
California Gull
Thayer's Gull
Lesser Black-backed Gull
Black-legged Kittiwake
Northern Pygmy-Owl
Berylline Hummingbird
Costa's Hummingbird
Lewis's Woodpecker
Tufted Flycatcher
Black-billed Magpie
American Dipper
Varied Thrush
American Tree Sparrow
Golden-crowned Sparrow
Evening Grosbeak

Other Vertebrates

Exclusive of Fish

Compiled by Allan H. Chaney

Alligators

Alligator—Ponds, resacas, streams; South Texas except coastal.

Turtles

Snapping Turtle—Some permanent waters; Edwards Plateau.
Yellow Mud Turtle—Permanent waters with mud bottoms; throughout
Big Bend Mud Turtle—Rare, cattle tanks; Presidio County.
Desert and **Ornate Box Turtle**—Sandy plains, prairies, bottomlands; throughout.
Texas Map Turtle—Clear vegetated streams; central Colorado River basin only, Edwards Plateau.
Cagle's Map Turtle—Clear streams; Guadalupe River Basin only, Edwards Plateau.
Big Bend Slider Turtle—Muddy bottom ponds and streams; Brewster, Presidio, and Hudspeth counties.
Red-eared Slider Turtle—Muddy streams and ponds; throughout except Big Bend.
Zug's River Cooter—Clear streams and ponds; Pecos and Rio Grande drainages
Texas River Cooter—Clear streams; Guadalupe and Colorado river basins, Edwards Plateau.
Western Painted Turtle—Clear streams; Culberson and El Paso counties.
Texas Tortoise—Dry brushlands and sandy areas; South Texas to Val Verde County.
Spiny Softshells (2)—Rivers, lakes, ponds; throughout.
Stinkpot—Muddy bottom streams and ponds; eastern Edwards Plateau.

Lizards

Mediterranean Gecko—Introduced, commensal with man in buildings; South Texas, Val Verde, Brewster, and El Paso counties.
Texas Banded Gecko—Rocky areas; throughout except eastern Edwards Plateau and eastern South Texas.
Reticulated Gecko—Dry rocky areas; Presidio and Brewster counties.
Green Anole—Commensal with man, spreading; eastern and lower South Texas and Del Rio.

Collared Lizards (2)—Rocky areas; Balcones Escarpment to El Paso.
Reticulate Collared Lizard—Sandstone rock outcrops; Eagle Pass to McAllen.
Longnose Leopard Lizard—Desert flats; Big Bend to El Paso.
Texas and **Southwestern Earless Lizard**—Rocky areas; throughout to Cameron County.
Spot-tailed Earless Lizard—Desert washes; Trans-Pecos.
Plateau and **Southern Earless Lizard**—Brushlands and road margins; Edwards Plateau to upper South Texas.
Keeled Earless Lizard—Sandy savannahs and dry brushlands; Laredo east to the Gulf.
Rose-bellied Lizard—Brushlands and rocky areas; South Texas.
Mesquite Lizard—Commensal with man, in mesquite trees; South Texas.
Crevice Spiny Lizard—Rocky areas; Edwards Plateau to El Paso.
Blue Spiny Lizard—Rocky areas; Del Rio to McAllen.
Twin-spotted Spiny Lizard—Dry areas; Trans-Pecos.
Texas Spiny Lizard—Woodlands; throughout, Big Bend to Brownsville.
Prairie and **Fence Lizards**—Many habitats; throughout.
Canyon Lizards (3)—Rocky canyon walls; Del Rio through Big Bend.
Tree Lizards (2)—Trees and rocky areas; Trans-Pecos, Edwards Plateau, and along Rio Grande to Brownsville.
Desert Side-blotched Lizard—Desert flats; Trans-Pecos.
Texas Horned Lizard—Open terrain; throughout.
Mountain Short-horned Lizard—Forests; Davis and Guadalupe mountains.
Round-tailed Horned Lizard—Dry, open, rocky terrain; Trans-Pecos, western Edwards Plateau, Zapata County.
Texas Spotted Whiptail—Rocky grasslands; throughout except Hudspeth and El Paso counties.
New Mexico Whiptail—Sandy washes; El Paso Valley.
Gray-checkered Whiptail—Dry rocky areas; Presidio County.
Chihuanhuan Spotted Whiptail—Open area habitats; Big Bend to El Paso.
Desert Grassland Whiptail—Open grasslands; El Paso Valley.
Plateau Spotted Whiptail—Dry rocky flats; Big Bend.
Trans-Pecos Striped Whiptail—Dry rocky foothills; Trans-Pecos.
Prairie-lined Race Runner—Open sandy areas; South Texas to Del Rio.
Colorado Checkered Whiptail—Rocky flats; Trans-Pecos.
Marbled Whiptail—Desert flats; Laredo to El Paso.
Laredo Striped Whiptail—Open dry areas; Rio Grande basin, Laredo to McAllen.
Ground Skink—Oak woodlands; Edwards Plateau and eastern South Texas to Willacy County.
Short-lined and **Four-lined Skinks**—Many variable habitats; throughout except Guadalupe Mountains.
Great Plains Skink—Sandy and loamy soils; throughout.
Variable Skink—Debris piles; Davis and Guadalupe mountains.
Western Slender Glass Lizard—Sandy coastal soils near water; coastal South Texas.
Texas Alligator Lizard—Rocky woodlands; Edwards Plateau and Brewster County.

Snakes

New Mexico and **Plains Blind Snakes**—Variable moist habitats; throughout.
Trans-Pecos Blind Snake—Rocky areas near water; Del Rio to El Paso.
Diamondback Water Snake—Ponds, tanks, and streams; throughout from Big Bend east.
Blotched Water Snake—Ponds and streams; Davis Mountains, Big Bend, Edwards Plateau, Starr County, NE South Texas.
Texas Brown Snake—Variable habitats; South Texas.
New Mexico Garter Snake—Near water; El Paso.
Checkered Garter Snake—Near water; throughout.
Blackneck Garter Snake (2)—Near water; Trans-Pecos and Edwards Plateau.
Ribbon Snakes (4)—Near water; throughout from Big Bend east.
Texas Lined Snake—Under debris; Edwards Plateau and Duval, McMullen, and LaSalle counties.
Eastern Hognose Snake—Variable habitats; eastern Edwards Plateau and northern South Texas.
Mexican and **Dusky Hognose Snakes**—Variable habitats; throughout.
Regal and **Prairie Ringneck Snakes**—Woodland; Trans-Pecos and Edwards Plateau.
Racers (3)—Variable habitats, open areas; Davis Mountains, eastern South Texas, and eastern Edwards Plateau.
Western Coachwhip—Open areas; throughout.
Whipsnakes (4)—Variable habitats; throughout
Western Rough Green Snake—River thickets; throughout except Big Bend to El Paso.
Speckled Racer—Resaca and river thickets; Cameron County.
Texas Indigo Snake—Variable habitats; South Texas from Del Rio east.
Big Bend Patchnose Snake—Rocky lowlands; Big Bend to El Paso.
Texas and **Mountain Patchnose Snakes**—Rocky areas; throughout.
Trans-Pecos Rat Snake—Rocky areas; El Paso to Uvalde.
Great Plains Rat Snake—Variable habitats; throughout.
Texas Rat Snake—Variable habitats; South Texas and eastern Edwards Plateau.
Baird's Rat Snake—Rocky outcrops; Big Bend and western Edwards Plateau.
Glossy Snakes—Sandy and dry open habitats; throughout except Edwards Plateau.
Sonoran Gopher and **Bull Snakes**—Variable dry habitats; throughout.
Gray-banded Kingsnake—Dry rocky areas; Trans-Pecos east to Edwards County.
Prairie Kingsnake—Coastal brushland and open pasture; eastern South Texas to Willacy County.
Desert Kingsnake—Variable habitats; throughout.
Texas Longnose Snake—Friable and sandy soils; throughout except central Edwards Plateau.
Ground Snakes (2)—Open terrain under rocks and debris; throughout.
Black-striped Snake—Under debris; Lower Rio Grande Valley.

Western Hooknose Snake—Under debris in arid open regions; Trans-Pecos and Edwards Plateau.
Texas Night Snake—Under debris in various habitats; throughout.
Northern Cat-eyed Snake—Near water; coastal South Texas and Hidalgo County.
Blackhood and **Devil's River Blackhead Snakes**—variable habitats; Val Verde, Brewster, Presidio, Pecos, and Jeff Davis counties.
Flathead Snake—Under debris and rocks; Brewster County, Edwards Plateau south to McAllen.
Plains and **Texas Blackhead Snakes**—Under debris and rocks, variable habitats; throughout.
Southwestern Blackhead Snake—Under rocks and debris in dry areas; Webb County, Trans-Pecos, Edwards Plateau.
Rough Earth Snake—Under rocks and debris; Coastal South Texas to Willacy County.
Trans-Pecos and **Broad-banded Copperhead**—Woodland and rocky habitat; absent from South Texas and west of Davis Mountains.
Western Cottonmouth—Near ponds and rivers; eastern Edwards Plateau.
Texas Coral Snake—Variable habitats; Pecos County east and south throughout.
Massasaugas (2)—dry and sandy grasslands; Trans-Pecos except Big Bend, South Texas.
Western Diamondback Rattlesnake—Various habitats; throughout.
Mojave Rattlesnake—Desert and foothills; Big Bend to El Paso.
Prairie Rattlesnake—Prairies and rocky areas; Trans-Pecos.
Blacktail Rattlesnake—Rocky desert areas; Edwards Plateau and Trans-Pecos.
Banded and **Mottled Rock Rattlesnakes**—Rocky cliffs of higher elevations; Edwards Plateau and Trans-Pecos.

SALAMANDERS

Lesser Sirens (2)—Isolated ponds and resacas; South Texas.
Barred Tiger Salamander—Isolated ponds; South Texas and Trans-Pecos.
Black-spotted Newt—Isolated ponds; coastal counties of South Texas.
Texas Salamander—In springs; Balcones Escarpment.
White-throated Slimy Salamander—around springs and caves; Balcones Escarpment.
Blind Salamanders (3)—Springs and caves; Extreme eastern Balcones Escarpment.
San Marcos Salamander—Springs; Hays County, Balcones Escarpment.
Cascade Caverns Salamander—Cave; Kendall County, Balcones Escarpment.
Valdina Farms Salamander—Sinkhole; Medina County, Balcones Escarpment.

TOADS AND FROGS

Mexican Burrowing Toad—Rare around Falcon Lake; Starr and Zapata counties.
Hurter's Spadefoot—Temporary water on sandy plains; South Texas.
Couch's Spadefoot—Temporary water in variable habitat; throughout.

Plains Spadefoot—Temporary water in variable habitat; South Texas and Trans-Pecos except Big Bend.
New Mexico Spadefoot—Temporary water in grasslands; Trans-Pecos and western Edwards Plateau.
White-lipped Frog—Near water; Hidalgo and Starr counties, South Texas.
Eastern Barking Frog—In crevices and under limestone rocks; Edwards Plateau.
Cliff Chirping Frog—Cracks and crevices in limestone cliffs; Edwards Plateau.
Spotted Chirping Frog—Wet rocky areas; Big Bend.
Rio Grande Chirping Frog—Moist areas; Cameron and Hidalgo counties, South Texas.
Woodhouse's Toads (2)—Lowland ponds; Trans-Pecos and coastal Lower Rio Grande Valley.
Gulf Coast Toad—Various habitats near water; throughout from Brewster counties, south and east.
Great Plains Toad—Temporary water; Brewster County north and west to border.
Texas Toad—Temporary water in lowlands; throughout.
Red-spotted Toad—Under stones near water; throughout except eastern South Texas.
Green Toads (2)—Under debris and rocks in various habitats; throughout.
Giant Toad—Ponds, lakes, resacas; Lower Rio Grande Valley.
Blanchard's Cricket Frog—Edges of streams and lakes; throughout except west of Big Bend.
Green Tree Frog—Pond and lake shores; coastal South Texas.
Canyon Tree Frog—Rocky canyons and streams; Big Bend and Davis Mountains.
Mexican Tree Frog—Cities and near woodland ponds; Cameron and Hidalgo counties.
Gray Tree Frog—Trees near temporary water; eastern Edwards Plateau.
Spotted Chorus Frog—Ditches and temporary pools in grasslands; eastern Edwards Plateau and South Texas.
Strecker's Chorus Frog—near water in various habitats; eastern Edwards Plateau and Kenedy, Brooks, and Willacy counties in South Texas.
Great Plains Narrowmouth Toad—Ditches and pools, grasslands; throughout except El Paso Valley.
Sheep Frog—Sandy brushlands and coastal plains; eastern South Texas.
Bullfrog—Permanent waters; throughout except Presidio and counties north.
Rio Grande Leopard Frog—near water in various habitats; throughout.

MARSUPIALS

Opossum—Woodlands, cities and farms; South Texas and Edwards Plateau.

SHREWS AND MOLES

Desert Shrew—Brushlands and deserts; throughout.
Least Shrew—Grasslands; South Texas.
Eastern Mole—Sandy soils; eastern South Texas.

Bats

Ghost-faced Bat—Caves; Big Bend, Edwards Plateau, South Texas.
Mexican Long-nosed Bat—Cave; Chisos Mountains.
Hairy-legged Vampire Bat—Caves; Val Verde County.
Little Brown Myotis—Rare, deserts; Hudspeth County.
Yuma Myotis—Caves and crevices; Trans-Pecos.
Cave Myotis—Caves; Trans-Pecos and Edwards Plateau.
Fringed Myotis—Caves and crevices; Trans-Pecos.
Long-legged Myotis—Caves, crevices, buildings; Trans-Pecos.
California Myotis—Wooded canyons, caves, buildings; Trans-Pecos.
Small-footed Myotis—Deserts, caves, buildings; Trans-Pecos.
Silver-haired Bat—Caves and buildings; Davis Mountains; Edwards Plateau.
Western Pipistrel—Caves and crevices; Trans-Pecos.
Eastern Pipistrel—Caves and crevices; Edwards Plateau, South Texas.
Big Brown Bat—Woodlands, caves, buildings; Trans-Pecos.
Red Bat—Woodlands; throughout.
Seminole Bat—Woodlands; Edward's Plateau, South Texas.
Hoary Bat—Woodlands; throughout.
Northern Yellow Bat—Palm trees; Lower Rio grande Valley.
Evening Bat—Woodlands; Edwards Plateau, South Texas.
Spotted Bat—Crevices; Big Bend, El Paso Valley.
Townsend's Big-eared Bat—Caves and crevices; Trans-Pecos.
Pallid Bat—Crevices and buildings; Trans-Pecos, Edwards Plateau.
Brazilian Free-tailed Bat—Caves and buildings; throughout.
Pocketed Free-tailed Bat—Caves and crevices; Trans-Pecos.
Big Free-tailed Bat—Caves and crevices; Trans-Pecos.
Western Mastiff Bat—Caves and buildings; Trans-Pecos.

Carnivores

Black Bear—Rare, forests; mountains of Trans-Pecos.
Raccoon—variable habitats except deserts; throughout.
Coati—Rare, woodlands along Rio Grande; throughout.
Ringtail—Brushlands and rocky areas; throughout except South Texas.
Long-tailed Weasel—Rare, variable habitats; throughout.
Badger—Grasslands and deserts; throughout.
Spotted Skunk—Variable habitats; throughout.
Striped Skunk—Variable habitats; throughout.
Hooded Skunk—Rare, woodlands and rocky areas; Trans-Pecos.
Hog-nosed Skunk (2)—Varied habitats; throughout.
Coyote—Varied habitats; throughout.
Kit Fox—Deserts; Trans-Pecos.
Gray Fox—Woodland, brushland, rocky areas; throughout.
Mountain Lion—Rare, canyons and brushlands; throughout.
Ocelot—Rare, thick brush; South Texas.
Jaguarundi—very rare, thick brush; South Texas.

Bobcat—Brushlands and rocky areas; throughout.

RODENTS

Rock Squirrel—Rocky areas; Trans-Pecos, Edwards Plateau.
Mexican Ground Squirrel—Sandy grasslands and brushlands; throughout.
Spotted Ground Squirrel—Sandy grasslands and deserts; throughout except Edwards Plateau.
Texas Antelope Squirrel—Rocky areas of deserts; Trans-Pecos.
Gray-footed Chipmunk—Forests; Guadalupe Mountains.
Fox Squirrel—Woodlands and cities; Edwards Plateau, South Texas.
Black-tailed Prairie Dog—Prairies; Trans-Pecos.
Desert Pocket Gopher—Friable and sandy soils; Trans-Pecos.
Plains Pocket Gopher—Grasslands; eastern Edwards Plateau.
Botta's Pocket Gopher—Varied soils desert to montane; Trans-Pecos and western Edwards Plateau.
Yellow-faced Pocket Gopher—Alluvial soils along streams; Trans-Pecos and Lower Rio Grande Valley.
Texas Pocket Gopher—Sandy soils; South Texas.
Mexican Spiny Pocket Mouse—Palm and brush thickets; Lower Rio Grande Valley.
Silky Pocket Mouse—Varied dry habitats; throughout.
Desert Pocket Mouse—Sandy deserts; Trans-Pecos.
Rock Pocket Mouse—Rocky areas; western Trans-Pecos.
Nelson's Pocket Mouse—Rocky slopes; Trans-Pecos.
Hispid Pocket Mouse—Varied habitats; throughout except western Trans-Pecos.
Banner-tailed Kangaroo Rat—Grasslands; northern and western Trans-Pecos.
Ord's Kangaroo Rat—Sandy deserts and grasslands; Trans-Pecos and western South Texas.
Padre Island Kangaroo Rat—Sandy grasslands; eastern South Texas.
Merriam's Kangaroo Rat—Deserts and grasslands; Trans-Pecos.
Beaver—Wooded streams; throughout.
Plains Harvest Mouse—Grasslands; Trans-Pecos, Edwards Plateau.
Western Harvest Mouse—Grasslands and deserts; Trans-Pecos.
Fulvous Harvest Mouse—Grasslands; throughout except western Trans-Pecos.
Cactus Mouse—Low rocky deserts; Del Rio to El Paso.
Deer Mouse—Varied habitats; Trans-Pecos, eastern Edwards Plateau.
White-ankled Mouse—Woodlands and brushlands; throughout.
Brush Mouse—Rocky montane slopes; Trans-Pecos.
Encinal Mouse—Rocky woodlands; Trans-Pecos, Edwards Plateau.
Pinyon Mouse—Rocky pinyon-juniper slopes; Guadalupe Mountains.
Rock Mouse—Rocky peaks of mountains; Trans-Pecos.
Texas Mouse—Rocky juniper associations; eastern Edwards Plateau.
Northern Grasshopper Mouse—Grasslands; throughout except Big Bend.
Southern Grasshopper Mouse—Grasslands and deserts; Trans-Pecos.
Southern Plains Woodrat—Deserts and brushlands; throughout.
White-throated Woodrat—Desert brushlands; Trans-Pecos.

Mexican Woodrat—Rocky elevated areas; Trans-Pecos.
Northern Rice Rat—marshlands; coastal northern South Texas.
Coues' Rice Rat—marshlands; Lower Rio Grande Valley.
Hispid Cotton Rat—Tall grasslands and fields; throughout.
Yellow-nosed Cotton Rat—Tall grasslands; Big Bend and Davis Mountains.
Mexican Vole—Open forests; Guadalupe Mountains.
Muskrat—Drainage ditches; El Paso.
Black Rat—Cities; Lower Rio Grande Valley.
Norway Rat—Cities; throughout.
House Mouse—Cities and farms; throughout.
Porcupine—woodlands in rocky areas; Trans-Pecos, Edwards Plateau.
Nutria—Marshes, ponds and streams; South Texas, Edwards Plateau.

RABBITS

Black-tailed Jack Rabbit—Open areas in varied habitats; throughout.
Eastern Cottontail—Open brushlands and woodlands; throughout except western Trans-Pecos.
Desert Cottontail—Open plains and deserts; throughout except coastal South Texas.

EVEN-TOED UNGULATES

Collared Peccary—Brushlands and desert; throughout.
Elk—Forests; Guadalupe Mountains.
Mule Deer—Deserts, brushlands, forests; Trans-Pecos.
White-tailed Deer—Varied wooded habitats; throughout.
Pronghorn—Prairies; Trans-Pecos.
Big-horned Sheep—Rare, rocky terrain; Big Bend and adjacent areas.
Bison—Reintroduced to prairies; Trans-Pecos.

EDENTATES

Nine-banded Armadillo—Woodlands and brushlands; Edwards Plateau and South Texas.

—

References:

Chaney, Allan H., 1982 revised 1990, **Keys to the Vertebrates of Texas Exclusive of Birds**. Biology Department, Texas A&I University.
Dixon, James R., 1987, **Amphibians and Reptiles of Texas**. Texas A&M University Press.
Schmidley, David J., 1977, **The Mammals of Trans-Pecos Texas**. Texas A&M University Press.

LOCAL REFERENCES

Arnold, K.A.—**T.O.S. Checklist of Birds of Texas**. Rev. 1984: Texas Ornithological Society.

Bomar, G.W.—**Texas Weather**. 1983: University of Texas Press.

Chaney, A.H.—**Keys to the Vertebrates of Texas**. 1982: Caesar Kleberg Wildlife Research Institute.

Davis, W.B.—**Mammals of Texas,** Bulletin 41. 1974: Texas Parks and Wildlife Department, Austin, TX 78744 ($2.63).

Kutac, E.A.—**Birder's Guide to Texas**. Rev. 1989: Gulf Publishing Co.

Lane, J.A. and H.R. Holt—**A Birder's Guide to the Texas Coast.** Rev. 1988: American Birding Association, Colorado Springs, CO.

Loughmiller, C. & L.—**Texas Wildflowers: A Field Guide**. 1977: University of Texas Press.

Oberholser, H.C.—**The Bird Life of Texas**. 1974: University of Texas Press.

Peterson, R.T.—**Field Guide to Birds of Texas**. 1963: Houghton Mifflin.

Peterson, R.T., and E.L. Chalif.—**A Field Guide to Mexican Birds**. 1973: Houghton Mifflin.

Schmidly, D.J.—**The Bats of Texas**. 1991: Texas A & M University Press.

Wauer, R.H.—**Field Guide to Birds of the Big Bend.** Rev. 1985: Gulf Publishing Co.

Weniger, D.—**Cacti of Texas and Neighboring States: A Field Guide.** 1984: University of Texas Press.

Wills, H.S., and M.M. Irwin—**Roadside Flowers of Texas**. 1961: University of Texas Press.

NOTES

NOTES

NOTES

AMERICAN BIRDING ASSOCIATION
Membership Application

All memberships include six issues of **Birding** magazine, monthly issues of **Winging It,** ABA's newsletter, member discounts offered by ABA Sales, and full rights of participation in all ABA activities.

Membership classes and dues:

- ❑ Individual $30 / yr*
- ❑ Family $37 / yr*
- ❑ Century Club $100 / yr
- ❑ Library $35 / yr*

US & Canada only; all others, add $7.00

Application Type

- ❑ New Membership
- ❑ Renewal

Member Information

Name ______________________________

Address ______________________________

____

____

Phone ______________________________

Payment Information

- ❑ Check or Money Order enclosed (US funds only)
- ❑ Charge to VISA / MasterCard (circle one)

Account Number ______________________

Exp Date ____________

Signature ______________________________

(a $1.00 handling fee will be added for use of credit card)

Sent this completed form with payment to: **ABA Membership**
PO Box 6599
Colorado Springs, CO 80934

RGV 1/92

Other Birdfinding Guides in the ABA/Lane Series

A Birder's Guide to Southeastern Arizona (1989)

A Birder's Guide to Southern California; 3rd ed. (1990)

A Birder's Guide to Colorado (1988)

A Birder's Guide to Florida (1989)

A Birder's Guide to the Texas Coast (1988)

A Birder's Guide to Churchill (Manitoba) (1988)

These and many other publications are available from:

INDEX

Abbreviated Table of Contents

E

F

Abbreviated Table of Contents

Abbreviated Table of Contents

N

O

P

Abbreviated Table of Contents

Q

R

S

Abbreviated Table of Contents

Abbreviated Table of Contents

Y

Z